Unrecognized States

D1615008

LIVERPOOL JMU LIBRARY

3 1111 01375 8568

To Keith and Emma

UNRECOGNIZED STATES

THE STRUGGLE FOR SOVEREIGNTY IN THE MODERN INTERNATIONAL SYSTEM

NINA CASPERSEN

polity

Copyright © Nina Caspersen 2012

The right of Nina Caspersen to be identified as Author of this Work has been asserted in accordance with the UK Copyright, Designs and Patents Act 1988.

First published in 2012 by Polity Press

Polity Press
65 Bridge Street
Cambridge CB2 1UR, UK

Polity Press
350 Main Street
Malden, MA 02148, USA

All rights reserved. Except for the quotation of short passages for the purpose of criticism and review, no part of this publication may be reproduced, stored in a retrieval system, or transmitted, in any form or by any means, electronic, mechanical, photocopying, recording or otherwise, without the prior permission of the publisher.

ISBN-13: 978-0-7456-5342-6
ISBN-13: 978-0-7456-5343-3(pb)

A catalogue record for this book is available from the British Library.

Typeset in 10.5 on 12 pt Times NR
by Toppan Best-set Premedia Limited
Printed and bound in Great Britain by MPG Books Group

The publisher has used its best endeavours to ensure that the URLs for external websites referred to in this book are correct and active at the time of going to press. However, the publisher has no responsibility for the websites and can make no guarantee that a site will remain live or that the content is or will remain appropriate.

Every effort has been made to trace all copyright holders, but if any have been inadvertently overlooked the publisher will be pleased to include any necessary credits in any subsequent reprint or edition.

For further information on Polity, visit our website: www.politybooks.com

CONTENTS

CONTENTS

ACKNOWLEDGEMENTS

This study began with a focus on the dynamics of conflicts involving unrecognized states, but transformed itself into an attempt to understand these 'places that don't exist' in international relations: how do they survive, what kind of entities evolve in the context of nonrecognition, and how that evolution affects attempts to reach a peaceful solution. In my attempt to answer these challenging questions, I benefited immensely from discussions with a number of colleagues. Thanks to Kristin Bakke, Eiki Berg, Helge Blakkisrud, Stacy Closson, Svante Cornell, Thomas de Waal, James Harvey, Antje Herrberg, Daria Isachenko, Pål Kolstø, Donnacha Ó Beacháin, Scott Pegg, Gareth Stansfield, Stefan Wolff, and everyone else who has helped with ideas, suggestions, and useful criticism. Also thanks to my colleagues at the Richardson Institute for Peace and Conflict Studies and to my students at Lancaster University who have over the years challenged, and sometimes defeated, my arguments on unrecognized states. Any remaining mistakes are, of course, my own.

I would like to express my gratitude to the Economic and Social Research Council for its financial support which enabled me to conduct the research for this book (grant code: RES-000-22-2728). The book, moreover, relies heavily on fieldwork and this was made a lot easier by the considerable support I received from a number of people. In Armenia and Nagorno Karabakh, I would like to thank Khachatur Adumyan, Armine Alexanyan, Robert Avetisyan, Gegham Baghdasaryan, Masis Mayilyan, Tevan Poghosyan, and Levon Zourabian. In Azerbaijan, I would like to thank Arzu Abdullayeva, Tabib Huseynov, and Fariz Ismailzade. Also thanks to Laurence

Broers, Jonathan Cohen, and Sabine Freizer, who helped me set up many of the initial contacts. In Croatia, I would like to thank Nikica Barić, Marina Lipovšćak, Saša Milošević, Petra Radić, and the staff at the archive of the Croatian Memorial-Documentation Center. In Serbia, I would like to thank Mile Dakić, Filip Švarm, and Jelisaveta Vukelić. I also owe a lot of gratitude to all the people I interviewed; this book would not have been possible without the information and insights they provided me with.

Some of the arguments presented in this book have previously appeared in articles published by *Survival* (August 2008), *International Spectator* (December 2009), and *Nations and Nationalism* (April 2001), and in a chapter in the edited volume *Unrecognized States in the International System* (Routledge, 2010). I am grateful to the editors and anonymous reviewers who helped me refine my thoughts. Finally, thanks to Louise Knight and David Winters at Polity Press, and to the anonymous reviewers, for believing in this project and for their many useful suggestions which have turned this into a much better book.

I dedicate the book to my partner Keith and to our beautiful baby daughter Emma.

1 INTRODUCTION

When I first visited an unrecognized state, Nagorno Karabakh, it was with some trepidation. The British Foreign Office warns against all travel to the region and the statelet is frequently described as a criminalized ethnic fiefdom. This is an image common to most unrecognized states. Unrecognized states are the places that do not exist in international relations; they are state-like entities that are not part of the international system of sovereign states; consequently they are shrouded in mystery and subject to myths and simplifications. All this leaves a first-time traveller, especially one with a career in international relations, a little bewildered and perhaps even a little worried, but also fascinated. But what first struck me on this trip to Nagorno Karabakh was the sense of normalcy. The border guard glanced at my passport, asked a few questions about the purpose of my visit, and let me cross the de facto border without further delay. The journey then continued along a—for the Caucasus—remarkably pothole-free road towards the 'capital' of Stepanakert.

Although its capital looks more like a dusty provincial town than a capital city, Karabakh certainly has the semblance of a state: its own flag, army, and government; basic public services such as health and education; and it even provides basic amenities for the intrepid traveller, such as hotels and a few restaurants. Nevertheless, unrecognized states are not like other states; they have achieved de facto independence, but have failed to gain international recognition or are recognized by a few states at most. They insist on their right to self-determination, but are faced with the stronger principle of territorial integrity. Unrecognized states exist in the shadows of international relations, in a kind of limbo, and the renewed outbreak of war is an ever-present risk and defining feature of their existence. Yet somehow these entities manage to survive, and even develop. This raises important questions about the nature of sovereignty and statehood. Unrecognized states are predominantly situated in highly volatile regions, and are themselves the product of violent conflict. In addition to Nagorno Karabakh (Azerbaijan), there are a number of such entities in the current international system, including Abkhazia and South Ossetia (Georgia), Somaliland (Somalia), Northern Cyprus (Cyprus), and Transnistria (Moldova). There are also a large number of historical examples of unrecognized states that have now either gained independence or, more frequently, been defeated militarily and reintegrated into their 'parent states'. These include: Biafra (Nigeria, 1967–70), Chechnya (Russia, 1991–94, 1996–99), Republika Srpska Krajina (Croatia, 1991–95), Eritrea (Ethiopia, 1991–93) and Tamil Eelam (Sri Lanka, 1986–2009). Unrecognized states may until recently have represented largely forgotten conflicts,[1] but events in Kosovo, South Ossetia, and Abkhazia have now sparked significant international interest. Kosovo's recognition provided encouragement for the leaders of other unrecognized states who argued that an important precedent had been set. As the then-president of Nagorno Karabakh put it, 'If the world community is ready to recognize the independence of[...]Kosovo, I think it will be very hard for them to explain why they don't recognize Nagorno-Karabakh.'[2] Moreover, it provided Russia with an instrument for reasserting influence in its 'near abroad'. Vladimir Putin already in 2006 had warned, 'If someone believes that Kosovo should be granted full independence as a state, then why should we deny it to the Abkhaz and the South Ossetians?'[3] On 7 August 2008, Georgia's president Mikheil Saakashvili unwisely responded to Russian provocations and launched an attempt to retake South Ossetia by force.[4] This gave Russia the needed pretext: under the guise of protecting the civilian population and acting under its peacekeeping mandate, the Russian Army quickly defeated the Georgian forces and on 27 August Russia announced its recognition of South Ossetia and Abkhazia. President Medvedev argued that independence could not be denied to these entities when it had been granted to Kosovo: 'You cannot have one rule for some and another rule for others.'[5] This move caused consternation in Western capitals, and it announced that after lying dormant for several years, the game of recognition had returned to global politics.

The relevance of unrecognized states—or in some cases partly recognized states—has therefore never been timelier. Yet we have very little understanding of how they operate; they remain 'black boxes' and anomalies in a world of sovereign states. This book provides a much-needed comprehensive analysis of unrecognized states, but it is not only about unrecognized states; it is a book about sovereignty and statehood. How do these anomalies survive in a system of sovereign states? How does the context of nonrecognition affect their attempts to build effective state-like entities?

Anomalies in the International System

The post-1945 world has often been described as being neatly divided into sovereign states, each wielding supreme power over a clearly defined territory.[6] Earlier international systems included overlapping sovereignties, colonies, and trusteeships, but this has given way to a world in which 'there are states and there is little else'.[7] As Stephen Krasner has pointed out, 'the language of diplomacy, the media and the street portrays nothing other than a world of fully sovereign states',[8] and Robert Jackson similarly argues that 'we take it for granted that the surface of the earth is portioned into territorially differentiated independent countries and we act accordingly'.[9] But although the current international system is clearly built on sovereign states, and these are the units that enjoy both rights and responsibilities, a number of territories do not fit into this system. The reality is a lot more complex, and unrecognized states are not the only entities that challenge the classical view of sovereignty.

Unlike what they often look like on a map, borders are often poorly represented by a clearly defined line.[10] Even where borders are not contested, as they still are in a number of cases, they may still be blurred, gradual, and fluid: authority gradually diminishes as we move from the centre to the periphery and border regions can include miles of territory over which the effective sovereign authority is unclear or blurred. For example, the border agreement between Yemen and Oman establishes a 10-kilometre-wide border zone, which reaches 5 kilometres into the sovereign territory of each state. Within this zone, 'neither Party may erect or maintain any fortifications, installations, military camps or the like'. On each side of the border we therefore find zones of diminished sovereignty.[11] Even when it comes to their most important function—defending borders and ensuring the survival of the state—sovereign states are not necessarily as clearly delineated as we might expect. For example, both the U.S. and Russia have long-term, or even perpetual, leases for military bases on foreign soil, such as the Russian navy base in Sevastopol, Ukraine, and the U.S.

navy base in Guantanamo Bay, Cuba. In both cases, we can talk about a form of residual sovereignty. The U.S. lease of Guantanamo Bay was a condition for the withdrawal of U.S. troops from Cuba after the Spanish-American war at the turn of the nineteenth century. The Cuban government claims that the lease is invalid under international law and that the treaty that established the lease should be declared void. The present Cuban authorities have, therefore, refused to cash all but the very first rent cheque—and Fidel Castro argues that this was cashed by mistake.[12] Sevastopol was home to the Soviet Black Sea Fleet and following the breakup of the Soviet Union, Moscow refused to recognize Ukrainian sovereignty over the port. The dispute was finally resolved in the 1997 'Peace and Friendship' treaty, which confirmed Ukrainian sovereignty over Sevastopol but, in a separate treaty, established the terms of a twenty-year renewable Russian lease of land and resources. As a result, Sevastopol is now home to both the Ukrainian Naval Force and Russia's Black Sea Fleet and the navies co-use some of the city's resources. In April 2010 the lease was extended for another twenty-five years with an option to prolong it for five additional years.[13]

The international system also contains a number of autonomous territories, which similarly illustrate that sovereignty is neither always exclusive nor absolute. One sees this in the example of the Channel Islands, which are British Crown Dependencies, and the Faroe Islands, which are a constituent country of the Kingdom of Denmark. These entities enjoy a distinct constitutional status and come close to being *de facto* independent states. They do not, however, control defence and foreign policy and therefore cannot be said to be fully independent, nor do they (currently) make claim to separate sovereignty.[14] The same is true for territories such as Puerto Rico (U.S.) or the Cook Islands (New Zealand) that have the status of associated territories, which is a status short of independence with certain functions, including international representation, carried out by another state.[15] Puerto Rican citizens have automatic U.S. citizenship and enjoy some of the protections offered by the U.S. Constitution. The local government has little or no participation in international affairs, and although it enjoys considerable internal autonomy, this is not absolute and restrictions remain. The Puerto Rican population has, however, repeatedly declined either to become integrated into the U.S.—as a U.S. state—or to gain full independence.[16] The position of the Cook Islands falls closer to an independent state: they are fully self-governing and can for most purposes be considered independent, even in the conduct of foreign affairs.[17]

The classical view of sovereignty is, perhaps more surprisingly, also problematized by a number of entities that are recognized as independent states. This is most obviously the case in states where an international administration has been established in the aftermath of a violent conflict. For example, the so-called High Representative retains the final say in Bosnia, and has the power to dismiss elected officials and impose laws, while Kosovo's independence is supervised by a UN Special Representative.[18] But even states that have not been engulfed by devastating wars do not always fully conform to the classical view of sovereign states as exclusive authorities. It is worth remembering, for example, that until the 1980s the British Parliament formally had to approve certain kinds of legislation, including constitutional amendments, in Canada, Australia, and New Zealand.[19] The international system also contains a number of mini-states such as Andorra and Monaco that are members of the United Nations,[20] but lack an independent defence policy. According to the 1993 Andorran Constitution, France and Spain—as the co-princes of Andorra—have to approve treaties involving internal security and defence, diplomatic representation and judicial representation, and they also retain the right to appoint two of the four members of Andorra's Constitutional Tribunal.[21] Similarly, Monaco's defence remains the responsibility of France.[22] These states are recognized, and are members of the international system of sovereign states, but they are not autonomous, since external actors are not excluded from domestic authority structures.[23] An even more puzzling anomaly is the Vatican City. The Holy See—as the Government of the Vatican City—maintains diplomatic relations with 178 states; it is a member of various intergovernmental organizations and has observer status in the United Nations; yet it fails to meet many of the normal criteria for statehood. The Vatican does not, for example, have a permanent population, and its claim to effective government would be undermined by the fact that Italy carries out a number of its governmental functions, such as policing of St Peter's Square and the supply of water.[24] But the most curious example is the Order of Malta, which has embassies in fifty-nine countries and issues diplomatic passports recognized by other states, yet does not control any territory—and has not done so since 1798, when Napoleon drove the Order from Malta.[25]

A number of authors have argued that not only these anomalies but states more generally fall short of the classical view of sovereignty. Joel Migdal, for example, asserts that the state is undermined from above, from below, and laterally: its capacity and autonomy are being diminished by international organizations, such as the European

Union, by international laws, for example on human rights, by globalization, by multinational corporations, and by several other factors, all of which challenge the idea of the state as the supreme sovereign entity.[26] These forces have a greater impact on weak states that were badly equipped for exercising their authority to begin with and some states consequently exist almost in name only. A quasi-state, in the words of Robert Jackson, is 'independent in law but insubstantial in reality and materially dependent on other states for its welfare'.[27]

The classical view of sovereignty as absolute and covering a clearly delineated territory is therefore at best an approximation. States are not always clearly delineated, sovereignty overlaps, and some states are barely able to fulfil the functions of sovereign statehood. The result of the latter is the existence of large territories that are, if not ungoverned, then certainly areas of limited governance. These territories include, but are not limited to, the tribal areas of Pakistan and Afghanistan, large parts of Yemen, and most of Somalia. And it is from such territories that unrecognized states often emerge.

States That Don't Exist

Unrecognized states have their origins in self-determination conflicts and are denied recognition because they are seen to violate the principle of territorial integrity. This sets them apart from the other anomalies, which are accommodated by the international system of sovereign states as they are not seen to violate it.[28] Additionally, an unrecognized state is defined as follows:[29]

- The entity has achieved de facto independence.
- Its leadership is seeking to build further state institutions and demonstrate its own legitimacy.
- The entity has sought, but not achieved, international recognition.
- It has existed for at least two years.

These criteria emphasize nonrecognition while also implying that a level of institution-building has taken place. This may be of a limited nature but it indicates that these entities are at least attempting to look like, and function as, states. The leadership is making a claim to independent *statehood*, and they have achieved the first level of state-building: territorial control.[30] The criteria, including the requirement that it has maintained de facto independence for at least two years, also exclude more ephemeral entities, such as various minuscule islands that have at different points declared themselves to be independent states. One of the more imaginative examples of this is the Republic of Boon Island, a tiny island off the coast of Maine, which declared independence in 2003. Boon Island citizenship can be acquired for $25 and government offices are for sale from the American Lighthouse Foundation.[31] Distinguishing between unrecognized states and these more curious entities may be relatively straightforward, but the difference between unrecognized states and other entities is often more subtle.

Failed States and Contested Territories

Unrecognized states are often seen through the same prism as another popular post–Cold War concept: failed or failing states. The two types of entities are not unrelated in that they often result from similar conflicts and wars, but although they have certain similarities, it is important to distinguish between the two concepts, which in some ways are polar opposites.

Ever since Somalia's collapse in the early 1990s, failed states have been high on the international security agenda. These states are unable to govern effectively and this lack of internal sovereignty is deemed to produce a dangerous hole in the international system of sovereign states which then fills with variations of disorder: conflict, war profiteering, terrorism, and piracy.[32] Unrecognized states are often born out of state collapse or extreme state weakness and represent areas of state failure in the sense that the central state has lost control over the territory. It is therefore not surprising that unrecognized states are often grouped with failed states, especially since some of the more well-known cases, such as Chechnya, actually came fairly close to the image of an anarchical entity. Most unrecognized states do not conform to this image, however; most manage to achieve a degree of statehood and even the largely unsuccessful cases are rarely completely anarchical. The same can, however, be said about 'failed states'. As I. W. Zartman points out, a failed state is not necessarily characterized by a situation of anarchy,[33] and in many cases it would be more accurate to speak about areas of limited statehood[34] or about 'black spots'.[35] New forms of authority are likely to emerge as alternatives to or replacements for the central control that has failed: in Somalia pockets of authority were established at an early stage and the 'ungoverned' tribal areas in Pakistan have also seen the emergence of various shadow states.[36]

Even though neither failed states nor unrecognized states therefore represent the complete absence of control, there is still an important difference between them: unrecognized states lack the international recognition that serves to bolster failed and failing states and helps protect them from complete collapse and external invasions. Although their origins are similar and they both demonstrate that sovereignty is divisible, unrecognized states and failed states represent different sides of the coin.[37] Failing states, or quasi-states, enjoy external sovereignty without internal sovereignty,[38] or with only a limited degree of internal sovereignty, while unrecognized states manage to survive without external sovereignty and are at least making claims to having achieved internal sovereignty. Quasi-states enjoy independence without self-reliance, but are propped up by external sovereignty.[39] Unrecognized states, on the other hand, enjoy no such protection; norms of nonintervention do not apply to them and self-reliance, especially in a military sense, is therefore crucial for their survival.[40]

Insurgent States, Black Spots, States-Within-States

It is relatively easy to distinguish between failed states and unrecognized states, conceptually, but the line between unrecognized states and other forms of 'para-states' can be harder to draw.[41] Defining unrecognized states in terms of their de facto independence, their attempt at institution-building, their aspiration for de jure independence, and their lack of international recognition leaves us with a number of borderline cases.

First, the requirement for de facto independence and *territorial control* excludes cases such as Western Sahara (Sahrawi Arab Democratic Republic, SADR),[42] which otherwise has a number of similarities with the unrecognized states analysed in this book. The SADR only controls around 15 per cent of the territory it claims, with the rest being under Moroccan control.[43] Despite being recognized by seventy states and a member of the African Union, Western Sahara cannot therefore make a claim to de facto independence. Unrecognized states frequently make claims to more territory than they actually control. The Nagorno Karabakh Republic, for example, continues to claim the district of Shahumyan, which is under Azerbaijani control,[44] while Somaliland claims all the territory of the former British Somaliland, even though the northeastern region of Maakhir in 2007 declared itself a separate, unrecognized autonomous state within Somalia and the Sool region remains disputed.[45] However, cases do control at least *two-thirds of the territory* they claim, including the territory's *main city* and *key regions*. This criterion also excludes a number of separatist movements, such as in Aceh (Indonesia), that have not (yet) managed to exert sufficient political control over the desired territory to qualify as de facto independent. These are, however, likely candidates for future unrecognized states.

Other areas are even further from being unrecognized states, such as the territories that Bartosz Stanislawski describes as 'black spots'. The central government is no longer able to impose effective control over these territories and regional warlords or anarchy reign.[46] Even where a regional warlord dominates, these 'black spots' lack the kind of territorial control that characterizes unrecognized states. The 'insurgent states' described by Robert McColl are of a similar nature: these parallel states may be able to provide basic public services, but they only control limited territory, which they use as a base for trying to overthrow the government.[47] Rather than seeking internationally recognized independence, which is a central driving force for unrecognized states, insurgent states seek to change the system in the existing state, while 'black spots' seek invisibility; they prefer to be 'forgotten islands of international disorder'.[48]

This does not mean that the formal *declaration of independence* is necessarily decisive. There are a few cases that have not formally declared independence yet *function as independent entities* and display *aspirations for independence*.[49] These are cases of 'incremental secession'.[50] Prominent examples include Taiwan, the Kurdish Autonomous Region in Iraq until the Transitional Administration Law was signed in 2004,[51] and Montenegro prior to its independence from Serbia-Montenegro in 2006. Simply excluding such entities from the definition would overlook the possibility that the absence of a formal declaration of independence can be a strategic attempt to increase room for manoeuvre and the prospect for international support. Such considerations were seen in Abkhazia, which only formally declared independence in 1999, even though it had been de facto independent since 1993. Eritrea likewise only declared independence in 1993 following an independence referendum, but it had been de facto independent since 1991 and its aspirations were clear. Entities that have not formally declared independence may function similarly to those who have; the same issues tend to be salient in their internal politics and they face similar challenges. The main difference is a greater chance of international engagement and greater flexibility when it comes to their maximalist goals. These differences are not insubstantial and do affect the kind of statehood that the entities are able to develop; these cases therefore provide an interesting contrast. The cases analysed in this book will, however, not include what could be termed 'states-within-states'; that is, regions that maintain a very high level of independence, but still recognize the central government and do not make separatist claims. These include cases such as the Ajara in Georgia (until 2004), Nakhichevan in Azerbaijan, and Puntland in Somalia.[52] What distinguishes these entities, apart from their lack of aspiration for independence, is that their de facto statehood often exists with the tacit approval of the central government, due to the need for political support or to economic interests in the region. This is crucial since it means that there is no external threat to their de facto independence.

Finally, there is the criterion of *nonrecognition*. Where does this leave cases that are recognized by some states? For example, Taiwan is recognized by twenty-three states while many other states have unofficial relations with the entity. In comparison, unrecognized states such as Nagorno Karabakh and Somaliland are not recognized by any states; the Republic of Northern Cyprus is only recognized by its kin-state, Turkey; while Abkhazia and South Ossetia are recognized by their patron state, Russia, and three other states. Another significant borderline case is Kosovo, whose 'supervised independence' has been recognized by seventy-four states.[53] Its status as a fully recognized state is, however, far from complete: Kosovo is unlikely to become a member of the United Nations in the near future due to Russian obstruction of this goal, and the entity's international administration retains the final say. This international presence minimizes Kosovo's internal sovereignty but it also makes the entity's existence less precarious. Russia's recognition of Abkhazia and South Ossetia raises the possibility that this form of partial recognition by one or more major powers could emerge as a more stable form of statehood. Depending on the number and calibre of recognizing states, these entities will function more like fully recognized states or more like completely unrecognized ones. Since this study is interested in the effect of nonrecognition, its main focus will be on entities that are completely unrecognized or only recognized by their *patron state*, and at the most a *few other states* of no great significance.[54] Borderline cases will, however, be included as contrasting examples of entities that have a somewhat different position in the international system, yet have important similarities.

Definition and Universe of Cases

A more precise definition therefore looks as follows:

- An unrecognized state has achieved de facto independence, *covering at least two-thirds of the territory to which it lays claim and including its main city and key regions.*
- Its leadership is seeking to build further state institutions and demonstrate its own legitimacy.
- The entity has declared formal independence *or demonstrated clear aspirations for independence, for example through an independence referendum, adoption of a separate currency or similar act that clearly signals separate statehood.*
- The entity has not gained international recognition *or has, at the most, been recognized by its patron state and a few other states of no great importance.*
- It has existed for at least two years.

This leaves us with the following list of unrecognized states after 1991. The start date indicates when these entities achieved de facto independence. In some cases this coincides with the signing of a ceasefire agreement, but in other cases the achievement of de facto independence was more gradual and the date is therefore only approximate. Unrecognized states also existed during the Cold War: for example, Katanga (DR Congo), and Biafra (Nigeria), and a number of the contemporary cases came into existence before the end of the Cold War. The post-Cold War era, however, appears to present unrecognized states with different constraints and different possibilities. This will be further explored in the following chapter.

The relatively small universe of cases does not mean that other forms of entities, including other forms of 'para-states', are of no importance. These entities illustrate possible alternatives for the unrecognized states if full, de jure, statehood is not achieved. Reintegration through force may be the most likely outcome—as recently seen in cases such as Tamil Eelam, Chechnya and Republika Srpska Krajina— but the leaders of unrecognized states may, under the right circumstances, be willing to consider very loose links with their parent states, similar to Andorra or Monaco, or solutions along the lines of a 'state-within-a-state'. These different entities, which all question the direct link between internal and external sovereignty, therefore serve as an inspiration, and perhaps also as a warning.

Table 1. Unrecognized States after 1991

Name of entity	De jure 'parent state'	Population size
Abkhazia (1993–)	Georgia	214,016 (2003 census)[55]
Bougainville (1975–97)	Papua New Guinea	175,160 (2000 census)
Chechnya (1991–, 1996–9)	Russia	1,103,686 (2002 census)
Eritrea (1991–3)	Ethiopia	5,291,370 (2008 census)
Gagauzia (1991–4)	Moldova	155,646 (2004 census)
Kurdish Autonomous Region (1991–2004)	Iraq	4,690,939 (2010)[56]
Montenegro (2000–2006)[57]	Serbia-Montenegro	620,145 (2003 census)
Nagorno Karabakh (1994–)	Azerbaijan	134,862 (2005 census)[58]
Republika Srpska (1992–5)	Bosnia	1,435,179 (2009)[59]
Republika Srpska Krajina (1991–5)	Croatia	430,000 (1994)[60]
Somaliland (1991–)	Somalia	3,000,000 (1997)[61]
South Ossetia (1992–)	Georgia	72,000 (2010)[62]
Tamil Eelam (1986–2009)	Sri Lanka	2,126,449 (2004 census)[63]
Transnistria (1991–)	Moldova	555,347 (2004 census)[64]
Turkish Republic of Northern Cyprus (1974–)	Cyprus	257,000 (2006 census)[65]
Borderline cases		
Kosovo (1999–)	Serbia	1,805,000 (2009)[66]
Taiwan, or Republic of China (1971–)	People's Republic of China	23,120,000 (2009)[67]

The statehood of unrecognized states is, moreover, highly unstable and they tend to move in and out of the above-mentioned categories; therefore what was once an unrecognized state can become a state-within-a-state, or perhaps a 'black spot', and vice versa. For example, Chechnya was an unrecognized state in the periods 1991–94 and 1996–99, a 'black spot' during the Chechen wars, and now, with the Russian authorities again in control, it comes closer to a 'state-within-a-state'.[68] The universe of cases is therefore by no means set and new cases are likely to emerge—if the leaders of contested territories manage to create basic institutions and establish territorial control, for example. The case of Chechnya also illustrates that at the margins it can be hard to differentiate between the categories; for example, when does a 'failed unrecognized state' become a 'black spot'?[69] This fluidity is important, and inescapable in definitions of unrecognized states, and it points to a lack of long-term sustainability.[70]

States Without Sovereignty

With unrecognized states defined, we can turn our attention to the questions their existence raises about sovereignty and statehood. Are unrecognized states sovereign? Are they even states? In a sense, the answers to these questions are obvious: they are not sovereign and are therefore not states. A traditional view of sovereignty would hold that without international recognition, without external sovereignty, any talk of sovereignty is nonsensical, and without sovereignty it makes no sense to talk about statehood. We find a parallel to this view in the constitutive approach to international law, which argues that a state is either recognized or it is not a state. As already illustrated with reference to the existence of anomalies in the international system, however, sovereignty and statehood are not necessarily that clear-cut and recent approaches have challenged the classical view.

In international relations theory, sovereignty has traditionally been seen as straightforward; as J. D. B. Miller put it, 'just as we know a camel or a chair when we see one, so we know a sovereign state'.[71] A sovereign state is commonly defined as being '*supreme* in relation to all other authorities in the same territorial jurisdiction' and '*independent* of all foreign authorities';[72] a state is sovereign if it is the exclusive and ultimate source of authority on its territory and sovereignty is therefore absolute. A state is either sovereign or not sovereign; it is the final authority or it is not the final authority, and we can therefore not talk about different degrees of sovereignty. As Alan James argues, 'sovereignty, like pregnancy, is either present or absent, never only partially realized'.[73] This view of sovereignty is an analytical assumption for the dominant theories in the field of international relations:[74] for neo-realists it is, for example, the logical condition of an abstract state, which allows it to be treated as a unitary actor.[75] Sovereignty is conceived of as indivisible, as a bounded whole, which means that the absence of external sovereignty (international recognition) undermines the meaningfulness of any other form of sovereignty.[76] Without independence it makes no sense to talk about supremacy; the absence of the former excludes the latter.[77]

This also has important consequences for the possibility of unrecognized statehood. According to the classical view, sovereignty is a fixed and exogenous attribute of states, and a state is therefore 'either sovereign, or it is not a state'.[78] The constitutive approach to international law similarly argues that recognition is a central element in the formation of a state; a state only becomes a state through recognition.[79] The argument is that international recognition confers rights that are core elements of statehood, such as the right to negotiate and conclude international agreements.[80] Unrecognized entities therefore cannot develop statehood.

However, recent research has increasingly problematized these approaches to sovereignty and statehood, arguing that sovereignty is multifaceted and statehood a matter of degree. Michael Cox and his colleagues argue that international relations studies 'has become a prisoner of its own simplistic understandings of how sovereignty has been exercised in practice'.[81] The view of sovereignty as fixed and indivisible has been criticized by authors who argue that sovereignty has a range of different and changing meanings.[82] There is, as Georg Sørensen contends, not one clear-cut sovereignty game for all states.[83] Constructivists such as Cynthia Weber argue that sovereignty is endogenous to the international system and produced and reproduced by the practices of states themselves.[84] Other authors have problematized the view of sovereignty as indivisible. This research is associated with Stephen Krasner, in particular, and his view that sovereignty has four different elements: (1) International legal sovereignty 'refers to mutual recognition'; (2) Westphalian sovereignty 'refers to the exclusion of external sources of authority both *de jure* and *de facto*'; (3) Domestic sovereignty 'refers to authority structures within states and the ability of these structures to effectively regulate behaviour'; (4) Interdependence sovereignty 'refers to the ability of states to control movement across their borders'.[85] International legal sovereignty was previously referred to as 'independence', and the English School referred to it as 'external sovereignty', while Westphalian sovereignty was termed 'supremacy' or 'internal sovereignty'.[86] The first two elements refer to authority, but the two additional elements—domestic sovereignty and interdependence sovereignty—introduce the importance of control or what we could refer to as *de facto* sovereignty; what is the state's capacity to, for example, control its territory and provide basic public services.[87] Other authors have referred to this form of sovereignty as positive sovereignty or empirical sovereignty; it is referred to as capabilities which enable governments to be their own masters;[88] or indeed as *statehood*. This form of sovereignty has by several scholars been described as a continuum; Robert Rotberg, for example, argues that based on state performance it is possible to distinguish between strong, weak and failed states.[89] So whereas authority may be conceived of as absolute, control or power is not; it is relative, it is a matter of degree. This introduces the possibility of different degrees of sovereignty, the possibility that domestic and interdependent sovereignty can be present to smaller or larger degree. Krasner moreover argues that the different elements of sovereignty do not necessarily go together; a state can have one but not the other.[90]

Sovereignty thereby ceases to be indivisible and it ceases to be absolute. There are different forms of sovereignty and they can be present to greater or lesser extent. According to this view of sovereignty, status, capacity and autonomy can be wholly, or partially, disconnected and this could be taken to mean that external sovereignty can exist without statehood *and* vice versa. Again, we can draw a parallel with debates in international law. Whereas the constitutive approach argues that recognition is essential for statehood, the declaratory approach separates the two and argues that recognition is not a requirement for the establishment of a state. Recognition simply acknowledges that a political entity has met the criteria of statehood.[91]

This book will ask if internal sovereignty can exist without external sovereignty—without international recognition—and, if so, what form does it take? The notion of internal sovereignty used in this analysis goes beyond formal authority and it also goes beyond a Weberian notion of territorial control—although the provision of security is crucial[92]—and includes the supply of basic public services and the enjoyment of popular legitimacy.[93] Krasner's study, while introducing the four different elements of sovereignty, is concerned with only Westphalian and international legal sovereignty,[94] and does not analyse the ways in which domestic and interdependence sovereignty vary— nor their links with the other forms of sovereignty. Jackson explored the possibility of a disconnect between external and internal sovereignty when he found that quasi-states enjoy external sovereignty, yet are unable to fulfil the functions of a sovereign state.[95] But can the reverse disconnect be found in unrecognized states? Can statehood exist without recognition, as suggested by the declaratory approach, and can unrecognized statehood therefore be placed on a continuum from strong to failed states? Or are the benefits of recognition so important that statehood without external sovereignty is impossible as argued by the constitutive approach and the traditional view of sovereignty? Or is it indeed the case that statehood without recognition is possible but takes a different form; that the disconnect is not complete? Krasner has argued that changes in the parameter of one form of sovereignty can lead to changes in others,[96] but has also suggested that the *absence* of one or more of the attributes conventionally associated with sovereignty, including recognition, does not prevent entities from operating perfectly well: nonrecognition does not condemn an entity to 'death and oblivion'.[97] Does the absence of external sovereignty therefore simply render internal sovereignty impossible, does it have no effect, or will it lead to a new type of internal sovereignty, a new type of statehood?

International Recognition

The defining characteristic of unrecognized states, the factor that determines their position in the international system and predominates in internal debates, is their lack of recognition. The policy of nonrecognition is therefore of crucial importance for the creation, development, and long-term sustainability of unrecognized states. The two approaches to recognition in international law—the constitutive and the declaratory approach—have already been mentioned; but how has the *practice* of international recognition been affected by effective statehood or its absence? This has changed considerably over time and has significantly affected the position of unrecognized states in the international system.

It is noteworthy that the issue of recognition 'simply did not arise in the earliest writings on international law'.[98] Sovereignty was, in its origin, merely the location of supreme power within a particular unit. It came from within and therefore did not require the recognition by other states or princes;[99] it would, in fact, 'entail an injury' for the sovereignty of a king 'to be called in question by a foreigner'.[100] Only around the middle of the eighteenth century did recognition begin to attract more detailed consideration, but the position was unchanged: the de facto existence of sovereignty was sufficient. There was no need for the recognition by foreign powers. From the nineteenth century on, however, new states only acquired international personality after they had been recognized by existing states; after they had been admitted into the group of 'civilized' states. Full statehood therefore became dependent on recognition, but this was extended to states that had demonstrated their capabilities for effective governance. How a state had become a state was of no importance,[101] and sovereignty therefore to a significant extent still came from within. The only exceptions were new states that were created at international peace conferences and therefore needed the help of already recognized states to achieve effective statehood. In these cases recognition was made conditional upon the acceptance of certain domestic political structures and policies, and 'the alternative to acceptance was nonexistence'.[102] Thus, the Treaty of Berlin of 1878 recognized Serbia, Montenegro and Rumania as independent states, but only after they had agreed to implement minority rights.[103]

The linking of recognition and ideological considerations became even more pronounced following the end of World War I. Recognition was now withheld from governments whose politics was found distasteful.[104] It was no longer without importance how independence had been gained. Woodrow Wilson's famous Fourteen Points speech to the U.S. Congress in 1918 had made national self-determination a primary consideration in the creation of new states.[105] In the speech he called for the impartial adjustment of all colonial claims with the interests of the subject populations having equal weight with those of the colonial powers. The dissolution of the Ottoman and Austro-Hungarian empires was, moreover, to result in the creation of new states along the lines of nationality.[106] There was, however, little general development of the principle of self-determination before 1945 and it was not recognized in the meaning of secession.[107] The 'self' in self-determination tended to be juridical and territory-focused rather than people-focused.[108] Even though the principle of self-determination had political force and led to demands for minority rights in newly independent states, it did not become the basis of the recognition of separatist entities. This is illustrated in the case of the Åland Islands, which in their demand for joining Sweden rather than the newly independent Finnish state invoked the right to self-determination. However, the Committee of Rapporteurs created by the League of Nations found in 1920 that the principle of self-determination was not applicable, and that it was anyway not 'properly speaking a rule of international law':[109] 'international law does not recognize the right of national groups...to separate themselves from the State of which they form a part by the simple expression of a wish.'[110] Similarly, 'lines of nationality' were by no means always followed when new states were created or borders adjusted. For example, the Treaty of Trianon, which was signed in 1920 between the Allies of World War I and Hungary, resulted in the Hungarian state losing about one-third of its ethnic Hungarian population.[111] The introduction of the principle of national self-determination did therefore not mean that empirical capabilities ceased to be of importance for the recognition of new states. On the contrary, the Montevideo Convention from 1933 required new states to have: a permanent population, a defined territory, an effective government, and the capacity to enter into relations with other states.[112] Effectiveness consequently remained more important than legitimacy.

The policy of recognition, however, changed markedly around a decade after World War I: recognized statehood had been primarily based on empirical capabilities or internal sovereignty; now it came to be based on juridical rights. The origins of the state may have been added as an additional criterion for international recognition following the end of World War I but it now became *the only* criterion.[113] This change was caused by the process of decolonization and the decision to recognize the newly independent states within their colonial borders (the principle of *uti possidetis*). As Jackson points out, 'to be a sovereign state today one needs only to have been a formal colony yesterday'.[114] Capacity to govern, or the prospect of developing such capacity, had no impact on international recognition; only the origins of the new states mattered.[115] In the United Nations (UN) resolution 1514 it specifically states, 'inadequacy of political, economic, social or educational preparedness should never serve as a pretext for delaying independence'.[116] Internal sovereignty had thereby ceased to have an impact on—let alone be decisive for—external sovereignty. As will be shown in Chapter 2, this shift was decisive for the emergence of unrecognized states.

For aspiring states without a colonial past the result of this change was a highly restrictive interpretation of the right to self-determination. This right excluded cases (1) in which force had been used or threatened, (2) which violated a colonial entity's right to self-determination, (3) which did not have the consent of the existing sovereign state or (4) where an apartheid regime had been established.[117] The first three of these points cover virtually all examples of separatist ambitions. In these cases, the existence of legitimate grievances and/or success in creating effective governance was not enough to override the principle of territorial integrity. As Samuel Huntington has argued, 'the bias against political divorce, that is secession, is just about as strong as the nineteenth century bias against marital divorce'.[118] Borders had become sacrosanct and once the process of decolonization was complete, the international map of sovereign states had been frozen.

There were, of course, exceptions to this general refusal to recognize secessionist entities. Recognition is, as Pegg points out, still by and large political in nature and remains the prerogative of an independent state.[119] As a result, pure self-interest and pragmatism sometimes result in a break with the very restrictive interpretation of the right to self-determination. A number of these exceptions were, however, interpreted within the restrictive framework. The independence of East

Timor was widely interpreted as a process of decolonization and it, moreover, had the consent of the Indonesian government, while the dissolution of the Soviet Union and Czechoslovakia occurred with the consent of the existing sovereign states. More problematic were the recognition of Bangladesh and of the former Yugoslav republics. In neither of these cases had the existing sovereign states consented to the separation and it was not a case of decolonization.

In the case of Bangladesh, recognition was granted, in part, on the basis of severe human rights violations. It was deemed to be a situation of a gross failure of the duties of the state, and Pakistan had therefore lost the right to rule. This form of secession is known as 'remedial secession', which means that entities have been governed in such a way that they, in effect, become self-governing territories and therefore have a status similar to colonial territories.[120] The argument for Bangladesh's status as a self-determination unit, which has the right to independent statehood, was further strengthened by it being geographically separate and ethnically distinct from the rest of Pakistan.[121] There are, however, indications that the UN did not treat it as a case of self-determination but rather treated the recognition of Bangladesh as a *fait accompli* achieved due to India's military assistance 'in special circumstances'.[122] The doctrine of 'remedial secession' was moreover opposed in scholarship, and subsequent state practice was, at least until Kosovo's recognition, undecided on the matter.[123] Territorial integrity therefore remained the defining principle of the international system; any separation against the declared wish of the parent state was still unacceptable.

Not even the recognition of four former Yugoslav republics in the early 1990s changed this state of affairs. These recognitions were couched in the language of state sovereignty, and in order to circumvent the problem of Yugoslavia's territorial integrity, the Yugoslav state was deemed to be in the process of dissolution.[124] There was therefore no existing sovereign state that could give its consent or withhold it, and despite Belgrade's vociferous—and military—objection to the recognition of the former republics, this was not deemed to be a case of unilateral secession. The reference to the dissolution of Yugoslavia was also used when Montenegro was recognized in 2006. As a former Yugoslav republic it had the same right as the others to secede and Serbia had, in any case, accepted the separation. From the point of view of territorial integrity, the recognition was therefore unproblematic.

Much more problematic was the recognition of Kosovo in 2008 by the majority of Western states. Kosovo had been an autonomous province in the former Yugoslavia and although this constitutionally involved a great degree of autonomy, the lack of republican status meant that the same argument for recognition could not be used. Also, Serbia was clearly not dissolving and it vocally opposed Kosovan independence. In 2003, the UN mission in Kosovo adopted the so-called 'standards before status' policy, which indicated that recognition as an independent state was conditional upon certain standards of effective and democratic governance. Similar requirements had also been attached to the recognition of the Yugoslav republics in the early 1990s,[125] but they had not been systematically or coherently applied and the main argument for recognition was, as noted above, found elsewhere. The 'standards before status' policy, however, indicated that empirical capabilities could again become crucial for recognition. This has become known as 'earned sovereignty': states earn their sovereignty by building effective, democratic entities.[126] Standards were, however, slow to develop and Kosovan impatience for independence grew. Meanwhile, attempts to reach an agreed solution with Serbia failed. In a 2007 report, the Special Envoy to the UN Secretary General, Martti Ahtisaari, recommended that Kosovo should be granted supervised independence. Kosovo would be recognized as an independent state, but an international overseer would still be present to ensure, in particular, that the new state lived up to its promises regarding democracy and minority rights.[127] Again, this could be taken to mean that empirical capabilities and the kind of state that was created had become increasingly important for recognition. However, in their decision to recognize Kosovo Western powers emphasized its alleged 'uniqueness' and only secondarily pointed to the experience of human rights violations and the commitment to democratic standards.[128] The justification was therefore similar to the one used for Bangladesh: a *fait accompli* arising from external intervention in unique circumstances. A shift in the policy of international recognition was therefore not announced, but other aspiring states nevertheless took note, as will be further explored in the following chapters.

Anarchical Badlands

The combination of traditional conceptions of sovereignty, the principle of territorial integrity, and the policy of international recognition significantly affects the common image of unrecognized states. The image that dominates in the media, in foreign ministries, and much of the academic literature is very much a negative one. These entities are commonly viewed as anarchical badlands that are founded on aggression and frequently also on ethnic cleansing; they are viewed as the antithesis of stable, orderly, sovereign states. This perception strengthens the case for nonrecognition; it is not only a question of the inviolability of borders; the statelets are deemed undesirable entities that constitute a security threat. Vladimir Kolossov and John O'Loughlin, for example, classified Somaliland as a 'pirate state' based on criminal-terrorist activities,[129] while Transnistria has been named, by a European Parliament delegation, a 'black hole' in Europe where 'illegal trade in arms, the trafficking in human beings and the laundering of criminal finance' is carried on.[130] Unrecognized states are widely perceived as criminal safe havens that specialize in the illegal traffic of goods such as weapons, drugs, and even radioactive material.[131] Several scholars, moreover, dismiss the claim that such separatist movements are based on popular will. As Amitai Etzioni puts it, 'a bunch of local autocrats hardly constitutes progress toward genuine self-determination'.[132] Such sentiments are echoed by the parent states of these entities; they consider the conflict part of their internal affairs and therefore claim the right to consider the separatist leaders 'bandits' under the domestic law of the state.[133] For example, Georgian president Mikheil Saakashvili asserted that Abkhazia's leaders 'have profited from illegal smuggling and contraband [and] now threaten to draw us all into conflict'.[134] The dominant image, therefore, comes very close to the 'blank' and threatening interior of failed states that Robert Kaplan described in his now infamous article, 'The coming anarchy'.[135]

There is certainly some truth to this view: shadow economies, weak to nonexistent institutions, and warlords did play a significant role following the cessation of violence, and continue to dominate in some of these entities. Chechnya between 1996 and 1999 is probably the best example of a largely anarchic entity dominated by infighting warlords. Valery Tishkov describes how the Chechen victory resulted in violence, 'chaos and demodernization', and the disintegration of civil institutions led to the 'proliferation of high-level criminal activities including hostage taking'.[136] Another case, which comes close to this image, is Republika Srpska Krajina, which struggled to create even the most basic institutions; the economy, insofar as one existed, was almost entirely based on smuggling and other forms of war profiteering; factional conflicts were prominent and the authorities lacked full control over the territory to which they laid claim.[137] Similar characteristics are found in other unrecognized states as well. Abkhazia's Gali region is, for example, riven by crime and violence,[138] while smuggling in the early years of Kurdistan's de facto independence may have provided as much as 85 per cent of the entity's revenue.[139] The context of non-recognition combined with institutional weakness provides fertile ground for criminal enterprises, and these entities are, as Walter Kemp argues, 'attractive environments for traffickers, profiteers and mercenaries'.[140]

The following chapters will demonstrate, however, that the image of unrecognized states as anarchical badlands is overplayed: they *are* generally weak, poor, and very corrupt, but this is not all that different from the countries of which they are formally part. Pål Kolstø argues that virtually all unrecognized states 'have a large shadow economy, often with intimate links to top state leaders',[141] but this is also true for many of their parent states. The context of nonrecognition and unresolved conflicts results in a complexity that is overlooked in most descriptions of these entities. For example, in the context of nonrec-ognition it is often difficult to distinguish illegal trade driven by crimi-nal intent from illegal trade driven by the need for survival. Abkhazia provides an example of this: due to the trade blockades imposed in the 1990s *any* international trade was illegal and the shadow economy provided the only means for survival. The shadow economy, thereby, also encompassed ordinary people surviving by selling something as innocuous as tangerines.[142] Consequently, the seemingly close connec-tion between unrecognized states and illegality should not necessarily be taken to mean that these entities are only founded on greed; that the conflicts are only driven by the vested interests of a few warlords. Nor should it lead to the conclusion that no form of statehood has evolved. The popular image of criminalized, warlord-controlled ethnic fiefdoms was perhaps a truer reflection of the situation immediately after the cessation of warfare, but developments in the situation of 'no war, no peace' have made it increasingly outdated.[143] The lengthy period of de facto independence has allowed the entities to build insti-tutions and they have, in many cases, also instigated political reforms. Such developments leave the idea of unrecognized states as failed states increasingly open to questioning. Their statehood may differ from the norm, but this is not the same as its complete absence.

The negative image of unrecognized states appears to be inferred from observations of the wartime situation, but this image has been reinforced by the framework used for analysing these entities. Much of the literature on unrecognized states has readily adopted the 'greed thesis', as presented by authors such as Paul Collier:[144] it is argued that intrastate conflicts are driven by opportunists who have an interest in maintaining the status quo since it allows them to make considerable sums in the shadow economy. Later versions of this argument allow for more nuances and for more complex interactions between greed and grievance, but these are often omitted from descriptions of unrecognized states.[145] But perhaps even more significantly, the image of anarchical badlands reflects a dichotomy often encountered in international relations theory between the rational and the meaningful— covered by the sovereignty principle—and the dangerous and anarchic;[146] unrecognized states are perceived as examples of the latter. As Jens Bartelson has pointed out, there is an inability to imagine an order not based on sovereignty,[147] and disorder is consequently assumed in its absence. Internal and external sovereignty are not seen as distinct types of sovereignty, but rather as 'complementary, always, coexistent, aspects of sovereignty'.[148] Thus, dominant conceptions of sovereignty prevent us from imagining the existence of internal sovereignty—the existence of statehood—without international recognition; a state is either sovereign or it is not a state. Some of the literature on unrecognized states has countered this image by arguing that these entities should be seen as 'states in all but name' or 'states-in-waiting'.[149] But this reflects the same dualism as described above; there is statehood or no statehood, order or disorder. It is conceivable that unrecognized statehood takes a different form than recognized statehood, however: that the absence of recognition does not render statehood impossible, but results in a different form of statehood.

Traditional conceptions of sovereignty have therefore had a significant effect on the ways unrecognized states are portrayed. A more straightforward explanation for prevailing simplifications, however, is the lack of research on the internal developments of these entities. They are 'informational black holes'[150] in more ways than one. Most research has focused on relations between the entities and their (de jure) parent states, with each side being treated as monolithic entities. While the issue of state building has received some attention,[151] the obstacles and opportunities provided by nonrecognition have not been systematically analysed, and very little research exists on the issue of political reform and popular legitimacy in the context of nonrecognition.[152] A few notable books have been written on unrecognized states: Scott Pegg first published his book *International Society and the De Facto State* and this was followed by Dov Lynch's *Engaging Eurasia's Separatist States*; by edited volumes from Tozun Bahcheli, Barry Bartmann, and Henry Srebrnik (*De Facto States: The Quest for Sovereignty*); and from Ian S. Spears and Paul Kingston (*States Within States*); and most recently by Deon Geldenhuys' *Contested States in World Politics*.[153] All five books make significant contributions to the research on unrecognized states, but they are all primarily focused on

LIVERPOOL JOHN MOORES UNIVERSITY
LEARNING SERVICES

the external relations of these entities and do not provide an in-depth analysis of their internal developments.[154] This is the objective of this book: to provide a comprehensive analysis of statehood without external sovereignty.

Unrecognized States in the Modern International System

This book presents an in-depth analysis of the politics of unrecognized states, focused in particular on the factors that enable them to survive and the kind of entities that result from the context of nonrecognition. It demonstrates how important internal dynamics are for the development of these entities, but these intra-communal dynamics also interact with the international system; internal politics is shaped and constrained by external factors, including by international norms and practices.

The analysis draws on several examples of unrecognized states, including Abkhazia, Chechnya, Nagorno Karabakh, Northern Cyprus, Republika Srpska Krajina, Somaliland, South Ossetia, Tamil Eelam, Transnistria, and Taiwan. These cases have a number of similarities when it comes to their initial creation, their subsequent development, and their formal position in the international system, but they also differ in important respects. Most notably, some have managed to create effective entities that appear to be states in all but name, while others remained notorious 'black holes' plagued by violent infighting. They also differ in terms of their degree of international isolation, their links with external patrons, and the kind of political systems that they have developed: some are consolidated democracies, while others have found it hard to move away from rule by authoritarian warlords. While this variation presents some analytical difficulties, it also allows the book to engage with broader issues, such as the link between internal and external sovereignty, the meaning of statehood, and anomalies in the international system. The book presents fresh primary research and challenges existing images of unrecognized states by engaging with, and rethinking, literature on sovereignty, statehood, and conflict resolution.

Chapter 2 covers the history of unrecognized states, explores their paths of creation, and discusses the security threats associated with these anomalies in the international system. Chapters 3 and 4 provide the main empirical analysis: how do unrecognized states manage to survive in the international system and what kinds of entities evolve in the absence of international recognition? Chapter 3 analyses the external sources of state building, while Chapter 4 focuses on the internal ones. Chapter 5 ties together the preceding analysis: what kinds of entities result from nonrecognition and to what extent do they challenge existing conceptions of sovereignty and statehood? Chapter 6 addresses the security concerns associated with unrecognized states and asks how these conflicts can be resolved. Chapter 7 concludes on the preceding analysis, which has found that internal sovereignty can exist without external sovereignty, but statehood without recognition takes a specific form and that these entities are not just like other states without the bonus of recognition. Nonrecognition comes at a cost, even if this cost varies from case to case, and it constrains the kinds of entities that can develop. These resulting tensions affect the long-term sustainability of unrecognized states and ultimately the prospects for peaceful outcomes.

2 STATES WITHOUT RECOGNITION

On 20 February 1988, the regional council in Nagorno Karabakh voted for the transfer of the Nagorno Karabakh region from Azerbaijan to Armenia. The council invoked the 'expectations of the Armenian population of Nagorno Karabakh' and appealed to the Soviet authorities to accept the redrawing of republican borders.[155] The Karabakh movement started out as a peaceful movement, but radicalization and militancy gained speed following anti-Armenian pogroms in Sumgait on 29 February 1988. Militant factions began to prepare for armed struggle and threatened to launch a guerrilla war if the demand for unification with Armenia was not met.[156] Full-scale warfare broke out following the collapse of the Soviet Union in late 1991, aided in no small way by the abundance of weaponry made available by the defunct Red Army. Military fortunes waxed and waned and the bloody war lasted for more than two years until a ceasefire agreement was finally signed in May 1994. The Armenian forces could portray themselves as winners: Nagorno Karabakh had, with the help of Armenia, managed to separate itself from Azerbaijan and had achieved de facto independence. Yet they had failed to gain recognition from any other states, and when the population was finally able to emerge from their shelters, the reality that met them was far from the nationalist promises of freedom, security, and prosperity. The infrastructure and economy were in ruins; promises of democracy had been replaced by warlord rule; the risk of renewed warfare was forever present; and the entity was facing international isolation.

This is a typical path of creation for an unrecognized state. Most of these entities emerged out of secessionist warfare. In most cases ethno-nationalism provided an important driving force, state break-down was often an important factor, and external assistance was crucial. But this pattern was not followed in all cases. Not all unrecognized states initially set out to achieve independence, civic nationalism was sometimes more important than ethno-nationalism, and not all of these entities could rely on the support of an external patron. These variations matter for our understanding of the emergence of unrecognized states. They affect the kinds of entities that are subsequently created and they have an impact on attempts to find a peaceful solution to those unresolved conflicts. Even though there are variations in their paths of creation, there are also important similarities. Contemporary unrecognized states result from the restrictive interpretation of the right to self-determination and the overriding principle of territorial integrity. This sets them apart from historical cases of unrecognized states and affects their position in the international system, and it also has an effect on the kind of security threats that are associated with their existence.

History of Unrecognized States

Unrecognized territories have existed at all times, but the reason for their lack of recognition has differed: from lack of empirical capabilities, to ideologically unacceptable regimes, to contravention of norms of territorial integrity. International recognition did not arise in the earliest writing on international law, as Chapter 1 explained.[157] Sovereignty came from within, and whether a state or principality was sovereign or not depended on the ability of the ruler to exercise supreme authority. All territories, all states, all principalities were therefore unrecognized, although we can of course speak of de facto recognition through diplomatic relations or other official links between states and other units. Once recognition became an issue in international law, and sovereignty therefore gained an external dimension, we can start speaking of territories that were denied recognition because they failed to live up to the criteria for external sovereignty. But the key criterion was empirical capabilities, the ability to exercise supreme authority. Not much had therefore changed: external sovereignty was denied to states, or other units, that had failed to create internal sovereignty. The way in which effective governance had been ensured, whether by force or by other means, and the kind of regime that had been established, were of no consequence.

The introduction of an external element to sovereignty did, however, lead to a time gap between the attainment of effective governance over a territory and the recognition of this fact, and an even more significant gap between the declaration of independence and the achievement of full sovereignty. The United States, for example, was only formally recognized as an independent state in the 1783 Treaty of Paris, seven years after independence was declared and two years after de facto independence was achieved.[158] This gap meant that there was often a period in which effective statehood existed without recognition, and territories that bear some resemblance to today's unrecognized states consequently emerged: territories that have achieved territorial control and a degree of effective governance, but are still awaiting recognition. Recognition was considered politically important in cases of secession,[159] but the question is if parent state acceptance was necessary for international recognition, or if the establishment of effective governance was sufficient. This was an issue when the former Spanish colonies in South America declared independence. These states maintained de facto independence for a considerable time without Spanish de jure acceptance of its loss of territory. As a result, the question of third-state recognition was raised, and in 1822 the U.S. decided to recognize Columbia despite Spanish protests. Crawford finds that no international legal consequences were deduced from the lack of parent state acceptance; it did not result in nonrecognition of the new states as long as effective independence had been achieved.[160]

Collective Nonrecognition: Ideology and Strategic Interests

It is not until after World War I, and the introduction of additional criteria for recognition, that we start to encounter collective withholding of recognition for reasons other than a lack of effective governance. As noted in Chapter 1, recognition came to be imbued with ideological considerations, but strategic interests and military alliances were often of even greater significance. The policy of collective nonrecognition first appeared as a principle of international law in the 1930s in connection with the Japanese attempt to establish the state of Manchukuo in eastern Mongolia. The region was seized by Japan in 1931; a puppet government, led by the last Quin emperor, was installed in 1932; and the Manchu State lasted until the defeat of Imperial Japan in 1945. The League of Nations declared that the territory rightfully belonged to China, and the U.S. articulated the so-called Stimson Doctrine, according to which 'a right cannot originate in an illegal act'.[161] The main objection to Manchukuo was that it was a puppet state and that it had therefore not achieved de facto independence: there was no prior independence movement and the main political power rested with Japanese officials. The illegality of its creation—through the use of force—was on the other hand not a categorical bar on statehood.[162]

The collective nonrecognition that was intended to follow was, in any case, far from complete: Manchukuo was recognized by Japan, El Salvador, the Vatican, Germany, and Hungary, and de facto by the Soviet Union. After the outbreak of World War II, the state was recognized by states allied with or under the control of Japan and Germany, including Poland, Rumania, Bulgaria, Finland, and Thailand.[163] Recognition was very much politicized, and the creation of a puppet state was deemed acceptable or unacceptable depending on whether or not the state in question was an ally. Other puppet states were also established during World War II: Germany created the independent state of Croatia (1941–45) on Yugoslav territory and the First Slovak Republic (1939–45) in Czechoslovakia. Recognition was again divided according to alliances, although Slovakia was accorded a degree of wider recognition prior to Germany and Slovakia's attack on Poland in September 1939.[164]

The puppet states of World War II differ in important respects from contemporary unrecognized or partially recognized states. First, they are called puppet states for a reason: their leaderships were externally imposed and they remained under heavy external influence,[165] and thereby lacked the de facto independence that characterizes contemporary unrecognized states, which, although often reliant on an external patron, also have strong indigenous roots.[166] Second, the reason for their lack of recognition differs. The recognition or nonrecognition of the puppet states was based on strategic interests that influenced whether the use of force by an external power was deemed an acceptable means of state creation. Military alliances were primary and nonallied states reportedly suggested that the Independent State of Croatia might be recognized after the war,[167] despite its lack of actual independence and despite the gross human rights violations committed by the regime. Once the dust had settled, effective control would still be decisive.

The legality of a state's creation became more important post-1945 and the nature of a state's regime and/or the use of force became reasons to deny recognition. For example, Ian Smith's Rhodesia was not recognized by any other state, despite the effectiveness of its governance, and was deemed an 'illegal racist minority regime' by the UN Security Council.[168] Collective nonrecognition was also used when South Africa refused to surrender its control over Namibia, which it had administered as a League of Nations Mandate Territory, and following the Iraqi invasion of Kuwait. In these cases the UN invoked a duty of nonrecognition, intended to prevent the consolidation of an unlawful situation.[169] In other cases, nonrecognition was not invoked but a number of states nevertheless withheld their recognition due to the way in which a state had been created or a border had been changed. Several states, for example, refused to recognize the Soviet annexation of the Baltic States and consequently still recognized Baltic diplomats as representatives of their former governments. This situation persisted until the restoration of Baltic independence in 1991.[170] Similarly, after the Korean War the claim of the Republic of Korea to be the government of Korea as a whole (both North and South) continued to be accepted by the Western bloc and North Korea was consequently denied recognition until 1991, when it was finally admitted to the UN.[171] Recognition or nonrecognition therefore depended on ideology and on strategic interests. External aggression, or more generally the use of force, was not necessarily a hindrance to the international recognition of border changes. For example, when Indonesia occupied East Timor in 1975, Australia supported the pro-Western Indonesian government, even though the UN did not recognize its claim to the territory and continued viewing East Timor as being a 'Non-Self-Governing Territory', and therefore insisted on its right to self-determination. Australia's recognition was an Indonesian condition for an agreement on the exploitation of continental shelf resources in the 'Timor gap', located between Australia and East Timor.[172]

In these cases, we are dealing with clearly functioning states; insufficient empirical capabilities are no longer the reason for lack of recognition. Denial of recognition was based on ideology or international norms; it was not the state as such that was opposed, rather the specific regime implemented or the extent of territory covered. When the point of contention is the nature of the regime rather than the existence of the state, other states have frequently withheld recognition from the government by not establishing diplomatic relations. The U.S., for example, refused to recognize the Soviet regime until 1934.[173] The (non) recognition of governments is no longer widely practised,[174] but has not disappeared completely from the international scene. The U.S. has, for example, still not established diplomatic relations with Pyongyang, but in 2005 the Secretary of State, Condoleezza Rice, stated that the U.S. does recognize North Korea as a sovereign state.[175]

Territorial Integrity and Nonrecognition

Contemporary unrecognized states, in contrast, have their origins in self-determination conflicts and are not denied recognition primarily because of the politics they espouse, or since they have resulted from an external aggression (although this sometimes plays a role as well) or because they lack the empirical capabilities required for statehood. They are denied recognition because they do not meet the criteria for the now very restrictive right to self-determination. With a few exceptions they are not former colonies, their de jure parent state has not agreed to the separation, and they have often used force to achieve their de facto independence.

The number of unrecognized states increased significantly following the collapse of the Soviet Union and the breakup of the former Yugoslavia, but this does not mean that they are only a post-Cold War phenomenon. Katanga (formally part of DR Congo), for example, existed between 1960 and 1963 and Biafra (Nigeria) from 1967 to 1970. However, the post-Cold War era arguably presents such entities with different constraints and different possibilities. Most unrecognized states are making a claim to national self-determination, but the post-Cold War world is not generally amenable to such demands. Secessionist conflicts are considered part of a state's domestic affairs and any international engagement with unrecognized states is therefore deemed unlawful, unless it has the consent of the parent state. Although this strict interpretation has been modified in practice, it does mean that conditions for unrecognized states are trying. On the other hand, it could be argued that unrecognized states are bolstered by the process of globalization, which makes it easier for them to obtain vital resources and which could therefore enhance their chance of survival.[176]

Although there are historical precedents, contemporary unrecognized states differ from them in important ways. First, unlike World War II puppet states they have achieved de facto independence based, at least in part, on local capacities. Second, their lack of recognition is linked to the very restrictive right to self-determination; it is neither based on lack of empirical capabilities nor on the political ideology the regimes espouse. Finally, their emergence and subsequent development is significantly affected by processes in the post-Cold War era. This can be further explored by looking at the paths of their creation, which have important impacts on the kind of entities that resulted.

Path of Creation

The term 'unrecognized states' groups together territories that may seemingly have little in common. What, for example, unites the high-tech world of Taiwan with the largely livestock-based economy of Somaliland or the violent chaos of the de facto independent Chechen state? The main things they have in common are their lack of international recognition and the situation of limbo in which they exist. But unrecognized states also have similarities when it comes to their path of creation: the emergence of these entities was in many cases associated with secessionist warfare and state breakdown; it was often driven by ideologies of ethno-nationalism; and it was significantly affected by both international actions and inaction. The politics of unrecognized states therefore tend to be shaped by four central factors: military victory, precarious existence, external dependence, and continuing attempts to legitimize the entity, both internally and externally. However, there are also important differences that affect the kinds of entities that result as well as their specific position in the international system.

Secessionist Warfare and State Breakdown

All unrecognized states are associated with armed conflict or warfare. In most cases this took the form of secessionist warfare, but in some cases the key dynamic was state breakdown rather than aspiration for independence. In yet other cases, the goal was irredentist rather than secessionist, but the goal of joining a kin-state has in most cases been replaced, at least in rhetoric, by a desire for independent statehood.

In the secessionist conflicts, the surprising thing is that the secessionists won. Thus, the South Ossetians managed to defeat the Georgian army; Armenian forces in Nagorno Karabakh gained the upper hand over Azerbaijan's ill-disciplined army. This military victory is a defining feature of these entities; it confers legitimacy on the leaderships and is frequently reified in the political discourse. War played a decisive role even in the few cases where we cannot really speak of secessionist warfare as the initial catalyst. For example, Somaliland resulted from the general chaos and dissolution accompanying the Somali civil war. The initial goal of the Somali National Movement was regime change, not secession, but following years of violence and war, it was pressured by its grassroots to declare independence[177] and at this point there was no longer a functioning Somali state to prevent it. The de facto independence of Taiwan similarly resulted from a civil war, not from a secessionist conflict. In 1949, the Nationalist Government retreated from mainland China to Taiwan and used the island as a base for their continued claim to the mainland. The government of Taiwan, or the Republic of China, sustained the claim that it was the sole legitimate government representing the whole of China.[178] Over time, however, Taiwan's de facto independent status was gradually consolidated. The 'one China' policy was abandoned and there was a process of indigenization.[179] Opportunity and an element of chance were therefore central to these cases, but the experience of war, if not outright secessionist war, remains a defining feature.

The intensity of the wars, however, varied significantly. The Transnistrian armed conflict was 'confined to a few hot spots',[180] and resulted in less than 1,000 casualties,[181] while around 1,000 people lost their lives in the 1991–92 South Ossetian conflict and around 500 people in the 2008 reprise.[182] War was much more severe in other cases. The conflict over Nagorno Karabakh, for example, lasted for over two years and at least 25,000 people were killed.[183] In Somaliland the two largest cities were bombed to rubble in 1988, killing an estimated 55,000 people.[184] If we look at entities that no longer maintain their de facto independence, the figures are even more harrowing. The thirty-year struggle to establish Tamil Eelam in Sri Lanka has cost the lives of an estimated 80,000–100,000 people;[185] the first Chechen war which led to the establishment of the Chechen republic resulted in the death of at least 46,500 people;[186] and the warfare and starvation associated with the conflict over Biafra in Nigeria was responsible for the death of up to 3 million people.[187]

Some of the wars that led to the establishment of unrecognized states were also associated with ethnic cleansing. The two Serb statelets in the former Yugoslavia, Republika Srpska and Republika Srpska Krajina, became synonymous with ethnic cleansing as the military forces engaged in a systematic campaign to homogenize the territory. The territory controlled by Republika Srpska Krajina had previously included very significant Croatian populations and even local majorities, but official documents from the entity argued in 1994 that it was now 95 per cent Serb.[188] Other wars have similarly resulted in very large numbers of refugees and internally displaced people. People have either been forced to flee their homes as part of a deliberate campaign or have fled as a result of the fighting. In the Caucasus, Georgia has accused both South Ossetia and Abkhazia of a policy of ethnic cleansing and the Azerbaijani government likewise asserts that Nagorno Karabakh was created through a policy of ethnic cleansing. The war over Karabakh forced over 750,000 Azeris to flee their homes,[189] and led the formerly Azeri-majority districts between Karabakh and Armenia to be virtually depopulated, while an estimated 352,000 people have become displaced due to the wars and fighting in South Ossetia and Abkhazia.[190] It is, however, important to note, first, that ethnic cleansing was not always one-sided. In the case of Nagorno Karabakh, the war also resulted in 353,000 Armenian refugees.[191] Second, the emergence of unrecognized states was not in all cases associated with ethnic cleansing. Transnistria and Somaliland do not, for example, share that legacy. But in the cases where it did happen and a large number of refugees and IDPs resulted, it clearly adds to the animosity between the unrecognized state and its parent state; it complicates attempts to find a peaceful solution; and it also affects attempts by the unrecognized states to gain international legitimacy.

These differing experiences of war have affected the depth of the emotional scars found among the populations, the level of mistrust, as well as the degree of physical destruction and therefore the difficulty of the task facing the leaders when trying to develop a functioning entity. In Transnistria, the level of destruction was fairly limited, while in a case such as Chechnya it was almost complete. War is, moreover, not only a characteristic of the past; it is also a likely future scenario. State breakdown or state weakness was a significant factor in most of these cases. It provided the opportunity that separatist movements were waiting for; it coincided with and was reinforced by the secessionist conflict and helps explain its success; or it led to the emergence of de facto independence and subsequent separatist ambitions. But the parent states may well regain their strength, as exemplified by Croatia's military victory in Republika Srpska Krajina, Russia's in Chechnya and, most recently, Sri Lanka's in Tamil Eelam. The victory over the parent states in these cases, therefore, did not result in sustainable peace. Rather, these entities exist in a situation that could be described as 'no war, no peace'.[192] Apart from occasional sporadic violence, this is no longer a case of armed conflict, but since a solution is still eluding negotiators, it is not a case of peace either. Unrecognized states are not protected by norms of nonintervention; extinction is a permanent risk and this tends to foster pronounced siege mentalities.

Previous Status

The previous status of the entities also differs and this affects their position in the international system; they are all seen to violate the principle of territorial integrity—but some more than others. A number of unrecognized states, such as Nagorno Karabakh, South Ossetia, Abkhazia, Chechnya, and Kosovo, were autonomous regions, or autonomous republics. When the federations of which they were part started dissolving in the early 1990s, they appealed to the international community for recognition. However, international recognition was reserved for union republics and was consequently denied—at least until 2008, in the case of Kosovo. The former autonomous institutions could be used as a basis for the creation of state-like structures; this arguably gave these entities a head start over entities that lack such an institutional foundation.[193] It should be noted, however, that the former autonomous regions and the de facto independent territories do not necessarily coincide completely, as the latter in most cases represent ceasefire lines, and as the territorial ambitions of the separatist leaders often went further than the autonomous region extended. Thus, if we compare the territory controlled by the Nagorno Karabakh Republic with the Nagorno Karabakh Autonomous region, we see that two of its former provinces are partly under Azerbaijani control, but that the entity holds seven additional districts between Nagorno Karabakh and Armenia. These districts ensure access to the kin-state and function as a military buffer zone. Moreover, the Nagorno Karabakh Republic continues to claim the Azerbaijani-controlled region of Shahumian, which was not part of the Nagorno Karabakh Autonomous region.

Other entities used to be (more or less well-defined) geographic areas centred on territories where the local ethnic majority differed from the national majority population. Thus, Republika Srpska Krajina and Republika Srpska were made up of territories with a prewar Serb majority population, territories with a significant Serb minority, *and* strategically important adjoining territories. The same is true for Northern Cyprus. Still other territories are primarily defined by geographical features. Transnistria, for example, was not an autonomous region in the Soviet Union and is constituted by territory on the left bank of the Dniester River. Finally, some of the unrecognized states have a past as recognized states. After decolonization, Somaliland (formerly British Somaliland) was an independent state for five days in 1960 and was recognized by thirty-five states.[194] On 1 July 1960 Somaliland joined the former Trust Territory of Italian Somaliland under an Act of Union, thereby forming the state of Somalia.[195] Even more interesting is Taiwan, which experienced a gradual process of de-recognition. Following the Chinese civil war, Taiwan was recognized as the legitimate representative of China and retained China's seat on the UN Security Council. However, when diplomatic relations with the People's Republic of China were restored in the 1970s, the majority of states transferred their recognition; as a result, diplomatic relations were cut off and in 1971 Taiwan lost its UN seat.[196]

A pre-existing institutional framework has been argued to be crucial in building support for independence,[197] and it certainly affects the task facing these entities after they achieve de facto independence. The previous status, moreover, affects their position in the international system, in particular their degree of isolation.

Legitimizing Ideology: Ethnic or Civic Nationalism

Pegg argues that unrecognized states are illegitimate no matter what kind of entities they manage to create,[198] but attempts to legitimize their de facto independence are still a major preoccupation. The main argument for independence put forward by unrecognized states has for a long time been the right to self-determination. As it reads in Abkhazia's 1999 declaration of independence, 'we appeal to the UN, OSCE, and to all States of the world to recognize the independent State created by the people of Abkhazia on the basis of the right of nations to free self-determination'.[199] This self-determination has, in most cases, been ethnically defined. Republika Srpska Krajina was, for example, proclaimed as a state for the Serbs. It was argued to be a defensive act that was necessary in order to protect the Serb minority in Croatia against what they argued to be the genocidal regime of President Franjo Tudjman.[200] It was also claimed that Republika Srpska Krajina was historic Serb land and this argument was used to refute accusations of aggression: the Serbs 'cannot be an aggressor in [their] own territory'.[201]

However, not all self-determination movements are ethnically defined, and some unrecognized states, such as Transnistria and Somaliland, encompass different ethnicities or clans and have adopted a more civic form of nation-building.[202] The Transnistrian population was in 1989 made up of 40 per cent Moldovans, 28 per cent Ukrainians, and 26 per cent Russians.[203] Since all three nationalities have 'ethnic homeland states' outside Transnistria, an ethnically defined nationalism could not form the basis of the entity's nation-building project. Instead, the authorities have tried to promote 'Transnistrianness' as a new and distinct national identity.[204] Somaliland is similarly diverse in that it is made up of several clans. The Isaaq clan is the largest, making up some 70 per cent of Somaliland's population,[205] but in order to retain unity and avoid internal strife, the authorities have been keen to promote an inclusive civic identity.[206] Given these demographic characteristics, both Somaliland and Transnistria have in their claims to independence focused on historic continuity, rather than national identity. Somaliland's leaders point to the existence of Somaliland as a British protectorate and to its five days of internationally recognized independence in 1960.[207] The Transnistrian authorities similarly stress continuity and historical rights when they argue that Transnistria gained its first statehood in 1924, which is 'earlier than Moldavia'.[208]

It is also important to note that the kind of nationalism espoused is not static: the strength of its ethnic elements can change over time. Most notable in this regard is the case of Taiwan. Initially, the government promoted a national identity based on (mainland) Chinese culture and suppressed movements toward expression of local Taiwanese culture, for example, by banning the use of the Taiwanese language. The promotion of Chinese culture was part of Taiwan's claim to mainland China and it presented Taiwan as the bearer of tradition. As the entity moved away from its 'one China' policy and a process of indigenization and democratization of the regime took place, however, a more ethnic Taiwanese form of nationalism emerged.[209] This suggests that both attempts to gain international favour and internal dynamics affect the kind of ideologies that are espoused.

Arguments for recognition that are purely based on self-determination fight a losing battle. It seems that the leaders of these aspiring states have realized the limits to such claims. Unrecognized states consequently combine self-determination arguments with a claim to a 'remedial' right to secession, arguing that the parent states denied them civil and political rights and that they were subjected to egregious abuses.[210] The proclamation of the Nagorno Karabakh Republic, for example, stressed the alleged 'policy of apartheid and discrimination pursued in Azerbaijan'.[211] The Transnistrian authorities likewise contend that they have a moral entitlement to self-determination since Moldova attempted to resolve the conflict through the use of force.[212] They further justify their decision to secede by pointing to alleged discrimination: 'After the adoption by Moldova's parliament of a series of discriminatory laws...the people of [the] Dniester region had no option but to seek adequate measures to protect their rights and human dignity.'[213] The leader of the Tamil Tigers invoked an even stronger claim when he asserted, 'Our people are subjected to unprecedented assaults. Arrests, imprisonment, and torture, rape and sexual harassment, murders, disappearance, shelling, aerial bombing, and military offensives are continuing unchecked.' 'The uncompromising stance of Sinhala chauvinism', he continues, 'has left us with no other option but an independent state for the people of Tamil Eelam.'[214]

In response to international developments following the end of the Cold War, unrecognized states are moreover increasingly making claims to having created effective, democratic state-like entities and are arguing that they have thereby earned their right to recognition.[215] Again this demonstrates that the legitimizing ideology is far from static. The following chapters will demonstrate how the rhetoric employed by unrecognized states, as well as the type of entities they are trying to create, respond to both internal and external demands.

International Actions

International developments not only affect the legitimizing ideology of unrecognized states, they also significantly affect their initial emergence. This is of course a paradox: unrecognized states originate in the restricted right to self-determination and the inviolability of borders, but despite unwillingness to recognize these entities and a tendency to isolate them, international actions remain crucial, both for their initial creation and for their subsequent survival.

Most surprising, perhaps, is the way in which measures implemented to try to solve the conflict over these contested territories, in particular the deployment of peacekeepers, have assisted the creation of unrecognized statehood. Peacekeeping forces not only delineate the entity's de facto border; they also help protect it. This effect is most evident when the peacekeepers are sympathetic to, or directly supportive of, the unrecognized states. For example, Georgia long complained that the peacekeepers stationed in Abkhazia and South Ossetia functioned as border guards rather than observers of the ceasefire.[216] Russian peacekeepers in Transnistria have similarly functioned as 'a second line of defence behind which the Transnistrian authorities may pursue their state-building project'.[217] However, similar effects can be observed where the peacekeepers do not seek to ensure the continued existence of the unrecognized state. In Cyprus, for example, the United Nations has helped entrench the de facto independence of the Turkish Republic of Northern Cyprus for more than thirty-five years.

It should be noted that peacekeepers do not always have this effect. The authorities of Republika Srpska Krajina had hoped that the UN peacekeepers would help preserve the status quo,[218] but they remained passive when Croatian forces retook control of the territory, even though it violated the ceasefire they were meant to uphold. In the case of Katanga the mandate of the UN peacekeepers explicitly included the promotion of Congo's territorial integrity and they were instrumental in ending Katanga's de facto independence.[219] Peacekeepers are, moreover, not stationed in all unrecognized states. There are no peacekeepers in Nagorno Karabakh, in Somaliland, or in Taiwan. In Nagorno Karabakh a military stalemate has ensured the continuation of a ceasefire for the last sixteen years; in Somaliland the absence of a functioning Somali state assists the survival of Somaliland despite the lack of an actual ceasefire; while in Taiwan the decision of the regime not to formally declare independence helps preserve the status quo by reducing the risk of a Chinese military offensive and the island in any case enjoys U.S. protection.

Other forms of international action can also help the emergence and survival of unrecognized states. In the case of Iraqi Kurdistan, an independence movement had existed for years, but the creation of 'no fly' zones in 1992—even though explicitly carried out on the basis of Iraq's territorial integrity—helped a de facto independent entity to emerge.[220] Kolstø and Blakkisrud have similarly argued that the EU border assistance, which was deployed to prevent dangerous goods from being smuggled over the Transnistrian de facto border, also helped consolidate Transnistrian statehood.[221] But the most important source of support comes from patron states. The large majority of unrecognized states are reliant on an external patron for military and economic assistance and would have been unlikely to emerge victorious without it. Nagorno Karabakh, Republika Srpska Krajina, and Northern Cyprus have been described as cases of foreign aggression— by Armenia, Serbia, and Turkey, respectively—and Transnistria's de facto statehood is argued to ultimately hinge 'on Russia's willingness to renew' its 'security guarantee'.[222] Events in August 2008 likewise made it abundantly clear that Russia provides an essential security guarantee for Abkhazia and South Ossetia. While these may be extreme examples, nearly all unrecognized states are dependent on some form of external support, not only for their initial creation but also for their survival as de facto independent entities. This situation has been described as states 'on the dole'.[223] Such dependence would seem to undermine their claims to independence, and unrecognized states are, consequently, often rejected as nothing but the puppets of external actors. Their survival and the nature of their development cannot, however, be reduced to this factor alone. As will be shown in the following chapters, unrecognized states often have access to other sources of external support and are keen to diversify. The position of unrecognized states in the international system and the forms of international engagement that are open to them are therefore important to their ability to entrench their de facto independence. And despite their common lack of recognition, we find considerable variation when international linkages are concerned.

International Position

In the case of collective nonrecognition, states are precluded from engagement that assists the illegal situation. The UN member states were consequently under obligation to refrain from 'lending any support or any form of assistance to South Africa with reference to its occupation of Namibia'. This included abstaining from 'entering into economic and other forms of relationship or dealings with South Africa on behalf of or concerning Namibia which may entrench its authority over the Territory'.[224] Secessionist conflicts are, in any case, classified as purely domestic affairs and the principle of noninterference therefore bars other states from providing assistance to the secessionist movements.[225] The international system of sovereign states is rigged to ensure that the parent state prevails;[226] it functions as a very effective gatekeeper to new entrants, and especially to entities that have been deemed undesirable. Even though the legal position of unrecognized states is less clear than the cases of collective non-recognition mentioned earlier,[227] the default position has therefore been non-engagement. But we do find some variation based primarily on security concerns, strategic interests and, secondarily, their path of creation. The position of unrecognized states consequently ranges from almost complete pariah status, in the case of Republika Srpska Krajina, to extensive engagement and membership of international organizations, in the case of Taiwan.[228] The cost of nonrecognition therefore varies significantly. In most cases, the unrecognized states are not actively opposed—the parent states, for example, rarely receive military backing—they are ignored; they are not part of the exclusive 'club of sovereign states' and there is significant unwillingness to engage in any activity that could be seen as endorsing them.

The Serb statelets in wartime Croatia and Bosnia were associated by the international community with the illegal use of force and ethnic cleansing. Their claims to self-determination were viewed as illegitimate and they were facing almost complete international isolation. Sanctions were imposed against the Federal Republic of Yugoslavia in May 1992 and this significantly reduced the supply of resources to the two entities,[229] and sanctions specifically targeting the statelets followed in 1993.[230] This isolation also affected international efforts to end the conflict. The mediators preferred to deal with leaders of recognized states and were often unwilling to engage with the leaders of the Serb statelets in Croatia and Bosnia. This position was made possible by viewing the conflict through the lens of ethnicity and monolithic representation; the local Serb leaders were thus regarded as the puppets of the Serbian president, Slobodan Milošević. Only once it became clear that intra-Serb consensus or control could not always be assumed, were the local Serb leaders reluctantly included in the peace talks.[231] While their demands for recognition were dismissed as illegitimate, there was consequently a hesitant willingness to engage with these entities, or rather their leaderships, in negotiations. Any other engagement, however, was regarded as strictly depoliticized and was limited to supplying humanitarian aid and deploying peacekeepers who were mandated to uphold ceasefires and protect 'safe areas'. When negotiations failed, the parent states were offered military support to defeat the Serb statelets.

The unrecognized states in the Caucasus also experienced blockades. The Commonwealth of Independent States (CIS) imposed sanctions on Abkhazia in 1996, including a full trade embargo, which meant that the illegal trading of agricultural products was the only means of subsistence for the inhabitants.[232] Border restrictions were partially lifted in 1999 and Russia formally lifted the blockade in 2008.[233] Armenia has since 1993 been subject to a blockade from Turkey, which has also had a detrimental effect on Karabakh, as Armenia constitutes its only link to the outside world.[234] However, the main international policy toward unrecognized states in the Caucasus has been to ignore them, however; apart from the very extensive involvement of external patrons, the Caucasus entities have seen little international engagement. The arguments of the parent states have largely been accepted—the entities are illegal, they represent a de facto occupation, they are based on ethnic cleansing and their leaderships lack any popular legitimacy—and international engagement is only undertaken if explicitly approved by the parent states,[235] and it is always deliberately depoliticized.[236] International organizations do not engage with the authorities and the involvement has therefore largely been framed as an issue of human security and grassroots development,[237] which is not problematic in relation to the principle of territorial integrity.

This almost complete lack of engagement constitutes a change from the situation in which the pre-1945 unrecognized states found themselves. In the nineteenth century, political contacts were established with the newly de facto independent South American states, despite Spain's resistance to their recognition.[238] Before World War I, nonrecognition had very little impact as long as effective control had been established and relations with unrecognized entities were also maintained in the interwar period and into World War II. China did not recognize Manchukuo, and argued that its existence violated its territorial integrity, but it still established official ties for trade, communications, and transportation,[239] and the U.S., which had spearheaded the collective nonrecognition of the entity, was keen to maintain its commercial interests in Manchukuo and actually increased its exports to it.[240] This situation changed following the outbreak of war, when relations became more sharply defined by military alliances. But the Independent State of Croatia, which was under significant German and Italian control, nevertheless established relations with neutral Turkey. It failed to achieve a formal trade agreement, but cultural relations were established, meetings were held with the Croatian Ambassador to Bulgaria, and Turkey clearly demonstrated its reluctance to cut off the entity completely.[241] International engagement was even afforded to separatist entities still involved in active conflict. Thus, the recognition of belligerency allowed external parties to maintain, or establish, commercial relations with separatist forces with either the approval of the parent state *or* if the belligerents had achieved the character of an organized government.[242] There was consequently a less clear dividing line between sovereign and nonsovereign entities.

The lack of international engagement with contemporary unrecognized states has important consequences. Unrecognized states are unable to obtain loans from international credit institutions; they are barred from membership of international organizations; international laws and regulations do not apply on their territories, which tends to discourage foreign investors; international markets are often closed to them; their inhabitants are unable to travel unless they can obtain (and are willing to use) passports from their parent states or external patron; and visitors are in some cases very actively discouraged from travelling to these unrecognized entities either through warnings on foreign office websites or legislation in the parent states which makes such travel an offence.[243]

Is this as significant as suggested by the constitutive approach in international law? Do these international rights and responsibilities constitute the *sine qua non* of statehood? First, as will be further explored in the following chapter, there are other sources of international support. We have already touched on the importance of an external patron, but a number of unrecognized states also receive significant support from a diaspora population, which can help fund their state-building project and at times provide the necessary expertise. Second, there are exceptions to the general rule of international isolation. Even in the case of collective nonrecognition some pragmatism is allowed for. The key is to refrain from relations that would imply the legality of the situation or help support it, but this does not extend to acts unrelated to the occupation, or acts that would harm rather than benefit the territory's population.[244] A similar distinction has allowed for the supply of humanitarian aid to a number of unrecognized states and the acceptance of travel documents from, for example, Northern Cyprus, deeming that these are 'no more than evidence of identity and not...recognition of a separate TRNC'.[245] But in some cases, due to economic or security considerations, the international engagement has gone a lot further and these unrecognized states consequently find themselves in a less isolated position.

The most notable examples are Somaliland and Taiwan. Somaliland's independence is supported by Rwanda, South Africa, and Zambia, but neighbouring states are strongly opposed and the entity remains completely unrecognized.[246] Even so, there has been a process of creeping international acceptance, which in some cases approaches de facto recognition.[247] Somaliland has developed 'functional relationships' with its neighbour Ethiopia; it has signed formal memoranda with Britain and Denmark on the repatriation of failed asylum seekers; EU and UN agencies have offices in Somaliland to manage their aid programmes; the Somaliland authorities have cooperated with Western intelligence services on counterterrorism; and Somaliland ministers and government employees are able to travel on Somaliland passports.[248] Moreover, international actors are not afraid to involve themselves in the domestic politics of the entity, which is usually an anathema when unrecognized states are concerned. Thus, the British Embassy in Addis Ababa funded a consultant to revise the electoral law for the 2005 elections[249] and sponsored a team of international observers.[250] This greater degree of international engagement can be explained by Somaliland's strategic position on the Horn of Africa, by fear of instability, *and* by the lack of effective opposition from Somaliland's parent state, Somalia. An even more interesting example is Taiwan. Taiwan remains recognized by twenty-three states, but even states that have switched their recognition to the People's Republic of China have retained links with Taiwan. The U.S. has a 'de facto embassy' in Taiwan, the American Institute in Taiwan (AIT), which is technically a private organization staffed by career diplomats who are officially 'on leave'. The Taiwanese counterpart in Washington, and twelve other U.S. cities, is known as the Taipei Economic and Cultural Representative Office (TECRO).[251] Similar links are found with other countries. Russia, for example, has a representative office in Taipei, and Taiwan has a representative office in Moscow; Japan has maintained nongovernmental, working-level relations; and there are unconfirmed reports of military collaboration between Singapore and Taiwan.[252] Similar, innovative arrangements have allowed Taiwan to join international organizations, almost as if it were a (recognized) state.[253] Under the name 'Separate Customs Territory of Taiwan, Penghu, Kinmen, and Matsu' (short form: Chinese Taipei) Taiwan participates in the World Trade Organization and the entity is also a member of the Asian Development Bank. In addition, Taiwan maintains extensive worldwide economic, transport, and trade links, and several states have enacted legislation to enable continued commercial relations.[254]

The principle of territorial integrity can therefore sometimes be trumped, or at least mediated, by other interests, but international engagement remains the exception rather than the rule and has tended to be ad hoc. Krasner argues that alternative arrangements in the case of Taiwan provide the 'functional equivalent of recognition',[255] but even though Taiwan has been ready to distort its de facto independent status and has not formally declared independence, the lack of recognition still comes with restrictions. This is one of the reasons why Taiwan has become one of the leading forces behind an attempt to open the international system to unrecognized states.[256] Not all international organizations will, for example, allow Taiwan to join: it is not a member of the United Nations, the World Bank or the International Monetary Fund and it only has observer status (as Chinese Taipei) in the World Health Organization (and then only on the basis of an invitation). When China gained admission to the Asian Development Bank—of which Taiwan is a founding member—Taiwan was allowed to remain a member, but despite its protests Taiwan is now referred to as 'Taipei, China'.[257] Also, many countries have restricted the entry of high-ranking Taiwanese officials as they are worried that any visit could be construed as a state visit and thereby as a de facto recognition of Taiwan. International engagement is significantly restricted by the fear of damaging relations with China and therefore remains conditional on the acceptance of the parent state.

Territorial integrity and thereby the acceptance of the parent state remains primary, even in these cases of more extensive international engagement. It is telling to compare this with the case of Macedonia, which was denied recognition by Greece due to a dispute over its name. However, the state's right to exist was not disputed and Greece's opposition did not prevent other states from establishing extensive relations. The state even joined the UN two years before recognition by the European Union was finally achieved.[258] Full external sovereignty is often not required by international organizations, which is also illustrated by the fact that several non-self-governing territories have been allowed to join. For example, Western Sahara is a member of the African Union; Bermuda and American Samoa are members of the International Olympic Committee; and Gibraltar is a member of Interpol (sub-bureau).[259] Even more noteworthy is the fact that India and the Philippines were founding members of the UN at a time when they were not still formally independent, and UN membership for Ukraine and Belorussia was also accepted, despite their lack of independent statehood, in a bid by the U.S. to improve relations with the Soviet Union.[260]

For other anomalies in the international system, sovereignty is not necessarily interpreted as 'either / or', either entirely present or absent. This reflects the view of sovereignty as multifaceted. For contemporary unrecognized states, however, sovereignty continues to be viewed as a dichotomy. These entities violate the principle of territorial integrity and parent states' approval is therefore deemed necessary for any form of engagement. Sovereignty is not a fact, it is 'a claim about the way political power is or should be exercised'; part of its function is to explain and justify political and economic arrangements 'as if they belonged to the natural order of things'.[261] The cost of nonrecognition for unrecognized states therefore depends on their ability to muster international goodwill and on the position of their parent state.

Security Implications of Nonrecognition

The relative international isolation faced by unrecognized states does not necessarily translate into a lack of international interest. Despite their often modest size, unrecognized states feature frequently in the international media and create headaches for international policymakers. This interest is explained in large part by the threat of instability and renewed warfare associated with these entities. Unrecognized states result from warfare, they tend to be located in volatile regions, and the risk of renewed instability is forever present. This was aptly demonstrated by the Russian-Georgian war in August 2008, and similar security concerns exist in other cases.

The security concerns associated with unrecognized states fall in two broad camps: (1) risks associated with porous borders and unregulated territories, and (2) the risk of renewed warfare over the contested territory. While the former is often overplayed, the latter—although it has rarely emanated from the unrecognized state itself—is much more serious.

Risks from Territories Outside Effective Control

As noted in the previous chapter, much has been made of the risk that these territories can turn into anarchical badlands. This image is very similar to that of failed states and implies that a vacuum in authority will quickly be filled by criminals who make immense profits from the smuggling of dangerous goods, including radioactive material.

Although smuggling certainly exists in a large number of unrecognized states, it has already been argued that this encompasses goods such as tangerines that represent no security risk whatsoever. In fact, EU border monitoring in Transnistria has found that the smuggled goods mostly consisted of frozen chickens and similar goods, not drugs and weapons.[262] International observers had for years warned that dangerous articles were smuggled across the border and described Transnistria as a criminal black hole,[263] so although we cannot rule out that such smuggling occurs elsewhere, the Transnistrian findings should serve as a caution against alarmist assumptions. The potential security risk associated with smuggling from, and through, unrecognized states is greater while the war is still ongoing. But, as will be demonstrated in the following chapters, once violence ceased the de facto authorities were actually able to exert greater control over the territory than is often assumed. This does of course not preclude criminal activity, as the authorities may be complicit, but it is still a different scenario than the out-of-control areas of the popular imagination.

Another threat that has sometimes been mentioned is that these territories can be used as a breeding ground for terrorists. Again, this is drawn from the presumed 'out-of-control' character of unrecognized states and the argument is made, in particular, by parent states. In 2001 the president of Azerbaijan, for example, argued that one should not distinguish between separatism and terrorism, since 'separatism is the mother of terrorism'.[264] The risk of terrorism in the case of Nagorno Karabakh is hard to substantiate, but there *are* examples of terrorism and other forms of violent acts emanating from or associated with unrecognized states. The main example of this is the case of Tamil Eelam, where the Tamil Tigers continued using terrorism against Sri Lankan targets in their ongoing attempt to consolidate and expand the de facto independence of the entity. Terrorist forces have, in some cases, come from outside the unrecognized state, or at least been financed by external sources. During the three years of Chechen de facto independence, Islamic extremists became increasingly prominent in Chechnya, and ever since Russia regained control of the territory they have used terrorist attacks to try to separate the territory anew. In other cases, the unrecognized states have themselves been the target of terrorist attacks. In Somaliland in 2008, at least thirty people were killed when car bombs exploded outside the Ethiopian embassy and UN offices in Hargeisa. Responsibility was claimed by the Islamist militant group Al-Shabab, which is challenging the transitional government in Somalia and has gained control over large parts of the state. Since then, Somaliland police have reportedly foiled several terrorist acts.[265] Terrorist acts can therefore also emanate from within the parent state. This illustrates that this form of violence in the majority of cases stems from the unresolved conflict; it stems from the ongoing dispute over territory rather than from the ungoverned status of the territory.[266] This brings us to the second form of security threat associated with unrecognized states: the risk of renewed warfare.

Risk of Renewed Warfare

Kolstø and Blakkisrud have convincingly argued that unrecognized states tend to be status quo players.[267] They won the first round of warfare and are trying to consolidate control over the territory they conquered and gain international recognition. They would therefore seem to have little incentive to start a new war. There are, however, exceptions. Unrecognized states frequently do not control all the territory to which they lay claim. Their de facto border in most cases represents a ceasefire and they may have ambitions for further territorial gains. Such territory could, in some cases, make it easier to defend the entity or could make it more economically viable. For example, Somaliland in 2007 captured the capital of the Sool region from Puntland forces,[268] and further violent conflict over the territory controlled by Somaliland cannot be ruled out. In most cases unrecognized states are, however, unlikely to be the initiator of renewed warfare; this role usually falls on the parent state.

The de facto loss of territory is often a significant burden on the parent state and their claim to the lost territory has not been abandoned. The parent states often hope that time is on their side: they hope that the unrecognized state becomes gradually weaker due to international isolation, while they themselves have the time to build up a stronger army. Inspiration for such a strategy can be found in Croatia's successful military offensive against Republika Srpska Krajina, Russia's brutal reintegration of Chechnya, and Sri Lanka's devastating attack on Tamil Eelam. Even though these conflicts are often described as 'frozen conflicts', war is never far away. Military exercises, preferably close to the front line, are a common occurrence; shootings across the front line are frequent; and both sides engage in bellicose rhetoric. Only in a few cases does the conflict actually appear frozen, with genuine cessation of violence: in Transnistria, there have been no reports of incidents resulting in casualties since 1992.[269]

The threats to security are therefore very real, but they tend to be of a different kind than the ones often attributed to unrecognized states. The risk of smuggling of nuclear material or the risk of these territories becoming terrorist havens is much smaller than the risk of a new and very bloody war over the contested territory. Chapter 6 will discuss what can be done to overcome this risk.

The Politics of Unrecognized States

A legacy of armed conflict and war is common to unrecognized states and their emergence was in all cases affected by both international actions and inactions. While the former is emphasized in the literature, the latter is often overlooked. Moreover, their paths of creation otherwise show significant variations: some unrecognized states are born out of secessionist warfare, others result from state-collapse; some used to be recognized states, others were autonomous regions, while still others were ill-defined geographical areas; some emphasize an ethnically defined identity, while others tried to mobilize their populations through a more inclusive identity. It is important to recognize this flexibility within the category of unrecognized states; it demonstrates that unrecognized states are far from being a static or completely homogenous category, and the differences matter for the position of unrecognized states in the international system and their ability to create effective statehood.

Although there are significant variations in their position in the international system—ranging from pariah status to extensive engagement—all unrecognized states are constrained by their lack of recognition. Without parent-state approval, international engagement is kept to an absolute minimum. Even in cases where the parent state does not function as an effective entity or where the unrecognized state has deliberately refrained from declaring independence—thus not violating the principle of territorial integrity—a number of doors remain closed. This sets contemporary unrecognized states apart from historical cases and from other anomalies in the international system.

Unrecognized states are only to a very limited extent accommodated by the international system of sovereign states; the dominant trend is one of isolation.

This raises questions about their survival: how do unrecognized states survive in the international system, and what kind of entity are they able to create? Somaliland has its own currency, army and government, and it also provides public services such as health and education.[270] But does this make a 'state in all but name', or does the lack of recognition render it something else? This is the focus of the following chapters.

3 SURVIVING IN THE MODERN INTERNATIONAL SYSTEM

Unrecognized states all find themselves in a position of limbo in the international system and their paths of creation also show striking similarities. Yet the fact of nonrecognition does not fully determine the kind of entity that is likely to evolve. A quick glance at a few examples demonstrates remarkable variation in stability, prosperity and level of development. Arriving in Taiwan's modern international airport, most travellers would for example fail to notice that this was anything other than a normal state. The airport is the world's fifteenth-busiest air freight hub and thirteenth-busiest airport by international passenger traffic.[271] The capital of Taiwan, Taipei, has seen substantial regeneration since the late 1980s. A light-rail network was built, environmental laws strengthened, and the city went from being an ugly, albeit wealthy, duckling of Asia 'to one of the region's most dynamic, comfortable and liveable cities'.[272] The few visitors who venture into the far reaches of the Caucasus Mountains and find themselves in Nagorno Karabakh would have quite a different experience and be struck by a couple of things in particular: by the entity's isolation and small size, by the tanks frequently transported through the streets, but also by the economic growth that has turned the capital into a veritable building site, and perhaps the large billboard depicting a mass wedding which was held with the purpose of revitalizing the entity's deteriorating demographics. Finally, when driving through Croatian Krajina the most noticeable features of the region are its remoteness, the rough beauty of its landscape, and a distinct lack of people. There are almost no traces of the state that was once proclaimed on this territory; no state institutions, no flags, no army. Only the many burned-out houses and empty villages point to the region's recent history of contested statehood and remind us of the failed project of Republika Srpska Krajina. Even before Croatian forces regained control of the main part of the territory, in August 1995, the claim to independence had a utopian, or perhaps dystopian, ring to it. Krajina had all the characteristics of a state: a territory, a population, and a government,[273] and several state institutions were created, but its four years of existence were marked by infighting, rampant war profiteering, and economic collapse. Former inhabitants argue that the entity was in fact a 'ghetto'.[274]

Some unrecognized states therefore come relatively close to realizing the separatist dreams of (de facto) independent statehood, security and prosperity, but in other cases the reality is markedly different. Despite this variation in their level of state-building, almost all unrecognized states manage to create the basic trappings of statehood: an army, a government, courts, media, a national anthem, a flag, licence plates, and perhaps a separate currency. Unrecognized states have, moreover, demonstrated considerable staying power and all make similar claims to having created effective, democratic entities. This chapter and the following analyse the process of state-building in unrecognized states: how do they manage to survive and what kind of entities evolve in the absence of international recognition: are they merely states-in-waiting that have reached different levels of state-building, or is there something qualitatively different about unrecognized statehood? The external sources of state-building are analysed in this chapter, while the following chapter focuses on the internal ones.

External Sources of Unrecognized State-Building

Unrecognized states may face a degree of international isolation, but are at the same time dependent on external forces for their survival: they rely on support from external patrons, diaspora populations, and other transborder linkages, and have sometimes even established limited relations with their parent states. These forms of external support come at a price, but they are essential for the survival of unrecognized states. The need to attract such support and the hope of achieving international recognition also affects the kinds of statehood that emerge from the context of nonrecognition. Self-justification is a key to their foreign policy,[275] and their statehood is renegotiated in view of external developments: how do they best make themselves worthy of recognition? Unrecognized statehood is therefore in some ways reminiscent of Alice in Wonderland: state identities are in flux and the entities are continuously trying to catch up with the white rabbit that is the international community.

State-Building: From Territorial Control to Effective Entities

State-building can be divided into a number of (frequently overlapping) phases.[276] The first step is to establish physical control over the territory covered by the state. This step has been achieved by all unrecognized states; it is a definitional requirement that they must enjoy de facto control over (most of) the territory they claim to rule. The second step is to establish a monopoly on the legitimate use of violence and credible military defensive capabilities. Unrecognized states have proven their ability to defend their territory, even if this may not be sustainable in the long term, but establishing a monopoly on the legitimate use of violence has often proved more difficult. The legacy of war has had a significant impact on the process of state-building in unrecognized states, and a number of them have struggled to establish control over warring warlords. Chechnya is infamous for the chaos created by infighting warlords, but Somaliland also suffered from heavy internal fighting in the early 1990s.[277] This second phase of state-building relates to a very Weberian understanding of statehood: a state is defined by its monopoly on the legitimate use of violence. There is more to state-building than this, however. It also involves the delivery of basic public services; not just security, but also services such as water and electricity supply and, more ambitious, health and education. This is based on the view that the state's authority is founded on a social contract between the ruler and the ruled; the state provides necessary services in exchange for loyalty.[278] This third phase concerns state capacity: the ability of the rulers to exercise their authority. In other words, it is about the creation of internal sovereignty. There is, however, one additional aspect to state-building, an aspect that may come into existence before the third phase, possibly even before the first and the second. Some term this 'nation-building',[279] others refer to it as the 'idea of the state'[280] or simply internal legitimacy.[281] The emphasis differs—is a sense of common identity, for example, required?—but all terms refer to the legitimacy of the state in the eyes of the population.

State-building can in all its phases beneficially be viewed as an interplay between internal and external forces. Jackson argues that when it comes to state-building, the international community can at most assist or hinder it, and I. W. Zartman likewise points to the importance of indigenous leadership,[282] but we should not overlook the ways in which statehood is affected by international norms and practices. Moreover, state-building requires resources and these will often have to come from external sources. As Zartman argues, 'States need some emergency pump-priming to get the machine started.'[283] This is especially the case if the starting point is a war-ravaged entity where the men with the guns rule and the economy is in ruins.

State-Building Through Self-Reliance?

The odds on survival are clearly stacked against some unrecognized states. Republika Srpska Krajina did not have autonomous institutions to build on, only municipal institutions that were far from well-developed. Moreover, the geography of the entity was hardly conducive to state-building. Republika Srpska Krajina consisted of three different regions: two of them were connected by a corridor, while the third, Eastern Slavonia, Baranja, and Western Srem, was connected to Serbia, but not to the two other regions. A former advisor to the Croatian president dismissed the territory as 'the Philippines on land'.[284] Odd-shaped countries are found elsewhere, but this kind of geography and the associated difficulty of free movement certainly impede attempts to impose central control. Republika Srpska Krajina was, finally, suffering due to the ongoing war in the former Yugoslavia; international sanctions that only excluded 'essential humanitarian supplies including medical supplies and foodstuffs distributed by international humanitarian agencies'[285] were imposed, and the supply of resources to the entity was consequently severely affected. State-building was therefore a tall order indeed, but the entity did have access to limited, if diminishing, resources from its kin-state and other entities in a similar situation, such as Abkhazia, somehow managed to pull through.

The situation in Nagorno Karabakh also shows a lot of similarities. The entity may have had institutions on which to build, but the reality facing people when they finally emerged from their shelters in 1994 differed markedly from what they had started fighting for in the late 1980s. They had managed to fight off Azerbaijan's control, but great losses had been suffered in the war, the entity's infrastructure was more or less completely destroyed, and poverty was severe. Daily life was more about survival than anything else. Given this starting point, it is indeed remarkable that the authorities, with some justification, are now making claims to being an effective entity.

A difficult starting point is therefore not an insurmountable obstacle to building a functioning entity. Moreover, if we look at Taiwan, which has a per capita GDP of $16,423 and is the world's leading producer of a range of IT products,[286] one could even argue that the lack of international recognition does not stand in the way of economic development and that lack of resources is not necessarily a problem. Most unrecognized states would, however, find it hard to emulate Taiwan's success—the entity was after all recognized for decades and enjoys the backing of the U.S. The mean tendency is probably closer to a case such as Somaliland, whose GDP per capita was estimated at only $226 in 2003.[287] As a comparison, South Ossetia's GDP per capita was in 2002 estimated at $250[288] and Abkhazia's was in 2001 estimated at $350.[289] The Abkhaz authorities argue that by 2009, it had increased to $2530.[290] Alexis Heraclides argues that many secessionist movements opt for self-reliance due to the high cost of third party involvement,[291] but this is often not an option for unrecognized states. The building of effective entities, capable of survival, brings with it the undeniable need for external assistance. This results in the paradoxical situation that external dependence is necessary in order for de facto independence—from the parent state—to be maintained.

Patron States

It is impossible to understand the creation and survival of de facto states without reference to external actors,[292] and the entities are, more often than not, dependent on support from a patron state.[293] The importance of neighbouring states for the escalation of separatist conflicts is increasingly recognized in the literature: neighbouring states who share ethnicity with a minority across the border may help incite separatist sentiments or offer military and financial support once such movements emerge.[294] The involvement of patron states is not predicated on the existence of ethnic ties, however, nor does it stop once de facto independence has been achieved; in some cases, it actually intensifies. Due to their lack of international recognition, unrecognized states are not spoilt for choice when it comes to attracting external support, and patron states therefore fill an important gap. Based on ethnic links and/or strategic interests, these states choose to support unrecognized states with diplomatic, economic, and military assistance. Such external support helps compensate for the lack of international recognition and significantly assists the process of state-building. Military support helps the entities achieve the first and the second phase of state-building—establish territorial control and impose a monopoly on the legitimate use of violence—while economic support is needed in order for authorities to build infrastructure, create governing institutions, and provide basic public services; that is the third phase of state-building. However, the degree of support received often leads to the accusation that these entities are nothing but the puppets of external actors,[295] or at least states 'on the dole'.[296]

Most attention has been given to the military support provided by external patrons. The continued survival of unrecognized states in many cases depends on exactly this kind of support. If the entities are unable to defend themselves, it does not matter how effective they have become at delivering basic public services. Vital military support is, or was, provided by Russia in the case of Abkhazia, South Ossetia, and Transnistria; Armenia in the case of Nagorno Karabakh; Turkey in the case of Northern Cyprus; Serbia in the case of Republika Srpska Krajina and Republika Srpska. In these cases, troops were deployed and assisted both in the initial military victory and in the subsequent defence of the unrecognized state. The precise role of the patron state is, however, often contested. Armenia argues that it only provides financial support for the armed forces in Nagorno Karabakh;[297] and Serbia similarly downplayed its involvement in the Serb statelets, arguing that they supported their ethnic brethren across the border but denied direct military involvement. Irredentist activities are usually denied due to the risk of international repercussions. In other cases, such military support is explained as 'peacekeeping'. This is the case in Transnistria, where the Russian peacekeepers still provide a vital security guarantee, even though Russian involvement was initially 'more by default than by design'.[298] The Russian military involvement in Abkhazia and South Ossetia similarly used to be legitimized as peacekeeping, but Russia has, since its recognition of the two entities, signed a deal with both of them that gives Moscow the power to guard their borders.[299] U.S. support of Taiwan does not include recognition of its independence—which has in any case not been declared—but it does include a security guarantee that has helped deter a Chinese military offensive. In addition to such more-or-less acknowledged direct military involvement or security guarantees, the armed forces of unrecognized states frequently receive significant funding from their patrons. Armenia, for example, acknowledges that it supplies substantial equipment and weaponry to the Karabakh army and its officers assist with training.[300]

Without this kind of support, unrecognized states would in many cases be unable to defend their de facto independence. However, the support from patron states goes beyond military support. They also help create effective entities, they help create functioning statehood. Armenia, for example, serves as a vital economic lifeline for Nagorno Karabakh; Karabakh uses the Armenian currency, its inhabitants use Armenian passports, and Armenia grants the entity a so-called inter-state loan, which in the first years after the war made up the vast majority of Karabakh's budget.[301] Armenia, moreover, provides the main market for products from Nagorno Karabakh and constitutes its only link with the outside world. In fact, when it comes to economy, culture, and defence, Nagorno Karabakh and Armenia can be seen as a single space.[302] Similarly, Russia has since 2002 provided the inhabit-ants of Abkhazia and South Ossetia with passports, it has paid local pensions, and has contributed significantly to their state budgets.[303] In the case of Transnistria, Russia is the source of (semi-)private invest-ments, it is a major market for exports, and it provides loans and credit, helps with pensions and has ensured the continued flow of subsidized gas, even in the face of nonpayment.[304] A final example is the case of Northern Cyprus, which remains completely dependent on Turkey for its economic viability: the Turkish lira is used in the entity, the head of the central bank is a Turkish citizen[305] and Turkey provides financial support in the form of aid, loans and subsidies.[306] In extreme cases, unrecognized states are so short on resources that patron states even manage their foreign relations for them. Republika Srpska Krajina's strategy for gaining international recognition was, for example, left almost entirely to Belgrade.[307] The Krajina ministry of foreign affairs was only formed in November 1992, nearly a year after independence was declared, and documents from the time describe how the ministry lacked even the most basic resources and had prob-lems recruiting professional diplomats or even people with a command of foreign languages.[308] They simply did not have the resources to fulfil this aspect of effective statehood.

Significant dependence results from such support: if the patron state decides to pull its resources, then even the basic survival of these enti-ties would be open to questioning. But the unrecognized states point out that they have few alternatives to their reliance on patron states: 'Who else will lend us money?'[309] Dependence on a patron state can therefore be seen as a function of international isolation: the more isolated the entity, the more important the patron state becomes. In some cases, such dependence does indeed appear to be reluctantly embraced and the image of a willing puppet should perhaps be replaced with that of a coerced puppet. There is a difference between being dependent on a 'patron state', due to isolation and lack of alternatives, and *wanting* it to be that way. For example, when Moscow's favoured candidate was defeated in the 2004 presidential elections in Abkhazia, it was described by a leading civil-society activist as a 'serious demonstration that we are not in Russia's pockets'.[310] In other cases, the linkages are of a much more voluntary nature and based on stronger ties. While the leaders of Republika Srpska Krajina in 1991 proclaimed their separation from Croatia based on the right to national self-determination, they did not proclaim a separate identity; their national identity was shared with the Serbs in Serbia proper. Such ambiguity when it comes to the claim to independence is found in a number of unrecognized states; for example in Nagorno Karabakh, South Ossetia, and Northern Cyprus. Many of these independence claims were initially more strategic than anything else; it was thought to improve their position at the negotiating table, or the goal of joining their kin-state was deemed even more elusive than the goal of independence. But over time this initial pragmatism has in some cases turned into gradual development of separate identities. Pragmatism can also work the other way around: relations with an external patron are in some cases guided primarily by the need for resources, and only secondarily by any form of emotional ties, but this form of dependence can also lead to ambiguity when it comes to the demand for independence. For example, the inhabitants of Transnistria in 2006 voted for Transnistrian independence and, at the same time, for 'future association' with the Russian Federation.[311]

Such close ties come at a price. It might help unrecognized states create effective entities, but it also detracts from the substance of their de facto independence. Patron states often exert significant influence over unrecognized states, either through the more or less explicit threat of withdrawal or through the targeted supply of resources. For example, in the case of Republika Srpska Krajina, the leaders knew that their most important audience was in Belgrade, not in the entity households, since their independent statehood along with their political careers were doomed projects without the support of the kin-state. If they did not follow Belgrade's tune, they knew that resources would simply be transferred to a rival leader.[312] Belgrade supplied most of its resources to the strategic region of Eastern Slavonia, and this resulted in a greater sense of security and less hardship in this region, but it also had a negative side: Eastern Slavonia became a haven for war profiteers who made fortunes from smuggling goods to Belgrade, which was after all only a two- to three-hour drive away,[313] and it was ruled with an iron fist by the paramilitary leader Arkan, whose job was to ensure Belgrade's continued control.[314] In the case of Abkhazia, Moscow resorted to bullying tactics when its preferred candidate lost the 2004 elections: it threatened to stop the transfer of pensions and issuing of Russian passports and closed the border, thereby cutting off Abkhazia's lifeline, until a power-sharing agreement was reached between the two candidates.[315]

The significant dependence on patron states—not just for the initial creation of unrecognized states, but also for their subsequent survival and development of effective statehood—makes it tempting to reduce unrecognized states to this factor alone; without a patron state, they remain but ephemeral phenomena. Support for such a case could be found in the relatively short-lived existence of Chechnya, which lacked a patron, and the two Serb statelets that saw a significant drop in patron-state support, or perhaps even in the recent demise of Tamil Eelam. It would, however, be a mistake to overlook some of the complexities characterizing the relationship between unrecognized states and their patrons. First of all, external dependence is often a two-way street, especially when a kin-state is involved.[316] A kin-state is likely to be somewhat constrained by shared ethnicity and the kin-state leader may be held politically responsible for the fate of the co-ethnics across the border. This limits their room for manoeuvre and their ability to control the unrecognized states. As the advisor to the Nagorno Karabakh president confidently puts it, the question is actually 'Who depends on whom?'[317] Nagorno Karabakh has great symbolic importance and Armenian leaders ignore the entity at their peril. The entity's leaders also have a more direct impact on Armenian politics and have on more than one occasion shown their potential power when it counts. In the late 1990s the Armenian president, Levon Ter-Petrosyan, was forced to resign after he agreed to a phased approach to the Karabakh conflict, rather than the package solution which the Karabakh leadership demanded, and the former president of Nagorno Karabakh, Robert Kocharian, took his place—the periphery had taken over the centre.[318] It would therefore be misleading to see Nagorno Karabakh merely as a state 'on the dole':[319] it certainly finds itself in a position of influence that would be the envy of most recipients of income benefits. Nagorno Karabakh is admittedly an extreme example, in which the patron-client relationship is almost reversed, but clients do fall out with their patrons and the relationship is not as one-sided as the puppeteer-image would have us believe. Such a process was also seen in the case of the self-proclaimed Serb entities in wartime Bosnia and Croatia; from being in a near-symbiotic relationship with the Serbian regime in Belgrade, the local leaders one by one fell out with their former benefactor and began to assert their autonomy.[320] Similar strains are even found in the case of Northern Cyprus, despite Turkey's recognition of the entity and its very extensive support. The Turkish Cypriots have, in fact, gone from complete loyalty toward Ankara to a more complex relationship and there are now significant forces in Northern Cyprus, including the entity's president, that advocate a loosening of ties with the kin-state.

Moreover, some unrecognized states manage through other means. Somaliland does not enjoy the support of a patron state nor did Bougainville, and although Taiwan and Iraqi Kurdistan benefit from a level of U.S. support, including a security guarantee in the former case, they are not propped up by their external backer to the same extent as some of the examples above. Even in cases of significant patron support, the level of support often fluctuates. Abkhazia and South Ossetia did not receive sustained support from Russia until Putin came to power, yet still they managed to survive. Much attention has been paid to patron states as the enablers of de facto statehood, but this should not lead us to believe that there are no other external sources of support. Such support will frequently come from diaspora communities, which play a crucial role in cases such as Nagorno Karabakh, Somaliland, and—until recently—Tamil Eelam, but this is supplemented by revenue stemming from other transnational sources, in particular licit and illicit trade and international aid.

State-Building and Globalization

When assessing the different sources of support for Nagorno Karabakh's state-building project, the presidential advisor commented that 'globalization is a trend which clearly strengthens our independence'.[321] Kurdistan's minister of extra-regional affairs similarly contends that in an earlier era, the Kurds would not have been able to rule a village, let alone a de facto state.[322] The most important factor that both refer to is their diaspora communities and the informational networks that enable them to closely follow developments in the unrecognized state and provide vital financial support.

The significance of diaspora communities has long been recognized in the literature on separatist wars and other forms of intrastate warfare. Most of the focus in this literature has been on how the

LIVERPOOL JOHN MOORES UNIVERSITY
LEARNING SERVICES

support from diaspora communities, often described as 'long-distance nationalists',[323] enables separatist movements and other insurgencies to arm themselves.[324] Such support, it is argued, makes it more likely that war breaks out and that it lasts for longer. The importance of diaspora support does, however, not end after the active war phase. It can also have an impact on state-building in cases where de facto independence has been achieved. In fact, this is arguably where it is likely to make the most significant contribution. Although diaspora communities have often sent volunteers to contribute to the military efforts and can assist with the supply of weapons—or more often financial support that enables the acquisition of weaponry—they cannot provide the kind of military support that a state actor can. Whereas a patron state can provide military guarantees, or at least significant backing, diaspora communities can provide vital economic support and know-how concerning the building of an effective entity. Contrary to the involvement of patron states, which is somewhat constrained by the principle of territorial integrity, diaspora support is rarely prevented by the countries in which the communities reside. Unless, that is, the separatist movement has been declared a terrorist organization, which is what happened in the case of the Tamil Tigers. This did not, however, put an end to diaspora support for the state-building efforts in Tamil Eelam: new organizations were formed that had less obvious links to the Tigers, and although these organizations were scrutinized by governments in, for example, Canada and the UK, the flow of funding was not halted.[325]

Diaspora support is one of the keys to the relatively successful process of state-building in Nagorno Karabakh: without the very generous support from the Armenian diaspora a lot less would have been achieved. Much of the country's infrastructure has been built or rebuilt with the help of diaspora money, including the road linking Nagorno Karabakh and Armenia proper and the entity's north-south highway.[326] This form of investment continues to this day: in 2009 the diaspora was expected to finance half of all public construction in the entity, including schools, hospitals, and water supply.[327] Moreover, the growing foreign investments, which the Karabakh authorities proudly point to, consist almost entirely of diaspora money. The entity's swankiest hotel is, for example, owned by Swiss Armenians while its main telephone company is owned by a Lebanese Armenian. The advisor to the Karabakh president proudly describes this as a 'globalized form of state-building';[328] and in the sense of being heavily dependent on diaspora involvement it is truly global in scope.

Diaspora communities have also played a crucial role in the formation of Somaliland and 'have been an important pillar of the Somaliland state-building project'.[329] This support is particularly significant since Somaliland lacks a patron state that it can rely on for help with these efforts. Somaliland has, as noted in Chapter 2, faced less international isolation than other unrecognized states, but it is important to note that international support was not forthcoming for its initial state-building efforts; the UN, for example, 'refused to engage constructively with Somaliland'.[330] Somaliland therefore needed alternative sources of external support and the Somaliland diaspora stepped in to fill the gap: it provided expert knowledge of how modern societies operate, and made monetary contributions thought to be worth up to U.S. $500 million a year.[331] The diaspora's economic role has taken a number of different forms: 'economic support for the livelihoods of extended family networks', which constitutes around 50 per cent of the total remittances and has helped lift people out of poverty; 'finance for public services and infrastructure', including health and education; and investments in property and multimillion dollar business, such as telecommunications.[332] The vital contribution from the diaspora has been recognized by the Somaliland government and further investments have been encouraged through tax breaks on certain types of imports, such as construction materials.[333] The case of Somaliland demonstrates that diaspora support is not only important in ethnically defined entities. Members of the Isaaq clan may be described as long-distance nationalists, but even non-Isaaq migrants who identify themselves with Somalia rather than Somaliland have contributed to the entity's development.[334] The Somaliland diaspora is primarily of a recent origin, and members of the diaspora therefore retain strong family links.

Tamil Eelam was another unrecognized state that due to its lack of an external patron relied heavily on support from the sizeable and relatively resourceful Tamil diaspora.[335] By the early 2000s, the Tamil Tigers had established an effective network for fundraising which covered at least forty countries,[336] and a lot of the money raised went into state-building projects in Tamil Eelam. Diaspora funds were especially important in the economic development of the entity, whereas the development of law and order relied less on external links.[337] Economic development became particularly important after the 2002 ceasefire agreement created a political space for focusing on social welfare and not just on security concerns.[338] The Tamil Eelam authorities not only made use of diaspora funds, but also of diaspora skills, and cooperated with Tamil NGOs such as the Tamils Rehabilitation Organization and the Economic Consultancy House, which both have strong diaspora links.[339] Like in Somaliland, the authorities recognized the importance of the diaspora community for the survival of the entity and in Hero's Day speeches the diaspora was urged to continue its support.[340]

Diaspora support is also vital in a number of other cases. In Iraqi Kurdistan, the diaspora provided the entity with skills and financial support and was particularly important in sponsoring cultural and educational activities.[341] In Abkhazia, important economic investments have similarly come from Abkhaz in Turkey[342] and the repatriation of the diaspora population is seen as a possible solution to the entity's catastrophic demographic situation. In order to encourage this, a Law on Repatriation was passed as early as 1993, and the authorities in 2002 established a State Committee on Repatriation whose task is to create incentives for the diaspora to resettle in Abkhazia. To this end, all taxpayers pay 2 per cent of their salary into a state fund. This shows the commitment of the authorities to repatriation and demonstrates that a diaspora population can serve a number of different functions when it comes to state-building projects. So far, however, these efforts have met with little success; less than 3,000 people have responded to the invitation. The Abkhaz diaspora tends to be well-integrated and a lack of knowledge of Russian, and sometimes Abkhaz, constitutes a barrier to their resettlement.[343]

Diaspora involvement is therefore highly significant in a number of unrecognized states. It can enable these entities to survive, even when they face international isolation and lack the support from an external patron, or it can reduce the dependence on an external patron by providing an alternative source of support. Like dependence on a patron state, however, this dependence may come at a price. The diaspora is, due to its lack of unity, a lot less likely than a patron state to intervene in internal affairs, but diaspora involvement has been deemed at times to relieve the government of its usual responsibilities.[344] Diaspora communities become responsible for fulfilling the social contract between the leaders and the population, and this affects the kind of statehood that develops. It is, moreover, frequently suggested that diaspora support empowers more radical forces within separatist movements; the argument being that since diaspora communities do not have to live with the consequences of conflict they are more likely to support maximalist positions and provide funding to leaders or parties who refuse to compromise.[345] In the case of Nagorno Karabakh this seems to be borne out by the frequently radical position of the

Dashnak party, which was founded by members of the Armenian diaspora in 1890 and continues to receive significant support from the diaspora community. This party played a key role in the radicalization and militarization of the conflict in the late 1980s, and the Dashnak leaders in Karabakh opposed the Armenian president, Ter-Petrosyan, when he attempted to negotiate a solution.[346] However, the reality is often a lot more complex than this 'radicalizing diaspora' image suggests. For example, most of the Armenian diaspora support in Karabakh has been apolitical; the diaspora has been reluctant to involve itself in internal politics and has instead focused on supporting the entity's state-building efforts.[347] In Somaliland, the diaspora has been a key factor in internal politics, but rather than promoting a radical, militarizing logic, the diaspora-led political parties in Somaliland have served as guardians of the entity's democratizing efforts and have, for example, called for the Security Committee, which currently enjoys sweeping powers, to be disbanded.[348] Diaspora involvement helps the survival of the entity, and therefore does have an impact on conflict resolution efforts, but this impact is not as straightforward as is sometimes suggested in the literature.

The effect of globalization is, moreover, not limited to diaspora support; transborder linkages are also of importance in unrecognized states, in particular in those without a sizeable or resourceful diaspora population. Transborder crime (as discussed in Chapter 1) has frequently been argued to be a significant factor in unrecognized states, and although the image of criminalized badlands has been overplayed, there is little doubt that the shadow economy has played a role in some of these entities, especially in the early stages of state-building. The shadow economy provided the unrecognized state with resources, and some of these resources found their way into the general economy and helped build up the entity. In the early years of Kurdistan's existence, for example, it is estimated that taxation and customs revenue generated by smuggling across the Turkish border earned the entity $750 million annually, providing Kurdistan with about 85 per cent of its revenues.[349] But the benefit of this to the process of state-building is contested. King adopts Charles Tilly's argument that the modern state system to a considerable extent evolved out of organized crime, and argues that similar processes can be seen in unrecognized states: 'basic networks, relationships, and informal channels that arose during the course of the violence, can replicate themselves in new, state-like institutions in the former conflict zones.'[350] Stacy Closson disagrees, and contends that such activities constituted an obstacle to the building of an effective state; the criminalized networks made it harder for the

authorities to impose their control.[351] The shadow economy is a double-edged sword for unrecognized states; it can help provide revenue
needed for state-building to succeed, but also risk empowering actors
who have an interest in relative disorder and it, moreover, risks damaging the entity's internal legitimacy. The Serb leaders had already before
the proclamation of Republika Srpska Krajina predicted that the
entity would have to survive on 'booty and state-controlled smuggling',[352] and war profiteers ensured that basic goods such as tooth-
paste, oil, and flour were available, albeit at highly inflated prices.[353]
It was therefore possible to sustain some form of normal life. Organized
crime, however, made little contribution to the growth of the entity's
economy; it merely enabled its basic survival and it gradually served
to undermine morale. A soldier in the Krajina army, for example,
noted that people fighting at the front deplored 'having to defend all
those smugglers and thieves who became rich overnight'.[354] The
authorities were seemingly aware of this problem, and the Krajina
parliament in 1995 asked the government to look into problems with
'the flow of goods and illegal trade'.[355] Some civilians were prosecuted
for their involvement in such activities[356] but impunity remained the
norm, especially for people higher up the food chain.

Other avenues are, however, available for de facto authorities to
finance their state-building efforts. The Tamil Tigers are believed to
have profited from large-scale selling of Tamil DVDs and telephone
cards,[357] and almost all unrecognized states are able to engage in some
form of international trade. Somaliland, for example, exports cattle;
Abkhazia exports citrus; and Karabakh exports include grains, carpets,
and watches. Due to their lack of recognition, this trade will be classed
as illegal, unless an export permit is obtained from the parent state,
but it differs from the kind of shadowy organized crime controlled by
the 'men with the guns' and it makes an important contribution to
state-building efforts. Only a few unrecognized states, such as
Republika Srpska Krajina, have been almost completely unable to
profit from some form of trade. The economy of Republika Srpska
Krajina was in ruins; the only functioning part of the economy was
agriculture, but Krajina was, due to international sanctions, only able
to export to Serbia.[358] Serbia's economy was similarly facing collapse
so this provided limited revenue. Republika Srpska Krajina tried to
get permission to export as an independent state, but this was rejected.[359]

In cases where patron states, diaspora communities, and international trade (be it legal or illegal) provide limited resources, there is an
additional source of transborder linkages that can help unrecognized
states survive: international aid. International organizations have gen-

erally been reluctant to provide development aid, as this could be seen to support separatism. Denise Natali, for example, describes how USAID staff members in Iraqi Kurdistan were forbidden to use the word 'development' in official communication as this could suggest U.S. support for greater Kurdish autonomy or even independence,[360] and an EU project to repair a dam was cancelled due to concerns about stimulating the region's autonomy.[361] Similarly, the UN was initially 'disparagingly hostile' to state-building efforts in Somaliland.[362] In the early 1990s foreign aid therefore virtually bypassed the entity and the lack of recognition later limited the aid available to short-term assistance.[363] Even though humanitarian aid does not directly contribute to the state-building effort, however, it does enable survival, and possibly frees up resources that can be used for state-building. We are, moreover, beginning to see a shift in the international dealings with unrecognized states, and development is now seen as a possible step toward stability and peaceful settlements. The World Bank began to engage in Somaliland in 2003[364] and the UN and the EU in 2004 launched large-scale development projects in Abkhazia focusing on basic infrastructure, hospitals, sanitation, and agricultural development.[365] Similar assistance was provided to Tamil Eelam as part of the ongoing peace process.[366] This involvement does not extend to willingness to help build up the unrecognized state's coercive apparatus, which is another important aspect of state-building, and it also depends on the absence of parent state objections. Although it vehemently rejects the unrecognized state's claim to independence, the parent state is not necessarily unwilling to allow such engagement, and may even itself offer limited linkages.

Parent States: Limited Relations?

The relative military weakness of the parent state has often been seen as a crucial factor enabling unrecognized states to survive,[367] but the parent state also has a more direct impact on the unrecognized state; through blockades and military incursions the parent state can make it difficult for the unrecognized state to survive, let alone develop an effective entity. However, in some cases the parent state allows the establishment of trade links and other forms of contact, which will make it easier for the entity to survive. This may seem like a curious strategy for a parent state to adopt; they are, after all, rejecting the separatist attempt and trying to re-establish control over their entire territory. According to international law, however, the parent state is still responsible for the welfare of this part of its population, and is parent obliged to take measures to protect it. Even very hostile states therefore tend to allow the supply of humanitarian aid to the unrecognized state and often permit patients from across the de facto border to receive emergency hospital treatments. Moreover, some parent states have seemingly realized that there is a limit to the 'smoke-them-out' strategy. For example, after initially insisting on complete boycotts, the Georgian and the Croatian governments both began opening up for limited relations. The Croatian government signed economic agreements with the Krajina leadership which included the opening of transport routes and the establishment of water and oil supplies to the entity.[368] The Georgian government similarly began cooperating with the Abkhaz authorities in the running of the Inguri hydro-power plant and the two sides in 2003 began talks on opening railway links. These negotiations were halted by the Rose Revolution later that year; they began anew in 2005 but failed to produce results. In 2009 the Georgian parliament passed the very restrictive Law on Occupied Territories, which made any form of engagement with the entities very difficult,[369] but a year later the Georgian authorities formulated a 'State Strategy on Occupied Territories: Engagement through Cooperation', which was followed by an 'Action Plan for Engagement'.[370] This has yet to be implemented and it remains unclear what approach will be given greater weight: the policy of engagement or the policy of isolation? A more consistent strategy of limited engagement has been pursued by the Moldovan government. In 1996, Chisinau, for example, offered to let Transnistria use Moldovan customs certificates, thereby allowing the entity to engage in licit trade.[371] As a result, thousands of vehicles cross the de facto border every day, many Transnistrian companies are registered in Chisinau and operate with Moldovan licences, and Transnistrian newspapers are sold in Chisinau kiosks.[372] Similarly in 2003, the Turkish Cypriot authorities opened the 'green line', thereby allowing for the free passage from Northern Cyprus to the rest of the island. Initially this resulted in a flood of people crossing the de facto border to work, shop, or just experience the other side, but numbers have since then declined.[373] The most extensive degree of engagement with the parent state is probably seen in Taiwan: a trade agreement gives Taiwan's agricultural products preferential access to the Chinese market, China is Taiwan's most important export market, and the majority of Taiwan's foreign investment goes to China.[374] After an absence of nearly sixty years, direct flights between China and Taiwan were introduced in 2008, resulting in an increase in tourist revenue for the island.[375]

The thinking behind such a strategy is that it will make it easier to reach a negotiated settlement,[376] and it has been pursued even in one of the most violent conflicts involving unrecognized states: the Sri Lankan civil war. Thus, the Sri Lankan state continued to provide public services, such as health and education, *within* Tamil Eelam. The de facto authorities, realizing that the Tamil population needed these services, did not attack the local civil administration even though they continued targeting the Sri Lankan armed forces and political leaders. In parallel with the services provided by the Sri Lankan authorities, the Tamil authorities started developing their own welfare programmes and, for example, provided primary health care and preschool education, thereby 'creating an element of division of labour'.[377] As part of the peace process, the leaders of Tamil Eelam and the Sri Lankan government even reached an agreement to jointly address humanitarian needs in the war-torn areas and 'use this as a precursor to substantive discussions on the core issues of power sharing and constitutional reforms'.[378]

This form of engagement is, however, not only problematic for the parent state, in that it risks prolonging the existence of the separatist entity that they want to reintegrate; it also creates dilemmas for the unrecognized state and may prove a significant challenge to its leaders. Engagement with the parent state, even in the limited form it has taken in the above cases, undermines the claim that the only options are 'independence or death'. Isolation plays into the hands of the leaders, at least in the short term, since it makes it easier to maintain a deferential population; this explains why the leaders of these entities are often vehemently opposed to having any relations with their parent state. They are worried about a form of creeping reintegration. If the parent state still takes responsibility for the welfare of its entire population, then it also makes it harder to claim that they have lost sovereignty over the contested territory. Moreover, if the unrecognized state relied on their parent state, this could lead to charges that their independence is merely 'imagined'.[379] In a number of cases, engagement with the parent state has, therefore, been opposed. The leaders of Republika Srpska Krajina would, for example, not even let Croatian representatives cross the Krajina land-border to take part in peace talks: they had to use a helicopter and leave as soon as the talks were over.[380] Later on when Krajina was facing desperate energy shortages, the entity's president still refused any cooperation with Croatia.[381] The Abkhaz leaders have similarly dismissed the Georgian re-launched strategy of engagement as a strategy of reintegration, in which they will take no part.[382] Finally, in Bougainville the supply of services by the parent state proved so controversial that it contributed to the outbreak of internal fighting.[383]

If possible, unrecognized states would therefore rather rely on alternative sources of state-building, and these are sometimes available to them. Unrecognized states are not completely barred from international engagement, but it is much more difficult for them to achieve than it is for recognized states. A number of these external sources of support are problematic and for wider international engagement they need goodwill; they need recognized states to be willing to dispense with the strict interpretation of the principle of territorial integrity. In order to improve their position in the international system, unrecognized states therefore try to create entities that are deemed worthy of engagement and perhaps even recognition.

Creating Internationally Acceptable Entities

The external dimension of state-building in unrecognized states is not only about resources and viability. It also affects the 'idea of the state': what kind of entity is likely to ensure external legitimacy? How do we best appeal to external audiences? Isachenko, for example, argues that the Transnistrian state-building project can 'be seen as a product of the international community just as much as an expression of local desires'.[384] Although it remains an elusive goal in most cases, the aspiration for de jure independence is maintained. However much we talk about globalization, erosion of the state, and the increasing irrelevance of territory, statehood remains the top prize; it legitimizes the struggle, guarantees protection for the inhabitants and prestige and power for the leaders. Even if this cannot be realized, unrecognized states still have an interest in appealing to the wider international community. Nonrecognition is, as noted in Chapter 2, not always associated with complete isolation, and a greater degree of engagement would enhance the prospects of successful state-building in the unrecognized entities.

Whereas the need for resources to enable state-building has remained fairly constant, the attempt to create entities that are deemed internationally acceptable has resulted in a great deal of flux. Strategies for gaining recognition are continuously being refined and renegotiated in view of changes in the international norms and practice of recognition, and over the last decade we have seen a gradual change from claims based on national identity and past grievances, to claims of having created effective, democratic almost-states. Through these claims, the leaders of unrecognized states are attempting to move away from associations with external puppeteers, shadow economies, and ethnic cleansing.

Changing Strategies

What is the best strategy for gaining international recognition? Well, aspiring states could resort to more or less subtle forms of bribery. Resource-rich Katanga, for example, tried—but failed—to bribe Costa Rican officials into recognizing the entity.[385] Promises of foreign investments are also said to have been behind Macedonia's recognition of Taiwan in 1999,[386] and Nauru reportedly requested $50 million for its recognition of Abkhazia and South Ossetia.[387] But aside from occasionally resorting to such economic sweeteners—which are beyond the means of most unrecognized states—the strategies adopted have been remarkably similar.[388] The main argument put forward by unrecognized states has, as argued in Chapter 2, combined a claim to national self-determination—based on historic links to a territory and a well-developed national identity—with a claim to a 'remedial' right to secession—based on alleged human rights violations. But this dual strategy has not been enough to ensure international recognition, and an emphasis on victimhood and vulnerability is, in any case, not necessarily the best strategy for an entity which wants to demonstrate its viability as an independent state. As the Biafran ministry of foreign affairs concluded in a confidential memorandum, 'the humanitarian approach has backfired. Ours now is the picture of a piteous starving sickly people non-viable and incapable of defending themselves from hunger and war.'[389]

By the mid-1990s, unrecognized states were, therefore, still looking for a recipe that might lead to international recognition, and decided to embark on a new strategy: they started emphasizing their alleged success in state-building and democratization, and these arguments gradually came to dominate over past claims to groupness and grievances. In addition to claiming a *right* to recognition, they now also argue that they have *earned* their sovereignty.[390] The speaker of the Nagorno Karabakh parliament, for example, argues that the entity has 'a serious basis for the international recognition of our sovereignty', 'we have held free elections for 16 years, law-enforcement bodies are formed, powers are divided, [the] army is under civil control'.[391] Pegg argues that such an external legitimizing strategy actually presents a hark-back to traditional views of sovereignty; that by focusing on their capacity to govern, these entities are 'playing yesterday's game'.[392] However, today's unrecognized states are not only proclaiming that they can govern, the entities are announcing that they share hegemonic international values ('not only are we the victims; we are the good guys, we are like you') and do not constitute a security threat. Such considerations were, as noted in Chapter 1, not completely absent from the traditional view. Minority rights were, for example, a precondition for the recognition of the states that emerged from the Ottoman Empire in the nineteenth century[393] and references were more generally made to 'civilization' as a criterion for international recognition.[394] However, this claim is now much more pronounced and specifically focused on democratic institutions.

The perception of an external incentive to build effective, democratic institutions is clearly illustrated in statements made by the authorities. For example, the foreign minister of Nagorno Karabakh argues that the decisive criterion for international recognition is viability,[395] and one of the leaders of Abkhazia, when asked why the entity should be recognized, responded that it had proven itself viable as a state.[396] The need for democratization is emphasized even more strongly. Thus in 2006 the president of Nagorno Karabakh, Arkady Ghukasyan, argued, 'People who have a very...democratic constitution...[who] strive for European standards, have more chances of being recognized by the International Community than others.'[397] On a very similar note, in 1999 the president of Somaliland, Mohamed Egal, publicly declared that international recognition depended upon adopting a multi-party system of democracy.[398] Finally, the process of de-recognition and the accompanying crisis of international legitimacy provided an important impetus for Taiwan to replace decades of authoritarian rule with gradual democratization.[399]

This emphasis on democracy directly reflects a shift in the international norms of legitimate statehood following the end of the Cold War.[400] Democracy came to be seen as the most legitimate form of the state[401]—and even as the cure for all ills[402]—and this normative shift was seemingly reflected in the conditions attached to the recognition of the former Yugoslav republics in the early 1990s: the first condition established by the European Community was the rule of law, democracy, and human rights. Other aspiring states took note of this linking of democratic statehood and recognition and it, along with NATO's military intervention in Bosnia, appears to have inspired them to embark on a process of democratization. The Karabakh leaders had on more than one occasion likened their cause to that of the Croatian and Bosnian Serbs,[403] but the former had by 1995 been expelled from the Krajina region while the latter were being bombed by NATO. At the same time, the Karabakh authorities were realizing that their military victory alone would not result in international recognition. Something more was needed, and the creation of democratic institutions came to be seen as the way forward. The hope was that if they recreated the entity as a democracy then Western voters would put pressure on their governments to recognize Karabakh or, at least, refrain from bombing it.[404] Since then, the international rhetorical emphasis on democratization—especially in U.S. foreign policy—increased further,[405] and the continued reference to the dangers posed by 'failed states'[406] has similarly made the entities keen to stress their ability to govern effectively. The EU accession criteria, as set out in the so-called Copenhagen criteria from 1993, point in the same direction by requiring new Member States to have established stable institutions 'guaranteeing democracy, the rule of law, human rights and respect for and protection of minorities'.[407] These criteria are again echoed in the conditions often attached to international aid: democracy and good governance. The dominance of such policies signals to the unrecognized states that to be part of 'us', to be part of the exclusive group of acceptable, sovereign states, state-building and democratization are required.

The statehood proclaimed in these entities has therefore been significantly influenced by international developments; or rather by *perceived* changes in international norms and practices of recognition. The resulting statehood forms part of an external contestation of identity: how do we want the world to see us? In their bid for international support the entities are often engaged in what has been termed a process of 'competitive democratization':[408] not only are they trying to demonstrate their own democratic credentials, they are also claiming to be more democratic than their parent states and they frequently describe themselves as 'islands of democracy' in otherwise authoritarian waters. The extent to which democratic reforms take hold can therefore be assumed to be affected by the degree of democracy found in the parent states, or in the region more broadly. Oleh Protsyk, for example, points out how the Orange Revolution in Ukraine and the democratic progress in Moldova served to highlight the Transnistrian regime's 'problem of democratic legitimacy' and served as an impetus for reforms.[409] Competitive democratization is particularly important to unrecognized states since the parent states always portray the regimes as illegitimate: in terms of their separatism, but also in terms of their (alleged) lack of popular support. Moldova has, for example, consistently raised this issue.[410]

Alternative: Turning Their Backs on the International Community

The assumption made by the unrecognized states is that if they build effective entities, if they introduce reforms, then they are more likely to receive vital support and may even gain international recognition. What happens, then, if an unrecognized state has given up on international support; if it has deemed that the only external support it is likely to get comes from its patron state, which cares little about the kind of entity that is developed? This was the case with Republika Srpska Krajina.

When the European Community's Badinter Commission in late 1991 invited applications for the recognition of states emerging from the former Yugoslavia, Republika Srpska Krajina, with the support of the Yugoslav Ministry of Foreign Affairs,[411] duly submitted its claim for independence. Based on already issued guidelines, this application was ignored by the Commission, and Croatia's independence was recognized instead, leading the Krajina leaders to more or less abandon the idea of international support. As the then-foreign minister of Krajina puts it, 'we were alone in the world'.[412] In an internal report from early 1993, Krajina's president, Goran Hadžić, notes that Krajina has previously been cooperative even when it came to UN resolutions they felt went against them, since this was thought to increase the chances of recognition, but he now advocates rejection as the best strategy.[413] Notwithstanding this policy of rejection, the Krajina rhetoric still prioritized effective statehood, popular legitimacy, and even democracy.[414] There are a couple of reasons for this. First, it points us to the importance of internal drivers of statebuilding. Second, it reminds us that there is a difference between rhetoric and substance. Both of these issues will be covered in the next chapter. But there is also a third reason: the holding of elections and the proclamation of popular legitimacy was seen to support the position of the Krajina leadership in their negotiations with Croatia;[415] it might not lead to international recognition, but the Krajina leaders were hoping to improve their prospect of surviving as an unrecognized entity, or at least to get a more advantageous deal in a negotiated settlement, and by pointing to popular legitimacy they could less easily be dismissed as warlords and this was felt to strengthen their position. Even if unrecognized states have given up on international recognition, they may therefore not be completely unaffected by international norms and values.

What if key external supporters do not subscribe to hegemonic international norms? At least one unrecognized state, Chechnya—or the Republic of Ichkeria—did not maintain its claim to democratic statehood. The entity held presidential elections in 1997 that international observers argued reflected 'the freely expressed will of the voters' and 'established a legitimate foundation for the new system of authority'.[416] However, the Chechen leader, Aslan Mashkadov, increasingly began championing Chechnya as an Islamic state rather than the democratic, secular state that had been proclaimed in the early 1990s.[417] This change in emphasis in part reflected pragmatic considerations regarding the need for external support.[418] Mashkadov was dependent on support from the Arab world and most of this support 'appears to have been channelled through Wahhabi organizations operating in Afghanistan, Saudi Arabia, and Qatar'.[419] The need for external support does not necessarily translate into an emphasis on effective, democratic statehood. If international recognition is deemed unobtainable, or immediate survival is a more pressing concern, then the support of a few external patrons may be substituted for general international acceptability, and these patrons may care less about the kind of entities that are created, or may make demands that do not reflect hegemonic international values.

More generally, it is questionable if the proclamation of democratic values is still seen as the most effective way of attracting wider international support, and perhaps even recognition. Unrecognized states had put their faith in the 'standards before status' policy for Kosovo which seemed to indicate that former autonomous provinces could be recognized *without* the consent of their parent state, *if* they had managed to create democratic, effective entities. However, Kosovo's recognition was not primarily based on such institutional standards. Its uniqueness was stressed, the experience of human rights abuses was emphasized, and democracy and minority rights were only given a secondary mention.[420] 'Status before status' had become 'standards then status' under international supervision, or—more cynically—'standards and then who cares about status?' In Nagorno Karabakh this meant that the leaders started talking a lot less about recognition and more about improving the status quo.[421] But even if they abandoned the goal of recognition, which would be difficult, this would not mean turning their back on the international community as they still stress the need for international engagement; it might, however, lead to a rethinking of strategies for attracting support.[422]

Depending on which audience unrecognized states appeal to, they may choose different strategies: the wider international community is one thing, an external patron is another, and an internal audience may have other demands and expectations still. This results in a possible discrepancy between rhetoric and substance, in a bid to please more than one audience at a time. External support is, in any case, not unproblematic for unrecognized states: it may enable their survival, but it also risks undermining their independence.

The Cost of Nonrecognition

Bougainville constitutes the sole example of an unrecognized state that managed to survive despite an almost complete lack of external support, and it did so due to the extreme resourcefulness of its inhabitants: the island's rivers were used to generate electricity, coconut oil was turned into fuel, weapons were homemade or taken from the Papua New Guinea army, and the rich soil was successfully utilized to supply basic food.[423] However, the price of complete isolation was high: thousands of people died due to lack of medical supplies, and although Bougainville eventually managed to—effectively—defeat the Papua New Guinea army and to sign a peace agreement that promises it an independence referendum, it never managed to create an effective state.[424] In the long term, unrecognized states cannot survive and turn themselves into effective entities without some form of external support for their state-building, but this can come in different forms and we see a trade-off between the different sources of support. Some unrecognized states have access to limited international engagement and therefore find themselves less dependent on external patrons. Other entities are provided with significant support from their diaspora populations, while still others receive some support from various other transborder linkages.

Due to the different amounts of external support available to unrecognized states, the cost of nonrecognition varies: for an entity such as Taiwan it is fairly limited, whereas it was very high for Republika Srpska Krajina. In order to survive in the long term, however, unrecognized states are dependent on either sustained support from a patron state or at least limited access to the international community, and both of these sources come at a price. Dependence on an external patron does not necessarily mean that internal sovereignty does not exist. Internal sovereignty is not a question of either-or, and recognized states are similarly dependent on international linkages—including sometimes for military defence—without this affecting their sovereign status. But recognized states often rely on a variety of international links, not just on a single patron. Moreover, they are not trying to justify their independence. Unrecognized states have in some cases been allowed more extensive international engagement, but this depends on the goodwill of the international community *and* the (at least tacit) approval of their parent states. Such acceptance may depend on the absence of a formal declaration of independence, as in the case of Taiwan, and it leaves the unrecognized states vulnerable. The parent state with which they are still nominally at war holds the key to their long-term sustainability, and their internal sovereignty becomes conditional on external developments. Nonrecognition is therefore associated with costs for all unrecognized states and the factors that enable these entities to survive also detract from the substance of their statehood.

External support is always problematic in unrecognized states; it affects the kind of statehood that develops and means that a claim to internal sovereignty will invariably be marked by ambiguities. Moreover, in their attempt to seek wider international engagement, or even recognition, the unrecognized states attempt to create entities that live up to real or imagined norms for acceptable statehood. The demands from an external audience, however, are not necessarily compatible with those made by an internal audience, and a difficult balancing act therefore ensues. This is the focus of the next chapter.

4 INTERNAL SOURCES OF UNRECOGNIZED STATE-BUILDING

' "Let us be us!" that is all.' This is how Gaspar Tamás describes the goal of contemporary nationalism; it 'destroys states...and fails to replace them with anything'.[425] However, in a recent speech to an audience drawn from the Armenian diaspora, the president of Nagorno Karabakh painted a very different picture: one celebrating an entity that has 'managed to recover from the wounds of the war and become [a] viable country inspiring pride to all the Armenians in different quarters of the world'.[426] The preceding chapter described how unrecognized states face external incentives to engage in a process of state-building, and may even have the resources to do so, but if these processes are driven primarily by concerns about external expectations then this could lead to charges that they are devoid of substance; that they amount to nothing but symbolic state-building. Lynch, for example, argues that unrecognized states 'may have the institutional fixtures of statehood, but they cannot provide for its substance'.[427] Unrecognized states may similarly make claims to democratic values but if this is solely driven by an attempt to please external audiences, then those results can be dismissed as a 'Potemkin democracy'.[428]

Unrecognized states cannot be reduced to their external dimension, however, and the success or failure of their state-building efforts also owes a lot to internal dynamics. Many of the wartime leaders of what were to become unrecognized states did not display any inclination toward state-building, let alone popular legitimacy. Yet King finds that 'the territorial separatists of the early 1990s have become the state builders of the early 2000s'.[429] The achievement of de facto independence to some extent changed their priorities, but it was not only the goal of recognition that led them to become committed state-builders. The persistence of an external threat also fosters a need for strong entities; it pushes unrecognized states toward de facto statehood and forces upon them an interest in institution-building. Modern statehood was, as Charles Tilly convincingly argued, based on the need for effective 'war machines'.[430] This was an important incentive behind state-building in these self-proclaimed states as well. The need for strong statehood is felt even more acutely in unrecognized states, since they exist in a situation of pure international anarchy without the protective norm of nonintervention.[431] There are therefore weighty reasons for unrecognized states to try to build effective entities, and these reasons go beyond the need to attract external support.

The creation of a strong entity that is able to defend itself requires the de facto authorities to consolidate the entity's coercive capabilities—they need to complete the second phase of state-building. But this is far from being a foregone conclusion. Several of the unrecognized states were initially characterized by a lack of central control, the dominance of irregular forces, and internal violence. How did some, such as Somaliland and Nagorno Karabakh, manage to create effective entities while others, such as Chechnya and Republika Srpska Krajina, were dominated by infighting warlords? If this hurdle is passed, state-building in unrecognized states becomes concerned with creating entities that are able to supply basic public services and that enjoy popular legitimacy, but this process is also significantly affected by the legacy of war and the context of nonrecognition. This chapter analyzes these efforts and the factors that potentially cause tensions: the prioritizing of security above all else, an emphasis on unity, and a tendency to promote ethnically exclusive forms of statehood. The goals of seeking international support and acceptability and creating entities that are able to defend themselves often overlap, but they at times pull in different directions. The result is an ambiguous and even schizophrenic form of statehood.

Ensuring Coercive Control: Avoiding Infighting Warlords

In the previous chapter, unrecognized states were—for the sake of simplicity—analysed as unitary actors with a single set of goals: attract external support and promote international recognition of the entity. But such collective goals are often overshadowed by the pursuit of narrow self-interests and these frequently run counter to the building of effective institutions. The problem is not so much that ethno-nationalism is anti-statist, as argued by Tamás,[432] but rather that warlords often thrive in a state of relative disorder. Kolstø and Blakkisrud use Mancur Olson's concept of the 'stationary bandit' to argue that state-building is in the interest of the leaders of unrecognized states, even if they are motivated by greed rather than collective interests, as it will give them a better basis for extracting resources: 'the vested interests of the one-time secessionists have turned them into state-builders.'[433] But although state-building may be in their long-term interest once in power, short-term interest in personal enrichment and power can result in debilitating infighting. Chechnya provides a striking example of an unrecognized state that very clearly failed in its endeavour to build an effective entity, even if such an outcome would have served both collective and individual interests. One of the key reasons for this collapse of statehood was the persistent infighting that characterized the Chechen entity. Such infighting has marred attempts at state-building in a number of other unrecognized states.

State-building was always unlikely to succeed in the case of Republika Srpska Krajina and its failure is most often explained in terms of external forces: the imposition of an international blockade and decreasing support from Belgrade. However, Republika Srpska Krajina was also killed off by intense elite rivalry. When Goran Hadžić became president in February 1992, a level of optimism was noticeable in the entity.[434] Many state institutions were created early on, including all significant government ministries; a constitution; parliament; an army; a police force; courts; a central bank that issued a separate currency; TV and radio channels and newspapers; educational institutions, including a university; and cultural institutions, such as a national theatre.[435] But less than two years later, the entity was approaching chaos: crime was rife, there was little or no central control, and the economy was collapsing.[436] Krajina's leadership was effectively split between the entity's two regions and Hadžić never managed to impose his control over the western part of the entity and could only travel to the capital Knin with strong escort.[437] Effective control in this region was largely in the hands of the minister of the interior, who controlled the police, but paramilitary groups also played a role.[438] These groups had access to very valuable war profiteering, including from trade with the Bosnian Muslim enclave in Bihać,[439] and the large sums involved may have allowed them to escape political control. In the eastern part of Krajina menacing warlords exercised a significant influence, especially Arkan and his paramilitary Tigers. Arkan was

officially an advisor to the president, but his influence extended far
beyond this role, and the region was even described as 'Arkan's private
state' or as 'Arkansas'.[440] This intense infighting and the lack of central
control undermined any attempts to create a viable entity, and it is
important to note that Republika Srpska Krajina failed *before* the
international blockade was introduced in 1993.

Similar obstacles were encountered in other cases. Shortly after the
withdrawal of Papua New Guinean forces in early 1990, Bougainville
descended into infighting and lawlessness.[441] Somaliland, similarly, saw
heavy internal fighting in the early 1990s and the control of the
Somaliland government, as a result, extended little beyond the
capital.[442] In the case of Kurdistan such infighting culminated in 1994
in a year-long bloody civil war between the Kurdish Democratic Party
and the Patriotic Union of Kurdistan, which effectively tore the entity
into two separate administrative zones.[443] Unrecognized states are
born out of warfare and it is not surprising that the context of weak
institutions and a surfeit of weaponry leads to violent power rivalries.
Even entities that initially manage to secure coercive control and create
a reasonably effective army are not immune to infighting. In Nagorno
Karabakh the civilian and the military leadership had in the first years
after the ceasefire almost exercised power in parallel, but the beginning
process of state-building led to a showdown between the president and
the commander of the armed forces, which culminated in an assassina-
tion attempt against the president and the arrest and imprisonment of
the army commander.[444] Different centres of power could no longer be
tolerated, and the beginning emergence of a functioning state also
meant that there was more to fight over. Capturing the state had in
the early years been associated with only limited advantages, but it
now came with real power.

Countering Infighting

Two unrecognized states, Chechnya and Republika Srpska Krajina,
failed spectacularly when it came to imposing central control, while
other cases struggled but managed to overcome this hurdle. What
explains this difference in outcome? In Chechnya, the attempt to
impose central control was hampered by the degree of destruction left
by the war, the failure to create a unified army during the war, and
the availability of external funding for the more extreme rivals to the
president, Mashkadov.[445] In the case of Republika Srpska Krajina, the
most obvious explanation is to be found in the geographic division of
the entity, which resulted in lack of mobility and lack of dependable

supply routes, but an even more important explanation can be found in the divided control over coercive resources. This was an almost direct result of Belgrade's divide-and-rule policy, which served to ensure the kin-state's continued influence in the entity. Such an instrument was made all the more powerful by Krajina's dependence on Belgrade; if Milošević became unhappy with his brethren across the border, he could always threaten to pull the plug, in which case the Serb entity would face a very rapid collapse.[446]

In other cases, infighting posed less of a challenge. Central control was, for example, quickly established in Transnistria, even though the entity initially had to rely on irregular forces made up of a combination of the embryonic national guard, paramilitary groups, and troops from the Russian 14th Army moonlighting for the Transnistrians.[447] One of the key reasons for this was the relatively short war that preceded the establishment of de facto independence. The power of the irregular armed forces simply did not have time to become entrenched.[448] But some entities that experienced prolonged and devastating warfare managed to avoid damaging infighting. In the case of Nagorno Karabakh, a number of factors seem to account for the success in imposing central control. Most notably, the army leadership had already during the war managed to subsume various militias, and these efforts had been helped, in no small part, by support from Armenia and from the diaspora. This relative cohesiveness of the army allowed one man to clearly emerge as Karabakh's strongman: the army commander and defence minister Samvel Babayan.[449] Aided by his very substantial wealth, Babayan enjoyed considerable autonomy. His power rivalled, and at times surpassed, that of the civilian leadership.[450] President Robert Kocharyan was not short on wartime credentials, but rather than challenging Babayan he appeared to accept his influential position, and the civilian leaders even helped promote a cult of Babayan the war hero.[451] Strongman leadership was possibly considered compatible with the need for speedy state-building, and the cult of Babayan helped confer legitimacy on the civilian leadership; Karabakh could be presented both internally and externally as the embodiment of military victory. Eventually this cult became difficult to control, but it still took years before open conflict emerged between the civilian and the military leadership. When at last it did, the president managed to impose civilian control over the armed forces—not a small feat for an entity that had emerged from wartime destruction only five years earlier. One of the decisive factors in this state-building success appears to be that the Karabakh conflict was primarily a bottom-up conflict. This provided the leaders with resources but also with constraints and may explain not only the reluctance on the part of other military leaders to engage in grabs for power but also the ability of the civilian leadership to undermine the power of the military leader: they could point to their popular mandate, which Babayan found it harder to demonstrate. Second, institutions were not entirely absent. Although very significantly weakened by the war, the entity did not implode and the army remained organized. Moreover, the years of 'no war, no peace' allowed the civilian regime to build institutions which increased its strength vis-à-vis the military commander. Third, Karabakh's external backers were supportive of the creation of statehood and the kin-state very clearly supported the imposition of civilian rule. Fourth, the perceived external pressures to present a democratic facade proved to be a powerful instrument in the hands of competing leaders.[452]

Kurdistan faced an even more significant hurdle in the form of a bloody civil war, but violence was brought to an end by a U.S.-brokered peace agreement. The agreement entailed an almost complete division of power: the two Kurdish parties each came to control a distinct region and the governance of Kurdistan was divided between two executives.[453] The stability was moreover reinforced by a U.S. pledge to protect the Kurds against possible aggressions by Saddam Hussein and by the increasing revenue stemming from the UN Oil-for-Food programme.[454] Whereas Kurdistan overcame threats to its internal stability through the institutionalization of divisions, Somaliland overcame such threats by building on social norms of consensus.[455] An inter-clan conference, which aimed to determine the 'destiny' of Somaliland, was organized in the town of Borama in early 1993, and the 150 delegates agreed on a security framework and a political system for the entity. The vast majority of decisions were by consensus, and included the demobilization and disarmament of clan militias, the creation of a new national army, and the transition to civilian administration.[456] As a result, by the late 1990s, most of the territory of Somaliland was under firm government control[457] and an effective entity, which was able to provide basic public services, was gradually created. Finally, in the case of Bougainville, attempts to create central control were hampered by an extreme lack of resources and pre-existing institutions, by the absence of a well-developed common identity on which the new leadership could build, and by their failure to convince the population that they had a plan for re-establishing security and good governance.[458] Only after years of fighting was central control finally established and this process was, just as in Somaliland, helped by the involvement of clan elders and chiefs.[459]

What enables unrecognized states to create largely orderly entities appears to be a mix of internal dynamics, external support, and international norms. The absence of significant wartime destruction clearly helps, but the cases also showed that this can be overcome. Similarly, if unrecognized states are able to build on pre-existing institutions and thereby avoid a dangerous institutional vacuum, they are in a better position to ensure central control. However, the case of Transnistria— which like Republika Srpska Krajina had no pre-existing institutions on which to build—demonstrated that this is not essential, and the case of Chechnya demonstrated that it is far from sufficient. Resources, more broadly, are clearly important for state-building, but when it comes to this initial phase of state-building it is as important how they are distributed. Of particular importance is whether external supporters finance competing warlords and militias. This stage of state-building has a much greater chance of succeeding if the external supporters back the incumbent leaders and refrain from divide-and-rule policies. The external dimension also matters in other ways for the establishment of coercive control. The above examples demonstrated that the perception of an external pressure to create a certain kind of entity can help empower civilian leaders against warlords and may dampen willingness to challenge incumbents. This, however, requires collective goals to be a priority for the leaders, which is by no means a given, and again brings us back to the distribution of resources: do the leaders depend on popular support for their political survival, or does it depend on other audiences, including external supporters? In a number of cases, bottom-up processes proved important in enabling this crucial phase of state-building. Separatist movements emerging from popular pressures would therefore appear to have a better chance of realizing their claims to statehood.

Dangerous infighting has thus been avoided in entities that either enjoy a high degree of homogeneity and have significant bottom-up pressures, or where such unity has been imposed by a sufficiently resource-rich leadership.[460] In Taiwan, unity was ensured in a top-down manner: the mainlander leadership imposed martial law, suppressed expressions of Taiwanese identity, and tried to ensure national unity through state-sponsored education and cultural programmes, and through two-year compulsory military service that combined military training with political indoctrination.[461] Unity in Somaliland was not imposed but achieved through bottom-up pressures,[462] but the risk of infighting and weakening of the entity still affected the kind of state-building process that followed; unity was given priority. This is a feature not just of Somaliland, but of unrecognized states in general.

However, while there is a risk of infighting, there is also a risk of too much unity: the factors that enable unrecognized states to overcome the hurdle of fractionalization also constrain the subsequent state-building process.

Building Effective, Legitimate Entities

Building a state-like entity at its most immediate level involves creating the symbolic attributes of statehood, such as a flag, a national anthem, national holidays, a head of state, and so on. Unrecognized states are making more ambitious claims than this. They claim to have created effective state-like structures that enable them to defend their territory and provide basic public services. The authorities in Transnistria, for example, argue that the entity has 'all attributes of a modern independent state', including '[its] own parliament, a central bank, courts, a modern democratic Constitution, army, police, border patrol, human rights monitors, a health service, public education system, environmental protection, tax collection'.[463] They are thereby claiming that they have all the necessary attributes of statehood *except* international recognition. Many observers were initially highly sceptical of these claims and tended to see the entities largely as failed or failing states. Kolstø, for example, argued that 'the modal tendency... is deficient state-building' and that the term 'quasi-state' is appropriate, since this is the category most of these states would fall into, were they ever to be recognized.[464] But the assessment of individual cases has gradually changed; Kolstø and Blakkisrud, for example, now argue that Transnistria has moved away from being a 'black hole' and developed 'something akin to full-fledged statehood (minus official recognition)'.[465] This process has, at least in part, been driven by a need for internal legitimacy.

Now it could be argued that popular legitimacy is a foregone conclusion in unrecognized states, unlike in weak recognized states,[466] due to the persistence of an external threat. A leader under pressure can always argue that the only alternative is reintegration into the parent state. Playing this card ensures, at least, a measure of insulation against popular dissatisfaction, especially if the achievement of de facto independence followed a bloody war. But this should not lead us to assume that the issue of popular legitimacy is unproblematic in unrecognized states. War heroes cannot necessarily count on unconditional support. Abkhazia's first president, Vladislav Ardzinba, was increasingly criticized, including for corruption, before he finally stepped down in 2005.

Internal legitimacy is important in unrecognized states, even if the leaders hold the entity in an iron grip and therefore do not depend on popular support for their continued hold on power. Most unrecognized states have less than one million inhabitants and the consequences of war, including the expulsion of a significant proportion of the population, has in many cases led to a demographic crisis.[467] This makes them vulnerable to emigration. Even South Ossetia's authorities put the population size at a minuscule 72,000, Nagorno Karabakh's population numbers 135,000 at the most, and Abkhazia's population is usually also estimated to be under 200,000.[468] Northern Cyprus is only slightly bigger with a population of 257,000, while Transnistria's population is estimated at just over 500,000.[469] But even larger unrecognized states or entities with no demographic crisis seek to avoid significant emigration, as it undermines the authorities' claim to majority support for independence and it makes it harder to mobilize an army of committed soldiers.

One way of convincing the population to stay and defend the entity is to offer generous public services. In Nagorno Karabakh, the authorities have tried to reverse the entity's negative demographic trend through a range of different measures: they have increased the level of social benefits, they offer substantial incentives for refugees to settle in underpopulated villages,[470] and they even organized a much-publicized mass wedding. In a bizarre ceremony, reminiscent of the Moon movement, 700 couples tied the knot and were awarded grants of $2,000, in addition to the $1,000 grant that all newlyweds receive from the government.[471] One year later, a baby boom was reported in the entity.[472] Legitimacy is, especially in a post-Soviet context, closely tied to social justice and fairness[473] and the economic argument has also played a central role in building support for Transnistrian statehood,[474] especially as Transnistrians 'almost uniformly believe Moldovans are significantly worse off economically than they are'.[475] This has, however, not completely eliminated the risk of emigration: the Transnistrian population has fallen from 770,000 in 1989 to an estimated 522,500 at the beginning of 2010.[476]

The ability of unrecognized states to buy popular support, however, varies significantly. It is one thing to move away from being a black hole and quite another to provide adequate public services, such as education and a health care system, let alone generous welfare payments. Some unrecognized states have wealthy external supporters or have generated their own economic development, while others struggle to raise enough revenue to keep the entity functioning. In fact, it makes little sense to try to compare the level of public services in cases as different as Taiwan and Somaliland. The context of nonrecognition creates incentives for state-building, and unrecognized states manage through external linkages to attract enough resources to maintain their de facto independence, but the level of resources available to them varies significantly and results in different levels of state-building. The more important question to ask is therefore if the context of nonrecognition constrains the process of state-building, regardless of the level of resources that the unrecognized states have access to, and thereby results in entities that differ from their recognized counterparts.

Lack of resources and the consequent inability to buy popular support does, moreover, not mean that resource-starved entities are necessarily devoid of internal legitimacy. First, the level of public services that really matters is relative; the unrecognized state may not be able to provide generous public services, or even adequate ones, but this is less of a problem if the same is true for the parent state. Again we find significant variation: Somaliland is clearly more effective than Somalia; Transnistria and Moldova do not differ much; while South Ossetia fails to match Georgia's level of state-building. Second, other sources of popular legitimacy are available. Legitimacy can stem from the initial victory and the ethno-nationalist goal, although this may to some extent be undermined if the promises of security and prosperity remain unfulfilled. The leaders of unrecognized states can, moreover, try to stave off such looming dissatisfaction by introducing political reforms.

Introducing Political Reforms

Rhetorical commitment to democracy is found in a majority of the cases, but popular legitimacy has traditionally been demonstrated through independence referenda, rather than through actual democratic elections. The leaders strive to present a united front and avoid the airing of internal divisions, so if elections were held they mostly served to confirm the ascendance of nationalists to power. The elections held in Chechnya in 1991, for example, followed what essentially amounted to an armed coup by Chechen nationalists and were marred by irregularities.[477] The Chechen nationalist leaders considered them to be a referendum on independence and their function was to demonstrate nationalist unity and popular legitimacy.[478]

Within the last decade or so, the emphasis placed on democratization has increased—but does this democratic rhetoric have any substance or is it directed at an external audience only? Isachenko, for example, argues that the Transnistrian regime in response to international pressures has worked 'diligently to create at least the facade of democracy by simulating such symptoms as having opposition groups and civil society'.[479] In the case of Nagorno Karabakh, the rhetoric of democratization was readily adopted after de facto independence was achieved, but the problem was that no one really knew what it entailed,[480] and the reality in the immediate postwar period was in any case very different. There was a lack of civilian control over the armed forces, and the army commander, Babayan, tended to exert his power through fear. A local journalist describes how drivers were afraid to overtake his car, fearing the consequences if they did so,[481] and there are stories of parents who sent their daughters away from the capital, Stepanakert, dreading what would happen if Babayan took a liking to them.[482]

Since then significant reforms have been introduced in Nagorno Karabakh,[483] and progress is also discernible in a number of other cases. We have consequently seen a process of gradual transition away from rule by authoritarian war heroes toward some form of proto-democracy. Somaliland for more than a decade appeared stuck in what Mark Bradbury describes as a 'seemingly endless political transition',[484] but in response to internal pressures and external threats to its de facto independence, democratization finally started moving along. Political parties were legalized in 2001,[485] district elections were held in 2002, presidential elections in 2003, and parliamentary elections in 2005. Despite lack of democratic experience and continued problems of government interference in the electoral process,[486] the outcome must be described as a success. Some international observers even described the 2003 elections as being among the freest and most transparent ever staged in the Horn of Africa.[487] When the first president of Somaliland, Mohamed Egal, died in 2002, power was smoothly passed to the vice-president and after a supreme court ruling the opposition accepted his victory in a very closely fought election.[488] Another example is provided by Abkhazia. For many years, Abkhazia seemed an unlikely candidate for democratization. The entity was left devastated after the war, violence occasionally still flared up, and the authorities were more than reluctant to loosen their grip on power. The first president of Abkhazia, Vladislav Ardzinba, was unopposed when he ran for re-election in 1999 and the opposition withdrew most of its candidates in the 2002 parliamentary elections in protest over the conduct of the campaign.[489] Things had changed by 2004, however, when the opposition candidate won the presidential election. Previously, the opposition had been weak, but an assortment of civil society organizations, the veterans' association, businessmen, and disgruntled former government ministers managed to wrest power from the incumbent regime. Despite high levels of tension, power was eventually transferred to the winning candidate. Change in leadership through contested elections is an important aspect of democratization but by no means the only one. The holding of elections has, however, been accompanied by increasingly pluralistic civil society and media.[490]

It would therefore seem that at least in some cases there is more to democratization than mere rhetoric, and a potential reason for this is the need for internal legitimacy. A crisis of international legitimacy provided an external impetus for political reforms in Taiwan, but the regime also had to become more in tune with local demands and concerns. As a result of de-recognition Taiwan received less international aid and the regime consequently needed to be able to extract resources from the population. The mainlander soldiers, who had made up the large part of the Taiwanese army, were moreover nearing retirement and it was therefore also necessary to be able to mobilize people for the defence of the island. A process of indigenization and democratization consequently followed.[491] Similarly, an important impetus behind democratization in Somaliland was the need to ensure internal stability. The protracted negotiations over the electoral law for the 2005 parliamentary elections led the opposition to threaten civil unrest if the elections were not forthcoming.[492] Finally, ethno-nationalism has been an important driving force in many unrecognized states and this has led to expectations of popular legitimacy. The advisor to the Karabakh president, for example, argues that the struggle for independence was a fight against tyranny and oppression, and 'without democracy, the Karabakh independence movement makes no sense'.[493]

Such reform processes have become increasingly feasible in the situation of 'no war, no peace'. After the homogenization caused by the war, or imposed during the war, pluralism gradually emerged and political differences as well as power struggles came to the fore. This pluralization was driven by economic problems and by popular dissatisfaction with the corruption and war profiteering associated with the authorities. In some cases, business interests played a significant role in the beginning process of democratization—most notably in Transnistria, where the Renewal (*Obnovlenie*) movement—associated with Transnistria's largest company, Sheriff—pressed for democratization and an end to isolation, and managed to win a majority in the 2005 parliamentary elections.[494] In Nagorno Karabakh, the emphasis on democratic rule had for years remained merely a proclamation, with little actual impact, but the overthrow of the army strongman and the imposition of civilian rule in 1999 created space for a political opposition to emerge. The unrest caused by the conflict breathed life into the democratic opposition, which had hitherto been embryonic. This opposition could use the democratic rhetoric employed by the authorities and turn it against them, and the 2000 parliamentary elections saw the first sign of genuine political pluralism.[495] The conflict between the civilian and the military leader thereby came to affect not only the process of state-building but also the process of democratization. The civilian leadership had consolidated power in the entity but this process acted as a catalyst for increasing pluralism, driven by dissatisfaction with the pace of democratization and the lack of socioeconomic progress.[496] Chechnya, on the other hand, illustrates how lack of state-building hampers any attempts at political reform. In response to the increasingly chaotic situation in the entity, and in an attempt to undercut his internal rivals, the Chechen leader, Mashkadov, abandoned the democratic rhetoric and instead championed the creation of an Islamic state.[497]

The question is, however, if meaningful democratization can even be promoted without internationally recognized sovereignty? In democratization literature this is, after all, frequently seen as a prerequisite.[498] Roland Paris convincingly argued that we know very little about the effect of democratization in countries that have recently experienced civil conflict, and he subsequently tried to rectify this,[499] but we know even less about the effect in unrecognized states in a context of 'no war, no peace'. Tansey argues that the obstacles to democratization encountered by unrecognized states are not tied to lack of recognition, but have much more conventional sources,[500] and it could even be argued that unrecognized states have a stronger incentive to democratize than recognized states. Not only are unrecognized states keen to demonstrate their democratic credentials to the outside world, there has at least historically also been a link between nationalism and democratization,[501] and leaders of unrecognized states could consequently be described as 'natural democrats'. Michael Lind, for example, contends that nationalism is a necessary condition for democracy,[502] Chaim Kaufmann argues that democratization is easier following ethnic partition,[503] and Margaret Moore finds that, 'self-determination may be necessary to secure the basic conditions for a well-functioning... democracy'.[504] That ethnic partition should facilitate democratization is, however, strongly refuted by Radha Kumar,[505] and several other scholars also dismiss the notion of a positive link between nationalism and democracy. Etzioni, for example, writes about a 'new and unproductive strain of self-determination' that undermines democracy.[506]

An analysis of Freedom House scores for unrecognized states would appear to confirm Tansey's view: nonrecognition does not appear to significantly affect democratization. Thus, unrecognized states span the entire spectrum from 'nonfree' (South Ossetia and Transnistria), through 'partly free' (Abkhazia, Kosovo, Nagorno Karabakh, Somaliland) to 'free' (Northern Cyprus and Taiwan).[507] Similar variation is found among their parent states: from nonfree (China, Somalia, Azerbaijan), through partly free (Georgia, Moldova), to free (Cyprus, Serbia). On the one hand, this shows that there is more to the proclamation of democratic values than mere rhetoric, which is important since dictatorships also frequently make democratic claims. On the other hand, it suggests that we should not exaggerate the effect of nonrecognition or ethno-nationalism; ethno-nationalist leaders of unrecognized states can become committed democrats, but not all leaders find democratization irresistible.

Even though we find significant variation when it comes to both state-building and democratization, we should not discount the effect of nonrecognition. In fact, the analysis given in the following section will demonstrate that lack of recognition, along with the path of their creation, has a significant impact on the kinds of entities that emerge. Sovereignty matters, both for state-building and for democratization.

Ambiguous Statehood

To say that nonrecognition matters is not to suggest that state-building and democratization has not taken place in unrecognized states—it has in fact reached surprising levels in some of them—but the impetus toward such reforms is counteracted by other forces. The authorities, for example, face a powerful temptation to create facade democracies, as a strategy for pleasing international audiences, while at the same time avoiding looming internal discontent. The unrecognized states have achieved different degrees of statehood and political reforms, but they face constraints that differ from those faced by recognized states; this suggests that they should not be seen as 'states-in-all-but-name'. Unrecognized states are torn between providing a strong state and an effective state, and between promoting unity, plurality, and diversity. The entities oscillate between these different identities and the cross-pressures may lead them to merely imitate recognized statehood.

LIVERPOOL JOHN MOORES UNIVERSITY
LEARNING SERVICES

Constrained State-Building

The lack of international recognition provides a powerful incentive for state-building, but this context also puts obstacles in the way; the most significant of which are associated with the legacy of war and the persistence of an external threat. The war often led to significant destruction, a shortage of resources, and infighting warlords, and although these can be overcome, what remains is a prioritizing of security. The resumption of war remains a very real possibility and a large share of revenues raised is therefore channelled into the defence sector.[508] The Transnistrian army is, for example, larger than Moldova's, even though Moldova has six times as many inhabitants,[509] and it has been argued that Nagorno Karabakh may be the 'world's most militarised society'.[510] The Karabakh standing army is estimated at 18,500 men and women, and the reserve force is said to be between 20,000 and 30,000 strong. This includes soldiers from Armenia proper, but with a population estimated at fewer than 135,000, we are nevertheless left with an astonishingly high percentage of people under arms. Taiwan's number of troops totals nearly two million (including 1.7 million in reserve) and although this is dwarfed by China's 3.5 million troops it represents no less than 8 per cent of the population. Northern Cyprus's troop total is 31,000, which is about half the size of its parent state's armed forces, but this still amounts to a very high 12 per cent of the population.[511] Somaliland's 15,000-strong standing army is, finally, seven times bigger than Somalia's.[512] Such prioritizing of the army creates an imbalance, as resources are taken away from other areas in need of development. Defence is seen as more important than education and health and such priorities in state-building risk undermining the internal legitimacy of the entity.

The channelling of resources away from other public services is not the only obstacle to effective state-building. The initial processes of state-building in many cases served the purpose of ensuring internal control—especially in conflicts that were not the product of bottom-up pressures—but this kind of state-building risks creating a 'hard state' rather than a 'strong state'.[513] When security and unity are prioritized, individual liberties tend to suffer. Martial law is tellingly still in place in many unrecognized states, even many years after the signing of the ceasefire agreement. In Taiwan martial law lasted for thirty-eight years and in Nagorno Karabakh it is still in place seventeen years after the ceasefire agreement. The Karabakh authorities are adamant that this is now largely symbolic,[514] but it does provide the authorities with the power to dispense with civil liberties. A more extreme example is found in Republika Srpska Krajina where the army played an important role in ensuring internal cohesion. It severely restricted people's ability to leave the entity and forcibly mobilized the adult male population; young men who had crossed the border into Serbia were in some cases forced on a bus back to Krajina where they had to join the army.[515] Restrictions are also found in unrecognized states that are more concerned with their international image, and in less immediate danger of a military offensive. In Somaliland the executive branch, for example, continues to operate a security committee that has sweeping powers of arrest and sentencing,[516] and the political process is also constrained by military priorities: voting does not take place in disputed districts, and security concerns led the upper house to postpone the presidential elections due to be held in 2008.[517]

Large defence budgets and the dominance of the military, including in the political sphere, is not unique to unrecognized states, being a common feature of postwar situations, but the tendency is reinforced by the context of nonrecognition: uncertainty and a looming external threat provide powerful arguments for militarization. What may develop is, therefore, a highly militarized entity that has a reasonably effective army but lacks effectiveness in other areas and chooses to restrict civil liberties. Although I therefore disagree with Tamás that these separatist regions are anti-statist—in some ways their lack of recognition and their precarious status result in highly committed state-builders—the context in which they find themselves significantly shapes and limits their statehood. The interaction of state-building and lack of external sovereignty constrains the statehood that is (or is not) created in these entities; nonrecognition is not only an incentive for state-building, it is also an obstacle.

Constrained Democratization

At first sight, there would appear to be fewer obstacles to democratization than to state-building in unrecognized states; a claim to popular legitimacy was, after all, integral to their rhetoric from the outset and a strong national identity is often believed to favour well-functioning democracy. But the prioritization of security above all else also has a significant effect on the introduction of political reforms. Nationalism and democracy are, moreover, 'joined in a sort of complicated marriage, unable to live without each other, but co-existing in an almost permanent state of tensions',[518] and it is therefore not surprising that Nicholas Sambanis finds that the effect of partition on

democratization is inconclusive.[519] The relationship between nationalism and democratization is less than straightforward and it is further
complicated by the context of nonrecognition.

We should therefore not be fooled by the strong rhetorical commitment to effective, democratic institutions that we find in unrecognized
states. Democratization is, first, not exempt from the problems facing
recognized states in transition: unrecognized states also struggle with
contested election results, limited political differences, lack of well-
established socioeconomic cleavages, and so on. One of the leaders of
the Nagorno Karabakh opposition, in his assessment of the level of
democracy in the entity, argued, 'We are not suppressed or beaten;
there is no violence, no blackmail. The opposition can appear on
TV etc. However, there is the issue of administrative resources.'[520]
Second, we find a tendency to prioritize form over substance. The
Nagorno Karabakh authorities are, for example, clearly familiar with
the basic requirements of a democratic system, but any move away
from an authoritarian system is reportedly considered proof of a well-
functioning democracy,[521] and the preoccupation with form over substance was illustrated with striking clumsiness when I observed the
entity's constitutional referendum on a freezing-cold December day in
2006. Upon returning from a long day of monitoring, I was presented
with a pre-written report which—unsurprisingly—endorsed not only
the referendum but also the constitution as being the epitome of
democracy. With a mild sense of alarm, I refused to sign this report,
as it was not based on observations I had made, and tried not to dwell
too much on the possible repercussions of this refusal. As it turned
out, the officials merely shrugged and asked if I wanted to submit a
separate report instead.[522] Their main concern was with the international image they hoped to convey and with a simplified, procedural
view of democracy—'we must have international observers'. To some
extent this reflects inexperience with the democratic process, but the
political reforms in unrecognized states are also subject to important
tensions, and facade democracy represents a tempting strategy for
negotiating these.

Two sets of tensions, in particular, affect and constrain democratization in unrecognized states. First, the political competition entailed
by democracy contradicts the nationalist claim to unity and homogeneous interests; the claim that the leaders speak for all Armenians, all
Turkish Cypriots, all Ossetians, and so on. Second, the concept of 'the
people' in self-determination movements is often ethnically exclusive
and there is, consequently, a tension between the 'ethnos' of self-
determination and the 'demos' of liberal democracy. Both tensions are

compounded by the context of nonrecognition: by the unresolved status of the entities and the perceived need for unity when faced with an external threat.

Etzioni argues that breakaway territories are often based on the denial of pluralism and the deliberate fostering of homogeneity. This undermines the prospects for democracy.[523] Political conflict is not merely normal in democracies, it is rather healthy,[524] and Paris reminds us that 'political contestation is no less a requirement of democracy than popular participation'.[525] But unrecognized states draw a lot of strength from the common identity they have fostered,[526] so why risk jeopardizing this by encouraging political divisions? There is a perceived need for unity and a fear that any divisions will weaken the entity. The proclaimed unity is, furthermore, central to their claim to self-determination, which is based on homogenous interests and aspirations. In some cases, this intracommunal consensus is largely imposed—a claim to self-determination can paradoxically be an authoritarian claim—and this only serves to make the leadership even more wary of the dangers posed by pluralism. The emphasis on unity is reinforced by the persistence of an external threat and the predominance of the military, and hence by the context of nonrecognition. This can lead to the creation of 'racketeer states',[527] in which the regimes exchange protection for loyalty: 'You do not have to think, we will protect you.'

Resulting from this tension is a situation in which political competition and debate is simultaneously encouraged and constrained. In Somaliland, the need for unity and avoidance of internal strife has undermined what are otherwise significant democratic achievements. The Somaliland authorities fear the apparent fragility of political consensus and have on more than one occasion restricted freedom of expression. In 2004 the Somaliland minister of the interior banned all organized debates on the potential impact of the Somalia National Reconciliation Conference,[528] and a weekly magazine that dared discuss the idea of Somaliland reuniting with Somalia was banned. The chairman of a media network and two journalists, moreover, spent two months in jail for having written about presidential corruption.[529] Unity is even institutionalized in the sense that only the three winning parties from the 2002 local elections have been allowed to field candidates for subsequent elections and they are, moreover, required to have significant support in each of Somaliland's six regions.[530] The authorities argue that such restrictions are needed, as a proliferation of parties could produce a fragmented and clan-based political system that might lead to instability and even collapse, as in the parent state Somalia.[531]

Similar concerns are used to justify the disproportionate power of clan leaders,[532] and the significant influence of an unelected upper house (the *Guurti*). Unity is, as the Director of Apsnypress in Abkhazia argues, 'often understood as agreement of opinion',[533] and such an interpretation will frequently be strongly encouraged by the authorities. In Nagorno Karabakh, the authorities have for years cultivated the perception that internal divisions constitute a threat to the entity's survival,[534] while unity in other cases is more directly imposed. The Transnistrian leadership, for example, accuses the opposition of being 'traitors' and 'fifth column'.[535] Any criticism of Transnistrian independence is framed as a threat to state security and 'offenders' were in the early years of the entity's existence given lengthy prison sentences.[536] Protsyk argues that the Transnistrian regime has 'chosen to severely restrict political competition in order to consolidate its hold on power and to maintain the appearance of public consensus on the issue of independence'.[537] But direct repression of dissent is not always necessary, as the opposition may be convinced to voluntarily curb its activities. The argument for unity is so powerful that unity is often ensured through self-imposed restraint. Immediately after the 2005 Transnistrian elections, the two main parties held a joint press conference at which they stressed the unity of their positions on the question of independence.[538] In the presidential elections the following year, the leader of the Transnistrian opposition did not run against the incumbent, arguing that it would risk destabilizing the state and 'for us the main priority is to resist external threats and to preserve Pridnestrovie [Transnistria] as a state'.[539] In the latest presidential elections in Nagorno Karabakh, all parliamentary deputies supported the regime candidate, citing the need for unity.[540]

Democratization in the context of a prevalent siege mentality clearly creates a number of contradictions; it makes it easier for the authorities to constrain and limit the process of democratization, and makes it more likely that the opposition will voluntarily curb its activities. Nevertheless, some developments have been seen in the years of 'no war, no peace', and pluralism has, contrary to Etzioni's claim, gradually emerged. For example, in Transnistria pluralism increased as the threat to the entity's statehood subsided,[541] and the political debate in the unrecognized states in the Caucasus is now often lively, whereas there was little or no political competition in the first elections. As the threat of war seemingly moves into the background, it becomes harder to justify an imposed unity and the goal of recognition and the promise of self-determination have been key factors in the gradual pluralization of the politics of unrecognized states.

Democratization in the context of a claim to national self-determination, however, raises another crucial question that presents significant dilemmas for the leaders of some unrecognized states: who are 'the people'? There is a tension between 'ethnos' and 'demos', between an ethnic and a civic definition of the people, and the former tends to be favoured.[542] This is an important argument raised by scholars who see nationalism and democracy as mutually hostile; in many cases, democratization is a privilege reserved for the majority. To be more specific, this emphasis on 'ethnos'—the prioritizing of collective rights—reflects a tension with liberalism rather than with democracy.[543] The tension is with *liberal* democracy. Consequently, the goal of national self-determination may favour a move towards popular sovereignty and the accompanying institutionalization of democratic procedures, but it is more difficult to reconcile with liberalism's emphasis on individual human worth and individual rights. The privileged position for the majority is compounded by the Soviet legacy that characterizes a number of unrecognized states. As Laurence Broers argues, this legacy brings with it a lack of comprehension of the possibility of a civic state; 'titular majorities expect the state to promote the symbols and interests of the titular nation'.[544] This is most problematic in the case of Abkhazia, since the Abkhaz only constituted 17.8 per cent of Abkhazia's prewar population, and even following the expulsion of the majority of Georgians from the region, the Abkhaz share of the population is at the most 44 per cent.[545] Nevertheless, 'crucial elements of democracy in Abkhazia' are for the ethnic Abkhaz only.[546] The Armenian and Russian minorities supported the Abkhaz fight for self-determination, with the Armenians even constituting almost a quarter of the Abkhaz army,[547] but they are nevertheless underrepresented in the political system structures; they each hold three seats in the thirty-five-seat Abkhaz parliament.[548] The main problem, however, is the Georgian returnees, who account for roughly a third of the population, and whom Georgia accuses Abkhazia of having disenfranchised.[549] Due to its prewar demographics Abkhazia may be an extreme case, but similar charges are raised against almost all unrecognized states.

Ethnic Democracies Running Out of Steam

It would therefore seem that unrecognized states—at best—tend toward a form of 'ethnic democracy', which Sammy Smooha defines as a non-civic form of democracy in which citizenship is extended to all, but the 'in-group' enjoys a superior position; it is a 'distinct but diminished type of democracy' propelled by ethnic nationalism,[550] which can be seen as a compromise between nationalism and democracy.[551] But this would overlook the context of nonrecognition, which, again, provides a potential catalyst for change. The hegemonic value that the entities are trying to emulate is liberal democracy, and the struggle for recognition may provide the necessary incentive to move toward a more civic form of democratization. As Allen Buchanan argues, precisely because secessionist entities crave international recognition, they may be more amenable to pressures for minority rights.[552] This is, for example, illustrated in the attempts by Somaliland to portray itself as a pluralistic multiclan entity, rather than as an entity dominated by the Isaaq clan.[553] This self-image of a multiclan entity appears to have taken root and is therefore not just for international consumption. Thus, when the first president of Somalia died, power smoothly passed to his vice-president even though he was from the small Gadabushi clan and had fought for Siad Barre against the Isaaqs.[554] The multiclan identity helps ensure internal consensus and stability and this is, in turn, thought to increase the chance of recognition.[555]

Moreover, the demographic facts in some of these entities require them to try to build broader alliances if they are to be able to demonstrate majority support for their cause. The Montenegrin leadership, prior to its independence referendum, was keen to create a Montenegrin identity that included the sizeable Albanian and Bosniak minorities. They recognized that ethnic Montenegrins did not by themselves constitute a majority and that they would therefore need the support of the republic's minorities.[556] Transnistria is another multi-ethnic unrecognized state that has grappled with its identity. The entity's population is made up of Moldovans, Ukrainians, and Russians, and the large proportion of Moldovans (estimated between 34 and 40 per cent)[557] makes it imperative for the regime to construct an identity that legitimizes its claim to separate statehood from Moldova and supports the purported majority backing for independence. The creation of an inclusive Transnistrian identity matters for both the external and internal legitimacy of the entity and has therefore been a priority from the outset,[558] although there is disagreement over the extent to which it reflects realities on the ground.[559] A similar combination of perceived external pressures to reform and lack of an outright majority has affected debates over identity in Abkhazia. Abkhazia's leaders vehemently deny allegations that Abkhazia's Georgian population has been disenfranchised,[560] and before Abkhazia was recognized by Russia, in August 2008, the entity's foreign minister, for example, argued that the leadership was doing 'everything we can' to integrate

Abkhazia's Georgian population.[561] Tensions between an ethnic and a civic understanding of the nation remain prominent, for example in the Abkhaz constitution,[562] which requires the president to be ethnically Abkhaz and speak Abkhaz, and there is a lack of mechanisms to counteract discrimination,[563] but it is not a case of clear-cut ethnocentrism.[564] The beginning attempts to forge a more inclusive Abkhaz identity should be seen as significant, as the Abkhaz leadership had explicitly used the argument of *national* self-determination to legitimize the entity's claim to independence. Concerns over international acceptability can instil a claim to national self-determination with a degree of fluidity.

Despite such examples of internal contestation of national identities, the possibility of adopting a more inclusive identity remains severely constrained; and it is once again the context of nonrecognition that provides both the impetus for and the obstacle to change. Kolstø and Blakkisrud point out that the absence of a recognized passport makes it harder to create a Transnistrian identity;[565] one of the symbols of inclusive identity is simply not available to unrecognized states. Even more important, demography is at the heart of these conflicts. The question, 'Who are the people?' has in many cases been left unanswered pending a solution on the issue of status. The reluctance to move away from an exclusive definition, not only of identity but also of the statehood that is being created, is moreover reinforced by the fear of renewed violence, and hence by the uncertain situation in which the unrecognized states find themselves. The Karabakh constitution, for example, contains a mix of 'ethnic' and 'civic' elements: the preamble establishes that the entity is a 'free, sovereign state of citizens with equal rights' and the constitution protects the freedom of religion (art. 26), but it also emphasizes that Karabakh realizes the dreams of 'our ancestors' and that this dream has been fulfilled 'with the power of unity of all Armenians in the world'. The constitution, moreover, recognizes the Apostolic Church of Armenia as the national church (art. 10) and establishes Armenian as the (sole) state language, although it guarantees the freedom of use of other languages (art. 14).[566] This kind of ambiguity does not differ significantly from constitutions adopted by recognized states founded by self-determination movements, and Karabakh's constitution is no more 'ethnic' than the constitutions initially adopted by the former Yugoslav republics. But the constitution is silent on one crucial point: the issue of citizenship, which is to be regulated by law. The authorities are keen to stress their tolerant attitudes and argue that they are, in principle, open to considering the return of Azeri refugees,[567] but this self-proclaimed tolerance cannot be realized until Karabakh's independence is ensured. As a consequence, the civic elements of the constitution remain largely symbolic, and Karabakh's leaders continue to reinforce the entity's homogeneous nature. The entity is caught between trying to portray itself as democratic and liberal, and at the same time protecting itself against any threat to its de facto independence. Similarly, a vocal constituency in Abkhazia argues that the mere presence, not to mention equal rights, of non-Abkhaz communities risks undermining the goal of independence and also poses a threat to the physical survival of the Abkhaz.[568] The entity is constantly preparing for renewed hostilities and this makes the Abkhaz suspicious of minorities: can they be counted on to defend Abkhazia?[569] The Abkhaz authorities are therefore engaged in a difficult balancing act: adopting more inclusive policies, with an eye to the entity's demographic crisis and international image, *and* strengthening the Abkhaz language, identity, and culture.[570]

Multi-ethnicity is not necessarily a problem for unrecognized states, but they struggle with minorities—or even pluralities—who share ethnicity with that of the parent state. Recognized states might also view such minorities with suspicion, but the unresolved status of unrecognized states and the fear of a military offensive make such worries more acute. Despite the professed multi-ethnic character of Transnistria, the question of what constitutes Moldovan identity has been highly politicized. The authorities insist that 'Transnistrian Moldovan' identity must be distinct from 'Moldovan Moldovan' identity and have for example imposed the use of the Cyrillic alphabet instead of the Latin alphabet used across the de facto border.[571] Moldovans are, moreover, underrepresented in political organs, and Protsyk argues that restrictions on political competition are directed, in particular, at potential challengers from the ethnic Moldovan community.[572]

Thus, the context of nonrecognition and the goal of national self-determination is a double-edged sword: it provides an impetus for democratic statehood but at the same time constrains it, or at least affects the form that we can expect to see. The upshot is that unrecognized states often run out of steam and find themselves in a seemingly perpetual transition; they make steps toward democratization but reach a plateau fairly early on and may even experience democratic setbacks. Kurdistan has been described as being 'caught in a transitional phase',[573] Kosovo as having achieved only a 'qualified political transition',[574] while democratization in Nagorno Karabakh seems unlikely to proceed further; a local analyst comments that democratization has now reached a sufficient level to create popular satisfaction.[575] Even in Somaliland, which has long prided itself as a democratic oasis in the Horn of Africa, the situation is assessed to have deteriorated since 2006,[576] and there are now increasing worries about the gradual introduction of one-party rule.[577] In 2006, elections to the upper house were postponed for four years as it was not possible to agree on how to distribute seats and choose members. In the following year three politicians were jailed for almost five months for trying to form a new political party.[578] The need for unity is prioritized and the resulting incomplete transition is reinforced by a growing perception that democratization may not provide a quick route to international recognition after all; whereas democracy was the buzzword of the 1990s and most of the 2000s, stability looks to be the key priority of the 2010s.[579]

Nonrecognition does therefore not constitute an insurmountable obstacle to democratization—democracy does not need sovereignty— but the process differs in important ways from that generally observed in recognized states. The lack of recognition and the need to create a self-sustainable entity creates important incentives for political reforms. What we find, even in a case such as Transnistria that is classed as 'nonfree' by Freedom House, is therefore not a closed autocracy: suppression of opposition coexists with elements of genuine pluralism and competition.[580] But nonrecognition also puts important obstacles in its way, as does the ideology of ethno-nationalism. The result is a tendency toward hybrid regimes. This does not mean the complete absence of political competition, but there is strong temptation to imitate democracy and ignore most of its substance. The prioritization of security leads to an emphasis on the need for a 'strong man' and makes it easier to curb opposition and insist on unity.

There are two noteworthy exceptions that are both classed as 'free' by Freedom House: Northern Cyprus and Taiwan. What explains this? First, the above analysis has identified a tendency, not a rule: nonrecognition does not determine the political system, but it does constrain it. Second, the starting point for democratization was much better in these two cases, as the state-building process was completed and democratization was therefore not hampered by state weakness. Finally, both of these entities have better relations with their parent states than many unrecognized states. China's military threat against Taiwan is muted as long as the island does not declare independence, and relations with the parent state have meanwhile improved considerably. Northern Cyprus has even less reason to fear a military attack from its parent state and increasing engagement characterizes relations between the two parts of the island. Democracy in Taiwan and Northern Cyprus is, in any case, not perfect. The Taiwanese authorities are criticized for limiting academic freedom and for putting increasing pressure on government critics 'and individuals whose activities could displease the Chinese authorities', while Northern Cyprus is criticized for having disenfranchised its Greek Cypriot minority population.[581]

Democratization in unrecognized states therefore generally points to a more pronounced form of 'ethnic democracy' than the one identified by Smooha. The status of the entities is precarious and the siege mentality is acute, and the form of regime that tends to develop is therefore even more defensive, and the issue of citizenship is still unresolved. It is, consequently, not only a question of a privileged position for the majority; significant groups may be permanently excluded from the process. In addition, the perceived need for unity also results in limitations for the majority's participation in the political process. The form of 'ethnic democracy' that is evolving in unrecognized states is, however, under considerable pressure, and appears less stable than the political regime Smooha identified in Israel. Due to the pressures of nonrecognition, the regimes may revert to being non-democracies, but they could conceivably also evolve in the direction of a less limited, more inclusive form of democratization. One of the factors that Smooha finds to be conducive to a stable 'ethnic democracy' is demonstrably absent in unrecognized states: noninterference on the part of the minority's external homeland and the international community. The risk of (military) interference by the parent state, and the desire for international recognition, lends a great deal of fluidity to the situation. The latter produces an incentive to create an entity that will meet with international approval, but the former fosters incentives for closing ranks behind the leader, for centralization and militarization and for exclusive statehood.[582]

Squaring the Circle of Unrecognized Statehood

Warlords can be turned into committed state-builders, but the legacy of war and the lack of international recognition put important obstacles in the way of effective state-building. Unrecognized states vary significantly in terms of the degree of their statehood—the degree of internal sovereignty that they have achieved—but they also face similar constraints. What tends to develop, regardless of the level of resources to which they have access, is a militarized entity that emphasizes unity, relies on a narrow definition of its identity, and is dependent on external support. These characteristics are not unique to unrecognized states, but they are strongly reinforced by the context of nonrecognition. Unrecognized states are, moreover, exposed to a number of countervailing factors: they strive for international acceptability, they need to create a militarily strong entity, and they must avoid a looming demographic crisis. If unrecognized states manage to overcome the risk of infighting warlords and create the unity necessary for state-building to proceed, a difficult balancing act therefore ensues: how is it possible to negotiate the often countervailing goals of international acceptability, de facto independence, and popular legitimacy?

How the unrecognized states decide to negotiate these tensions depends in particular on their access to resources.[583] If they have access to significant external resources and are therefore able to provide adequate public services, then they will, for example, be in less need of implementing genuine political reforms. Similarly, if they can rely on a resourceful external patron, then they may be tempted to reduce their attempts to achieve general international acceptability and therefore scale back their democratizing rhetoric. But the ability of the authorities to veer too far in one direction is significantly constrained. The different goals are not unrelated, and downplaying one of them risks jeopardizing the statehood that has so far been achieved. In order to ensure the continued survival of the entity, it may be tempting for the authorities to create militarized regimes that closely follow the tune of external patrons, but this would jeopardize their chances of international recognition and arguably also undermine any remnants of popular legitimacy. Most unrecognized states will therefore try to square the circle and achieve all of these goals at once, but this results in the ambiguous form of statehood outlined above; statehood that is at the same time independent and dependent, open and closed, pluralistic and homogeneous. And the question is if such unrecognized statehood can be sustained in the long term, especially if international recognition does not appear to be forthcoming.

5 RETHINKING SOVEREIGNTY AND STATEHOOD

> Without full access to the World Order, both the peoples of these *de facto* states and the international community at large suffer
> —Unrepresented Nations and Peoples Organization[584]

Critics might liken a comparative analysis of unrecognized states to the proverbial attempt to compare apples and oranges. After all, how can we compare the war-ravaged chaos of Chechnya to the relative stability of Nagorno Karabakh, not to mention the prosperity and advanced development of Taiwan? Comparing apples and oranges is, however, not as senseless as the expression suggests: both apples and oranges are fruits, after all, and they share important characteristics. The same is true of unrecognized states. They may differ in important respects, notably when it comes to their success in building effective statehood, but there are also important similarities. Statehood can exist without external sovereignty but it takes a specific form. This is not to say that all unrecognized states turn out the same way; the previous chapters clearly illustrate that this is not the case. Some unrecognized states do not stray far from the image of anarchical badlands while others manage to create surprisingly well-functioning entities. But lack of recognition matters, even in today's globalized world, and the conditions of their existence are consequently similar. Unrecognized states may, at some point of their existence, resemble failed or failing states, but their propensity both for failed and successful state-building differs from their recognized counterparts.

The context of nonrecognition combined with the goal of de jure sovereignty gives these entities a quality that is both ambiguous and transitory. Although some of these entities, such as Northern Cyprus, have survived for decades they are seen by others and (more important) tend to perceive themselves as temporary phenomena. The imagined transition is, however, based on a clear endpoint—only full, internationally recognized independence is deemed acceptable—and could therefore prove very long indeed. This refusal to compromise sets unrecognized states apart from other entities that challenge classic conceptions of sovereignty, for example entities such as Monaco and Andorra that have pragmatically accepted less than full sovereignty. The demand for full independence is often maintained by the unrecognized states even in view of limited viability and little chance of international support. Dogged determinism appears to be a key characteristic of these entities, or rather of their leadership, as was aptly illustrated when the then-president of Republika Srpska Krajina, Milan Martić, refused any form of cooperation with Croatia, even though energy supplies to the entity were running out, and declared that they would just have to use horse power instead.[585]

How sustainable is the status quo? Can unrecognized states continue living in a situation of limbo? Can they keep on balancing the often contradictory goals driving their statehood and what happens to their internal legitimacy and ability to defend themselves if recognition is not forthcoming? This sustainability is affected by both internal and external factors; it is affected by international norms and practices, but also by internal constraints. Is there a place for these entities in the international system and is this place acceptable to a domestic audience?

The analysis of unrecognized states therefore helps illuminate the nature of the system of sovereign states: the way in which it constrains, but also enables and accommodates, units that do not fit. Moreover, unrecognized states point to important mechanisms of state-building and its interplay with sovereignty and with popular legitimacy. Unrecognized states constitute a spectrum of entities—from failed to strong, or at least relatively effective, states—but this spectrum differs substantially from one of recognized states and this alerts us to central characteristics of both sovereignty and statehood.

State-Building and (Non)Recognition

In his characterization of para-states, Stanislawski argues that 'the lack of effective, recognized governmental control does not mean that these are ungoverned territories'.[586] Such territories represent alternative or contested sources of control, rather than its complete absence. The same is true for unrecognized states; they should not be dismissed as anarchical badlands, as black spots on the international map of sovereign states, but the degree of statehood that they have achieved differs significantly between the cases. Two conclusions can be drawn from this. First, that degree of statehood, or internal sovereignty, should be seen as a variable. This is already well established when it comes to recognized states,[587] but it is nevertheless worth reiterating that it is not a question of either / or: statehood or no statehood. Second, it alerts us to the fact that external sovereignty is not decisive for internal order; it is certainly not sufficient, but it is not necessary either.

This does not mean that recognition does not matter for the ability to build effective entities. International recognition limits external intervention and gives the states access to international material support, and it thereby provides a level of insulation against collapse.[588] Unrecognized states depend on external support for their survival, but such external support is much harder to obtain, and they are not protected by norms of nonintervention. If unrecognized states are unable to build an effective entity, then their continued survival is very much in question. In some ways, unrecognized states are, moreover, more likely than recognized states to experience the kind of fractionalization that is typical of failed states. In addition to the legacy of war, there is a lack of institutions and therefore of constraints on rivalling elites. The lack of recognition, moreover, creates an opportune environment for shadow economies, or as Thomas de Waal argues, 'virtually an incentive to become a rogue state',[589] and therefore provides rival elites with the resources needed to challenge incumbent leaders. Finally, the reliance on an external patron, which is found in most unrecognized states, makes it more likely that the control of key resources is divided. External patrons are not necessarily motivated primarily by the need for unity and may make use of internal divisions to increase their influence in the entity. This happened, for example, in Republika Srpska Krajina where the Serbian government used a divide-and-rule policy, and supplied rival leaders with both coercive and economic resources.

While nonrecognition therefore puts obstacles in the way of the creation of effective statehood, unrecognized states are in some ways in a good position to avoid dangerous infighting and succeed in statebuilding. They may lack the resources and institutions necessary to prevent criminalization, but unrecognized states tend to be relatively homogeneous, which reduces the risk of dangerous fractionalization. Internal cohesion is furthermore strengthened by the persistence of an external threat, and the leadership can make use of the legitimacy they have earned through their military success. Finally, the context of nonrecognition provides a powerful incentive for building an effective entity: an entity that can defend itself and which is deemed internationally acceptable. Unlike 'black spots', unrecognized states do not seek international invisibility,[590] they seek recognition and a place in the international system of sovereign states, and this affects their chances of clearing the hurdles to successful state-building.

Successful state-building seems to be most likely in unrecognized states that are the product of bottom-up conflicts; that receive significant external support; and where army cohesion has been achieved, often due to the sources of support available to the separatist movement. This is, of course, no recipe for escaping the chaos and violence of state failure, and the conditions that enable specific cases to make such a move are bound to differ, but it does nevertheless hold some important lessons for international efforts to rebuild states. First, it points to the importance of internal dynamics. State-building is not just about having enough resources; the failure or success of state-building in unrecognized states cannot simply be reduced to the presence or absence of an external patron. The distribution of these resources, leadership, and visions of statehood are all crucial and help avoid the problem of fractionalization. Second, although external sources of support were found to be important, we should not overestimate the importance of external guidance or underestimate local capabilities. Kaplan has even argued that the lack of international diktat is one of the reasons for the strength of the Somaliland state. 'Somaliland has constructed a functioning government from the bottom up, on its own, with little outside assistance'.[591] The good news is therefore that successful state-building *is* possible, even following near-complete destruction and very difficult circumstances. The bad news is that it is considerably easier in entities that share a common vision and identity, which is something that is not often found in recognized—but failed—states. Third, the analysis demonstrated the potential importance of international norms; home-grown initiatives may be more stable, but external dynamics *are* significant and can provide the needed impetus to successful state-building, even if international organizations are not directly involved. Policymakers should be aware of this interplay and supply appropriate carrots that appeal to the leadership or—if popular constraints exist or can be manipulated—to the general population. Finally, and perhaps most important, state-building in unrecognized states clearly demonstrates that de jure states are not the only possible unit for successful state-building, nor are they necessarily the best suited. This does not entail an argument for secession but it does provide added evidence for the need to look beyond the central government when attempting to rebuild a collapsed state.[592]

Some might counter that the factors enabling successful state-building in unrecognized states, such as external support and internal legitimacy, are very similar to the factors that are important in recognized states. This may be so, but external support is much more problematic in unrecognized states than it is in recognized ones. Moreover, the context of nonrecognition affects the internal legitimacy of the entities; it is aided by the persistence of an external threat and the ideology of ethno-nationalism, but is possibly undermined if recognition is not forthcoming and the authorities are unable to provide adequate public services, including a sense of security.

'States-in-all-but-name'?

In Chapter 1 I asked if unrecognized states are 'states-in-all-but-name', that is, entities that have all the attributes of statehood except recognition. Or is it the case that internal sovereignty cannot exist without external sovereignty? Is the cost of nonrecognition too high, such that it bars these entities from achieving effective statehood? What has been found in the preceding analysis is that the creation of state-like entities is indeed possible without recognition, but the lack of external sovereignty does constrain the form of internal sovereignty that develops. Despite significant variation in the degree of statehood achieved by unrecognized states, they share similar constraints and opportunities that set them apart from their recognized counterparts.

Unrecognized statehood is shaped by a series of dilemmas and tensions and acquires an almost Janus-faced quality; at the same time looking backwards and forwards, at the same time open and closed. It is the factors that enable unrecognized states to survive and clear the initial obstacles to state-building—such as centralization of resources, external support, internal cohesion, and lack of pluralism—that result in tensions and contradictions. The creation of statehood in unrecognized states is affected by two main driving forces: the goal of international recognition, or at least engagement, and the preservation of de facto independence. One of the reasons why the recognition-through-state-building formula has proved so popular is that it actually overlaps with the main priority of these entities: to survive. The struggle for recognition will, after all, face a significant, if not irreversible, setback if the leaders lose control over the territory to which they lay claim. Thus, no matter how much international favour Chechen leaders can manage to muster through tireless international lobbying, it all remains hypothetical as long as Moscow is in firm control of the region. Defending the de facto independence of the entity is primary, and the collapse of the Tamil-controlled areas in Sri Lanka has once again served as a warning against complacency and as a reminder that military defeat is never far away. Building strong, effective entities not only helps the entity's international image; it also makes them better able to defend themselves. The introduction of political reforms may similarly strengthen the entity and help stave off popular discontent.

Militarization or Civilian Control

The goals of survival and recognition therefore share a lot of similarities and they are both ultimately linked to the long-term survival of the entity, but they at times pull in different directions. The persistence of an external threat constitutes an important impetus for building a strong, effective state that is able to defend itself and which can therefore ensure the entity's survival, even without external support. Such an entity would ideally encompass more than just a strong army, but the legacy of war and the very immediacy of the external threat tend to foster a highly militarized form of state-building, predicated on the need for territorial defence. The resulting very traditional form of statehood, however, hampers the creation of a truly effective state by taking resources away from other areas, and it also undermines the other stated goal of the self-proclaimed states: the creation of a democratic entity.[593] Thus, while the rule of Samvel Babayan in Nagorno Karabakh seemingly served the initial survival and recovery of the entity, the commander's ruthless regime gradually became a thorn in the eye of the civilian leaders. The civilian leaders were perhaps most of all worried about their own lack of power, but they also appeared concerned with Karabakh's international image and with the obstacles the army commander posed to the creation of effective statehood.[594] As Zartman reminds us, the creation of a 'hard' state, rather than a 'strong' state, tends to be accompanied by the loss of willing allegiance and the legitimizing support of the population, and ultimately results in state weakening.[595] The problem goes deeper than just a strong role for the military, since this role, and the lack of criticism of it, is symptomatic of a strong emphasis on unity that makes it difficult to move toward genuine political reforms.

Unity or Pluralism

Internal cohesion is, as argued above, an advantage in the initial stages of state-building, but the perceived need for unity is hard to reconcile with the rhetorical emphasis on democratization and pluralism. This leaves the entities in a dilemma: the authorities gain a lot of strength from the internal homogenization and their often rigid interpretation of identity, yet are under pressure to allow for pluralism to emerge. This tension is most visible in ethnically plural entities such as Abkhazia and Somalia, which are torn between making a strong claim to national self-determination, based on the dominant communal group, and trying to avoid internal divisions and ensuring majority support for independence. There is thus a tendency toward a form of 'ethnic democracy',[596] but it is an unstable and ambiguous form of ethnically defined rule. These tensions between unity and pluralism or diversity are also noticeable in almost completely homogeneous entities such as Nagorno Karabakh, where the perceived need for internal cohesion and unity manifests itself in an emphasis on intra-communal consensus. State-building can be an effective way of ensuring internal cohesion, but this can be hard to reconcile with perceived external pressures to democratize and internal expectations of popular sovereignty.

There therefore appears to be a relatively small window of opportunity for the introduction of substantive political reforms in the context of nonrecognition. Democratization without improved prospects of international recognition risks subjecting the authorities to popular dissatisfaction, especially if they also fail to deliver effective statehood. As the leader of the Somaliland opposition warns, 'if democracy doesn't win recognition, people will look elsewhere'.[597] The authorities will therefore be tempted to emphasize the controlling aspect of state-building, or at least not progress further, but this risks undermining the entity's internal legitimacy, thereby leaving it weakened.

Dependence or Independence

Another source of tension is the external support on which unrecognized states rely. This support is vital for both the creation and subsequent development of unrecognized states, but it undermines their de facto independence and makes the claim to independent statehood less credible. Thus, if an unrecognized state relies on its parent state for access to the international market and perhaps even for most of its exports, then this raises questions about whether its independence is, in fact, imagined.[598] This is especially the case, if, as in Kurdistan, the unrecognized state actually reaches a political agreement with the parent state. As Natali argues, 'the processes that have helped create the Kurdish quasi-state have impeded its self-sustainability and independence'.[599] But parent state linkages are problematic even in the absence of such a formal agreement. Relations with China, for example, sharply divide the Taiwanese political parties.[600]

Reliance on a patron state is also not free of costs, and the patron-client relationship is therefore marked by tensions, even in cases where this dependence is largely desired—and not imposed. External dependence does not mean that internal sovereignty does not exist in these entities, as suggested by Katarzyna Pełczynska-Nałęcz and her colleagues;[601] internal sovereignty is not a question of either / or, and recognized states are similarly dependent on international linkages—including sometimes for military defence—without this affecting their sovereign status. Recognized states, however, often rely on a variety of international links, not just on a single patron. They are also not trying to justify their independence. The constraints associated with developing statehood in a context of nonrecognition means that a claim to internal sovereignty will therefore invariably be marked by a level of ambiguity. But the severity of this tension is not uniform: the level of dependence varies from case to case—and is, for example, much more obvious in South Ossetia than in Somaliland—and it varies over time. Dependence fluctuates, depending on the entity's access to alternative resources, including its position in the international system, and it also varies based on the preparedness of the patron state to keep up the subsidies or the willingness of the parent state to accept limited engagement. The linkages may consequently be of limited longevity.

Balancing Act

The result of the tensions outlined above is a difficult balancing act. In order to ensure the survival of the entity and further the goal of international recognition, the authorities must be able to maintain a strong defence but also have enough resources to provide basic public services; they must ensure popular support and internal cohesion while also keeping an eye on the international acceptability of the regime and their claim to independent statehood. It would therefore be tempting for the leaders of unrecognized states to downplay one of the goals and, for example, turn their backs on the international community and seek isolation. If unrecognized states were to seek the invisibility that is preferred by 'black spots', then this would significantly change the dynamics of their statehood. They would no longer feel the pressure to try to conform to international norms and would perhaps revert to a position that is closer to the popular imagination of these entities: warlord-controlled ethnic fiefdoms. Alternatively, the leaders might choose to opt for the guarantees provided by the external patron, instead of seeking international approval—or such a situation may indeed be imposed. The former has been contemplated in the case of Nagorno Karabakh and illustrated in calls for Armenia to formally recognize the entity and provide explicit security guarantees,[602] while the latter corresponds closely to what happened in the case of Abkhazia and South Ossetia. It is noteworthy that Abkhazia's recognition by Russia appears to have led to a hardening of positions on the return of refugees. The president has stated that returns are 'problematic' due to the risk of renewed warfare, and other officials concur that returns cannot be considered at this time 'because they could become a fifth column'.[603] Moreover, only people with an Abkhaz passport were allowed to vote in the most recent elections, thereby excluding most of the Georgian population.[604] Although the Abkhaz foreign minister still aims to increase the number of countries that recognize the entity,[605] the need for international acceptability has seemingly diminished and minority rights are therefore less of a concern.

Downplaying one of the goals, however, risks undermining the internal legitimacy of the unrecognized state and consequently its capacity for self-defence. The preceding analysis has shown that fear or ethnic solidarity is not enough to ensure popular support, and the authorities are likely to find that 'virtual politics' is insufficient when the stakes are high, when security or the future status of the entity are at stake. The fourth phase of state-building is not necessarily achieved and it can be reversed. The 'idea of the state'[606] presented by the authorities has in most cases been based on past grievances and prom-ises of a brighter future of security, prosperity, *and* recognition. This narrative has played a powerful legitimating role, but it constrains the manoeuvrability of the leaders and the introduction of political reforms could now come back to haunt them. The leader of the Somaliland opposition warns that the lack of progress in international recognition despite the introduction of political reforms might lead to disillusion-ment,[607] and one could imagine the authorities turning their backs on either democracy or recognition, or possibly both. But the question is, how will this affect the popular legitimacy that has so far served to strengthen the entity? Somaliland does not have enough resources to 'buy' support through effective services—resources are in fact drying

up—and there are already signs of growing extremism.[608] Choosing to
move closer to an external patron would also not resolve the tensions
of unrecognized statehood; it would likely cause popular dissatisfaction and would also deprive the leadership of the legitimacy afforded
to them by the continuing struggle for recognition. Moreover, this kind
of external dependence may well negate the de facto independence of
these entities. In the cases of Abkhazia and South Ossetia, the influence
of Russia is becoming increasingly pronounced, and the entities are
moving closer to becoming de facto—although not de jure—entities in
the Russian Federation.[609] It therefore appears that these entities are
more similar than we might have thought: they are facing similar pressures and similar balancing acts. In most cases, the authorities in
unrecognized states are therefore trying to 'square the circle': they are
trying to do everything at once, and the ambiguous and unstable statehood that characterizes unrecognized states results. But what does this
mean for the sustainability of unrecognized statehood? Are they transient phenomena, or can nonrecognition become a more permanent
status, perhaps even an alternative form of statehood?

Surviving as Unrecognized States

Statehood, or internal sovereignty, is therefore not ruled out by lack
of international recognition, but unrecognized states are nevertheless
not just like other states. On the one hand, nonrecognition comes at a
cost. Even in cases such as Somaliland, which is not facing complete
international isolation, the unrecognized status means that there is a
lack of bilateral technical assistance and loans, insurance companies
will not set up branches, the cost of living is higher since local companies cannot import goods directly, and international investors are
scared off by the lack of insurance and other forms of investment
protection.[610] Unrecognized states are continuously trying to find their
place in an international system that has no place for them, and they
consequently seem almost doomed to a transient existence, always
chasing the elusive goal of recognition. But nonrecognition on the
other hand provides important incentives for creating effective entities,
and today's globalized world may provide the international linkages
that enable it.

Unrecognized states are heavily reliant on external support, and this
could be said to leave them vulnerable: what if the external patron
withdraws its support, what if diaspora remittances dry up? Kolstø
and Blakkisrud point out that Transnistria's de facto statehood

ultimately hinges on Russia's willingness to renew its security guarantee, and comments that 'borrowed power is unstable power'.[611] The reliability of patron support is certainly a concern for unrecognized states: strategic interests can change and domestic and international pressures may lead even kin-states to rethink their priorities.[612] Although patron-state support is likely to fluctuate, it has in most cases been maintained for lengthy periods; kin-state leaders are often under domestic pressure to maintain the support and patron states likely develop vested interests in the entity. Even so, it does add an element of instability to unrecognized statehood.

Diaspora support has similarly been argued to foster a form of development that lacks a domestic basis and that is therefore unsustainable in the longer term. Concerns have, for example, been raised in Somaliland over the impact of remittances, which are argued to create a false economy and a new form of dependency that discourages efforts at local production.[613] Whether this is a problem depends on: (1) whether the remittances are accompanied by investments in local production, which they have been in a number of cases; (2) for how long the diaspora will sustain their support, especially if they do not benefit economically from their involvement. It is, after all, telling that international investment in unrecognized states often comes almost entirely from diaspora sources: investors without the emotional attachment would be unwilling to take the risk. Much has been made of the significance of ethno-national ties, but the longevity of such emotional ties may be limited. The sustainability of diaspora support would appear to depend on whether the external threat persists—even if the effectiveness of such arguments is also likely to wane over time—as well as the nature of diaspora: how important is the entity for diaspora identity? In the case of Nagorno Karabakh the survival of the entity has played a crucial role in revitalizing a diaspora community that has few personal links to Karabakh,[614] whereas in the case of Somaliland, individual family links are, for many, as important as collective identities in motivating continued support. The form of diaspora involvement is likely to differ in the two cases, and so is the sustainability of the involvement; diaspora support in the case of Somaliland may be less dependent on the fortunes of the entity, but can still persist for extended periods of time, since the diaspora population is relatively young.[615] Diaspora involvement that is less driven by 'long-distance' nationalism and more by personal ties could, however, lead to internal divisions as some groups benefit more than others; in Somaliland, it is especially the Isaaq clan that due to the higher socioeconomic status of its diaspora community has benefitted from remittances.[616] This could serve to undermine Somaliland's unity, as this clan is already the dominant group. Diaspora support therefore also comes with a price tag and its long-term sustainability will in some cases be open to question. It is, however, associated with fewer risks than reliance on the parent states for economic sustainability. Transnistria is, for example, clearly vulnerable since Moldova could choose to impose sanctions on its external trade, thereby undermining the sustainability of the status quo.[617]

Due to the insecurities associated with these forms of external support, unrecognized states are eager to diversify and to rely on self-generated economic growth, but this is almost impossible to sustain unless unrecognized states are allowed access to international markets. In terms of the supply of resources, status quo is therefore sustainable, also in the medium term. But it results in reliance on external patrons, diaspora populations, or even parent states—with the accompanying insecurities and threats to de facto independence—or requires unrecognized states to be allowed limited international engagement. These are constraints that do not necessarily bar long-term survival, so could unrecognized or partially recognized statehood become a more permanent status, and perhaps provide an alternative model for statehood, not just a curious exception? This depends to a large extent on whether prolonged nonrecognition can be legitimized internally; it depends on what happens to internal legitimacy if recognition is not forthcoming.

Nonrecognition in the Long Term?

International recognition may be the 'only way for the elites to fully enjoy the assets they have acquired'; it lures the leaders of unrecognized states with status, power, and—possibly—wealth.[618] The promise of international recognition has, moreover, been used by the leaders to legitimize their rule and excuse current hardship. The problem is that international recognition at some points starts to look like an unrealistic dream. Many unrecognized states have been de facto independent for more than a decade, but recognition does not look any closer. The bias against political divorce shows no sign of abating. Or does it? It could be countered that the Western recognition of Kosovo and Russia's subsequent recognitions of Abkhazia and South Ossetia have weakened the principle of territorial integrity: former autonomous provinces *can* be recognized without the consent of their parent state.

One could have imagined that these developments would have sparked optimism in other aspiring states, but the reaction was more subdued. The Karabakh authorities, for example, argued that the case of Kosovo set a useful precedent, and they welcomed the recognition of South Ossetia and Abkhazia,[619] but their attitude was otherwise surprisingly dismissive. They, in fact, argued that Kosovo's, Abkhazia's and South Ossetia's independence was not 'legitimate'; that it was 'not an acceptable form of recognition'.[620] Abkhazia and South Ossetia demonstrate that being recognized by a few states, even if one of them is a great power, does not guarantee an end to international isolation. Russia's growing influence in the entities, moreover, serves as a warning to other unrecognized states that are keen to protect their de facto independence. Kosovo is clearly in a more enviable position, but although the entity has been recognized by more than seventy states, its independence is still supervised, with the international administration retaining the final say, and the prospects of UN membership are currently slim. The Karabakh leaders therefore argue that these entities have not achieved 'full independence'[621] and ask—rhetorically— 'are Abkhazia and South Ossetia freer and more independent than they used to be, is Kosovo?'[622]

The assumed link between recognition and actual independence has seemingly been undermined, and this has led some leaders to question the value of de jure statehood. The struggle for international recognition has been central to the narrative employed by the Karabakh leaders for nearly twenty years, but they are now increasingly asking: What exactly is gained from recognition, especially if this recognition is only partial? Recognition is no longer associated with freedom and independence, unless this recognition is also accepted by the parent state, that is by Azerbaijan, and does not come with too many compromises.[623] In a time of territorial integrity, the price of recognition— or partial recognition—may be too high, it may not guarantee the independence and freedom that have been decisive goals for the Karabakh movement. As a result, the Karabakh authorities are now talking a lot less about recognition; it no longer dominates the official rhetoric as it did only a few years ago. Asked about this, the advisor to the president argues that Karabakh has overcome its 'nonrecognition complex' and can focus on other goals.[624] Status quo, not recognition, is argued to be the preferable option, at least in the short run.[625] The Karabakh authorities are, consequently, trying to describe nonrecognition not only as a more permanent status, but also as a more attractive proposition.

Other cases have similarly tried to come to terms with a status that falls short of full recognition. In Taiwan, the majority reportedly supports the status quo, rather than reintegration into China or declaration of independence,[626] and a *modus vivendi* with the parent state has developed. After the Annan Plan for Cyprus was defeated by the Greek Cypriot population in 2004, international engagement with Northern Cyprus has increased and some observers now speak of the 'risk' of Taiwanization: that Northern Cyprus, like Taiwan, could exist for the foreseeable future as an unrecognized but prosperous state.[627] An Abkhaz official similarly argued that the entity has all the independence it needs[628] and Vladimir Putin has declared that 'Abkhazia doesn't need to be recognized by any country other than Russia'.[629] Abkhazia has been recognized by only four states—Russia, Nicaragua, Venezuela, and Nauru—and seems unlikely to be recognized by more states in the immediate future. The international presence in Kosovo is, finally, close to open-ended; it is due to continue until the terms of the settlement are implemented, but this requires Belgrade's co-operation and is therefore strongly influenced by Russia's continued refusal to grant its recognition. It is therefore conceivable that both nonrecognition and partial recognition turn out to be a more permanent status than what was initially envisaged. Perhaps the system of sovereign states is beginning to lose its power. Even a case such as Transnistria, which has stepped up its campaign for international recognition, arguably provides further support for this view. Following the recognitions of Abkhazia and South Ossetia, the Transnistrian authorities announced that they needed to pursue broader international support in their quest for recognition.[630] Moscow had clearly snubbed Transnistria and sole reliance on the formerly supportive patron seemed ill-advised. However, some observers argue that the 'treaty on friendship and cooperation' which was proposed by Transnistria's president in April 2008 was a deliberate nonstarter.[631] The aim may have been to ensure international goodwill and keep internal discontent at bay, but the elite is in fact in no hurry to move away from the status quo.[632] Entities can seemingly survive without external sovereignty and possibly even prosper, and it has long been established that key actors might have an interest in the status quo since it leaves their economic activities largely unconstrained.[633] Models of statehood that depart from the usual paradigm are, as already mentioned, not new, and these entities have shown themselves capable of adapting to the globalized world. There is therefore not necessarily anything preventing them from acquiring a more permanent status— perhaps recognized by a few patron states.

But—and this is an important 'but'—such a change in strategy would be exposed to serious strain. Unrecognized statehood is based on a delicate balancing act, and abandoning the goal of recognition may well upset this balance. I would argue that there are serious problems with the sustainability of nonrecognition, due to both internal and external pressures. The Nagorno Karabakh leaders may, for example, be satisfied with the status quo, but what about the general population; it is one thing for the elite to change its strategy, it is quite another to bring followers along. The Karabakh authorities may be convinced that nonrecognition is an attractive option—or they may be forced to construct such a narrative due to the remote possibility of future recognition—but they have failed to convince the population, which still associates recognition with independence, prosperity, and above all, security. The population is reportedly worried that the status quo does not provide for their security; the war in Georgia made the risk of renewed warfare more real and the relative calm of the last seventeen years now appears more fragile.[634] The risk to the internal legitimacy of the entity is made worse by the fact that the leaders seem unable to imagine what nonrecognition as a permanent status would look like. When asked about their visions for Karabakh's future as an unrecognized state, they either become very vague or very specific ('we need better water supply').[635] Despite the existence of territories that challenge our usual conception of sovereignty,[636] there remains a strong tendency to view full, de jure sovereignty as the only attractive option. In the absence of externally recognized sovereignty, disorder and insecurity is assumed.[637] The goal of recognition, on the other hand, provides a powerful vision of statehood; one of security and prosperity. And it therefore legitimizes not only the entity but also the regime, especially when self-determination has been a central narrative from the outset. Observers of Transnistria likewise argue that it will have consequences for regime legitimacy if the authorities do not deliver the goal of international recognition,[638] but the status quo is also potentially under pressure from the business community, who resist the costs of nonrecognition.[639] Taiwan remains internally divided over which course to adopt: increasing engagement with China or independence; the status quo is only seen as preferable because the other options are considered too costly.[640] Abandoning widespread international recognition even presents problems for entities that have achieved partial recognition. Divisions, for example, persist within Abkhazia over the degree of dependence on Russia,[641] and Moscow still appears unsure of Abkhazia's continued loyalty and therefore seeks to impose its control in the entity.[642] Moreover, in an interview posted on the official Abkhaz website, the entity's president continues to emphasize 'the need to seek the recognition of an increasing number of countries, including from the Western community',[643] and the new Abkhaz foreign minister lobbies tirelessly for more countries to recognize Abkhazia as an independent state.[644]

Selling nonrecognition to an internal audience is fraught with difficulty. This suggests that the degree of popular constraint is crucial to whether the authorities will be able to change their strategy and pursue nonrecognition instead of recognition. In bottom-up conflicts we should therefore expect this to be more difficult, but even more top-down regimes are likely to feel the strain. Internal legitimacy is, as argued in previous chapters, important for the ability of unrecognized states to build effective entities that are able to defend themselves, and popular legitimacy is consequently important even in unrecognized states that have turned their backs on the international community and where the leaders largely depend on the 'men with the guns'. In Republika Srpska Krajina the creation of an effective entity which enjoyed popular support may, for example, not have had an immediate impact on the political survival of the rivalling leaders and they had abandoned the goal of international recognition, but it did affect the strength of the entity and hence its prospect for survival, and this was all the more important due to Krajina's complete international isolation. The leaders therefore maintained a rhetoric of popular legitimacy and the creation of effective institutions was an issue of political contestation.[645] A lack of internal legitimacy will not necessarily result in open revolt; the external threat serves to mute dissatisfaction and the coercive apparatus can be used to quell dissent. But it risks creating widespread apathy and emigration and it thereby weakens the unrecognized state. In the case of Republika Srpska Krajina, the mood in the armed forces became increasingly apathetic and fatalistic and former soldiers describe how the Croatian offensive in 1995 almost came as a relief.[646] This is clearly not the kind of attitude that helps the long-term sustainability of unrecognized states, and one can speculate that similar attitudes may have been found among the combatants in Tamil Eelam and contributed to the recent defeat. The Tamil Eelam regime was known for 'its intolerance of dissenting views and its violent practices' and although Pegg argues that this did not preclude popular support, such support was based on 'a combination of brainwashing, terror and helplessness'[647] and would perhaps more accurately be characterized as apathy.

There are therefore important internal obstacles to making nonrecognition a permanent status. They are further compounded by two significant external constraints. First, there is the external patron, which most of these entities rely on for their survival. If they move closer to this patron, they run the risk of losing their de facto independence altogether. Second, attempts by unrecognized states to create a place for themselves in the international system have so far been refused. The Unrepresented Nations and Peoples Organization (UNPO) has suggested 'opening the world order to de facto states' through trade and other forms of international cooperation,[648] but although we have seen increasing engagement with unrecognized states—often as part of a conflict resolution strategy—the cost of nonrecognition is still significant. Taiwan and Somaliland constitute partial exceptions, but even they find that important doors remain closed and engagement in these cases depends on, respectively, acceptance by the parent state and the absence of an effective parent state. UNPO's suggestion has therefore largely fallen on deaf ears, and suggestions that these entities should be allowed to join the United Nations are even less likely to be heard.[649] Such a suggestion in fact seems faintly ridiculous, but it is worth remembering that a large number of Krasner's anomalies, such as Monaco and San Marino, are in fact members of the UN. The international system of sovereign states therefore actively works against nonrecognition becoming a more permanent status. Very effective gatekeeping is built into the system, which consequently limits the existence of anomalies, not only through norms but also through the rules differentiating members from non-members.

Rethinking Statehood and Sovereignty?

Statehood without external sovereignty takes a specific form, but the question is if this should be seen as a new form of statehood, and indeed a new form of sovereignty. Unrecognized statehood is not a new phenomenon, and the current aspiring states have a number of predecessors. There may, however, be something qualitatively different about contemporary unrecognized states, or at least the ones that manage to create relatively well-functioning entities. Unrecognized states in the modern international system are born out of the very restrictive right to self-determination that emerged after World War II. This significantly constrains their prospects for long-term survival. The kind of statehood that emerges reflects the need to ensure external support while protecting their de facto independence and ensuring domestic backing. These entities are, moreover, very much the product of globalization, and although they often base their claim to independence on historic links and ancient identities, they also know how to operate in the globalized world. They survive through transnational networks—legal or illegal—and the authorities make use of the internet in their bid for international support, or in their bid for funding from overseas co-ethnics. The Transnistrian website Pridnestovie.Net, for example, promises to teach you '10 things you didn't know about Europe's newest country' and is a lesson in effective internet communication that many recognized states could emulate. Territorial control is still key to their statehood and Eiki Berg therefore rightly argues that the degree of deterritorialization associated with unrecognized states is limited,[650] but it is nevertheless central. The main key to survival for these entities remains good old military balance, but military strength alone can rarely sustain them indefinitely; they also need to preserve internal cohesion and they need to ensure that external support keeps on flowing. And the entities that manage this, without jeopardizing their de facto independence, are the ones that have adapted to the globalized system. In this sense, unrecognized statehood can be seen as a new form of statehood. It is certainly one that challenges conventional views of statehood; the absence of external sovereignty can coexist with a form of statehood that imitates traditional statehood, yet differs from it in important respects.

Does this type of statehood challenge dominant conceptions of sovereignty? It certainly challenges the more simplified notions of sovereignty, and the dichotomy that equals sovereignty with order and lack of sovereignty with disorder. Although most literature on sovereignty now adopts a far more sophisticated understanding, the dichotomy still informs much research on international relations, not to mention media reports on both failed states and unrecognized states. On the other hand, the mere existence of unrecognized states does not challenge the existing paradigm, the existing international system of sovereign states. As Krasner points out, the system of sovereign states is highly flexible and has a long history of accommodating entities that do not conform to our usual views of sovereignty; 'it has not pushed out alternative strategies, but rather has lived with them'.[651] It is noteworthy that unrecognized states do not set out to challenge or to reform the international system; they want to be part of it, they do not want to change it. They are not attempting to create a new form of statehood; rather, they want what others have, they want external sovereignty. This also means that they are generally not hoping that the international system will somehow accommodate their current status—like the protectorates and dependencies mentioned by Krasner.[652] They may try for such accommodation, but this strategy will be faced with both internal and external constraints. The status quo is consequently described as a transition; as a necessary, and possibly painful, step before the goal of full, de jure, independence can be achieved. The eagerness with which external sovereignty is pursued speaks to the power of the international system of sovereign states, and these entities very much see themselves as playing a zero-sum game: sovereignty or nothing—or as the de facto authorities often like to put it, 'independence or death'. Recognized statehood remains the top prize; it legitimizes the struggle, guarantees protection for the inhabitants, and gives prestige and power to the leaders.

Unrecognized statehood thereby challenges dominant simplistic conceptions of sovereignty and at the same time helps us understand how the international system of sovereign states works; it helps us to see the effect it has on units that do not fit. Anomalies still exist, but they have become a lot fewer. Daniel Philpott argues that although 'outsiders' in the international system are not considered legitimate polities entitled to full privileges, 'societies almost always trade, ally and negotiate' with them.[653] But this is not true in the current international system: outsiders are in many cases made 'honorary insiders', but those that are not are denied access to the privileged club of sovereign states. Krasner emphasizes that sovereignty lives with alternative strategies, but these strategies are now rare indeed, and the anomalies that do exist also tend to be treated almost as sovereign entities. Thus, states such as San Marino, Monaco, and Bosnia are allowed membership in international organizations even if it can be argued that they are not fully sovereign. Alternatively, dependencies or protectorates are treated as nonsovereign entities and as almost integral parts of their parent states. This was, notably, also the case for Kosovo until its declaration of independence in February 2008; its sovereignty was disputed and it was, in effect, treated as a nonsovereign entity. The dichotomy between sovereignty and nonsovereignty therefore also applies to these territories; there is no place for territories in between. Prior to decolonization, international law acknowledged two statuses: sovereign states and formal dependencies, but now only the former remains.[654] Despite all the talk of globalization and the waning power of sovereign statehood, absolute sovereignty and territorial integrity remain the guiding principles when it comes to substate anomalies, and international law is especially dismissive of secessionist movements which are 'meticulously excluded from the right to seek and be given support'.[655] At the state level, the power of the sovereignty paradigm appears inexorable, and newly created anomalies are therefore in flux, constantly trying to change their status.

Conclusion: Statehood Without Sovereignty

Lack of recognition does not render statehood impossible or meaningless, but the resulting statehood differs in important respects from recognized statehood. The entities remain caught in an ambiguous and largely transient position. Unrecognized states are not simply 'states in waiting', identical to recognized states aside from their lack of recognition. These entities therefore challenge dominant conceptions of sovereignty by pointing to the different forms that internal sovereignty can take, *and* demonstrate the continued power of the paradigm. There is not a complete disconnect between internal and external sovereignty, and this illustrates the strength of the sovereignty paradigm. Even in today's globalized world, it matters if an entity is recognized or not. This conclusion therefore takes a middle position between the declaratory and the constitutive approach to states in international law: recognition is not simply a formality. There is something qualitatively different about unrecognized statehood, but this does not mean that statehood is simply constituted by the act of recognition and therefore rendered meaningless without it.

The creation of statehood in these entities holds important lessons for international efforts to avoid state failure and assist in the rebuilding of collapsed states; it points to the significance of internal dynamics, emphasizes the potential importance of international norms as driving forces, and calls for state-building and external sovereignty to be partially disjointed—the central state may not be the most useful focus for state-building efforts. Unrecognized statehood is characterized by specific tensions and ambiguities that are unlikely to be found in recognized entities, but other forms of conflicting pressures will be found: tensions between external pressures and internal demands, conflicting demands from different communal groups, and so forth. What the analysis has shown is that state strength depends on more than access to resources, and for unrecognized states it is not just about the availability of external support. In order to build effective statehood following wartime destruction and a near-collapse of institutions, there is a need for a common vision; without a legitimizing idea of the state, an effective entity is unlikely to emerge. This is not a new argument,[656] but it has been downplayed in much recent literature that has focused on the need for security and capacity-building.[657] Moreover, the analysis demonstrated that fear or ethnic solidarities are not enough for long-term stability; other sources of legitimacy will be needed or popular dissatisfaction will prove a threat to the stability of the entity.

Intransigence is often a defining feature of unrecognized states, yet their statehood is by no means static; the tensions identified lend it an inescapable fluidity and these entities can also move in both directions on the spectrum between failed and fully functioning unrecognized states. Due to these tensions and the limited chance of recognition, the authorities of unrecognized states may be tempted to abandon the quest for external sovereignty; nonrecognition frequently serves narrow—often economic—interests. The emphasis on status quo can be used as a face-saving exercise when recognition is unlikely, and it can be used as a bargaining trick. Whether or not they will be able to make such a move depends on both external and internal factors. First, it matters if at least limited international engagement is available to the unrecognized state or if it can count on support from an external patron or other sources of external support. Second, it matters what kind of power relations we find within the entity and the type of internal legitimacy on which the leadership depends. If the leaders of unrecognized states abandon the struggle for recognition and the international system does not provide for an attractive alternative—or at least not one that competes with the promise of recognition—they expose themselves to popular dissatisfaction. This threatens the sustainability of the entity: people might choose to emigrate or apathy might spread and neither bodes well for the effective defence of the territory. In such a case the entity would become almost entirely reliant on external support; internal resources will prove insufficient for sustainability and the response of external patrons to the changed strategy therefore becomes crucial. We consequently see an interplay between internal legitimacy and the international dimension. This affects the sustainability of the unrecognized states, as well as the extent to which the authorities are likely to change their international strategies, and in which direction.

The manoeuvrability of the authorities is therefore constrained, but if nonrecognition is not enough, then which way will they move? Will they continue to insist on full recognition, and can they convince their population that this is a realistic option; will they move closer to their external patron; or will they start considering compromise solutions? The flexibility of demands, which is crucial for the prospect of conflict resolution, is affected by the sustainability of the statehood that has developed in the entities, as well as by the type of leadership that has emerged. This makes for an interesting interplay among sovereignty, statehood, and conflict, which will be explored in the following chapter.

6 MOVING TOWARD PEACE OR WAR?

My government, with the total commitment of our Armed Forces, has in an unprecedented humanitarian operation, finally defeated the LTTE militarily.

–Mahinda Rajapaksa, President of Sri Lanka[658]

On 16 May 2009, the Sri Lankan president announced the fall of the Tamil-controlled areas in the north of the country. Tamil Eelam had thereby followed unrecognized states such as Chechnya and Republika Srpska Krajina, and been forcefully reintegrated into the parent state. The defeat was hailed by the Sri Lankan authorities as the victory of legitimacy over terrorism and of humanitarian values over violence.[659] Yet other voices expressed concern over reported attacks against civilians[660] and the EU cautioned the Sri Lankan government that this was a time for reconciliation.[661] Reintegration through military means remains the most likely outcome for unrecognized states, but it is anything but peaceful and often has very little to do with humanitarian values. The second Chechen war, for example, cost the lives of an estimated 25,000 people,[662] while the Croatian recapture of Republika Srpska Krajina resulted in the exodus of around 200,000 Serbs.[663] Forceful reintegration entails the full-scale takeover of a territory, and built-up fears, years of intransigence, and growing appetite for revenge result in a significant risk of ethnic cleansing.

Military solutions to these conflicts often cause mild international consternation, but have few other repercussions, as long as it is done quickly.[664] Territorial integrity has been restored and this seems to be the primary concern, which in most cases outweighs humanitarian issues. The use of force is still considered acceptable, or is even 'the regularly anticipated response'.[665] Chechnya, for some years, proved an exception and Russia faced significant international criticism for its actions in the region,[666] but with the changed rhetoric following 9/11 and the casting of the conflict as one against terrorism, criticism largely subsided. Other parent states have taken note and adopted a similar rhetoric; the Azerbaijani leadership, for example, as early as October 2001 began talking about launching an 'antiterrorist strike' against Nagorno Karabakh.[667] One could therefore argue that the populations of unrecognized states have good reason to be fearful; a military attack is never far away and if—or when—it happens it is likely to be very bloody.

This does not mean, of course, that victory for the parent state is guaranteed. If the parent state underestimates the strength of the unrecognized state, then, rather than the quick takeover they were hoping for, we might see full-scale warfare, which could even draw in neighbouring states. The relative strength of unrecognized states is closely linked to the reaction of their external patrons, and this makes it hard for the parent state to estimate. The Croatian government assessed the situation correctly when they in August 1995 judged that Serbia would not come to the aid of its brethren in Croatian Krajina: no assistance was forthcoming from Belgrade or from the Serb entity in Bosnia and the entity's defences quickly collapsed. The Georgian president in August 2008 similarly appeared to gamble that South Ossetia's capital Tskhinvali could be recaptured before Russian forces intervened and that a quick takeover with limited civilian casualties would meet with international acceptance. As we now know, however, this played into Russian hands and showed that the external patron was far more central to the defence of the entity than the parent state appeared to have estimated. The president of Azerbaijan has repeat- edly threatened to launch a military offensive against Nagorno Karabakh,[668] but the outcome of such an offensive would depend not only on the military strength of the entity, which remains a largely unknown quantity—in Karabakh it is claimed that the entity has the strongest military in the region and would only need an hour to create chaos in Azerbaijan[669]—or on the strength of Armenia, but also on the possible reaction of Russia. The weapons stocks and determination on both sides combined with the risk of drawing in regional powers create an explosive situation and an all-out Azerbaijani offensive is often described as a 'nightmare scenario'.[670] Lack of information about the strength of these entities and the difficulty of predicting the reaction of external patrons make military 'solutions' a very risky strategy for the parent states, which even when successful often come with very significant human costs, and may not even result in lasting peace. The Sri Lankan government, for example, proudly proclaims that the Tamil Tigers are defeated and the war is over,[671] but experience from several intrastate conflicts shows that violence can soon resurface. In Chechnya the unrecognized state has long been defeated but instability persists along Russia's southern border and terrorist attacks have even reached the heart of the country. Resentment lingers and movements can regroup, especially if they still enjoy significant external support.[672] But this does not mean that it will not be tried. For many parent states it remains the preferred option; a military solution allows the authorities to maintain a unitary state without messy federal or confederal solutions.

Forceful reintegration is not the only possible outcome, however. A few unrecognized states, such as Montenegro and Eritrea, have joined the ranks of recognized states, while others were reintegrated peacefully through a negotiated settlement. The bloody war in Bosnia ended in November 1995 with the signing of the Dayton Agreement. This agreement denied recognition to Republika Srpska, but the statelet continued to exist as an entity in the reintegrated Bosnian state and enjoys wide-ranging autonomous powers, including the right to establish links with other states. It thus comes very close to being a 'state within a state', even if central institutions have gradually been strengthened. This agreement did not represent the end of conflict: voices within the Serb entity are still demanding secession and refusing integration, the Bosnian state is still far from well-functioning, and there are frequent calls for abolishing the entities.[673] But the agreement did put an end to violence. The 2005 Iraqi constitution similarly gives the Kurdistan region wide-ranging autonomous powers that—depending on how the constitution is interpreted—include its own government, internal security forces (essentially its own army), and the right to manage its own extensive oil and gas reserves. Tensions still remain, for example with respect to oil revenues, but the agreement has, at least for now, managed to maintain the territorial integrity of Iraq.[674] Liam Anderson finds that some form of federal arrangement is essential to a peace settlement involving unrecognized states, and autonomy arrangements have also characterized the agreements that ended the conflicts in Bougainville and Gagauzia. In the latter case, the degree of autonomy is fairly limited, but unrecognized states will generally demand extensive autonomy if they are to even consider reintegration.[675] While the proposed settlement for Northern Cyprus, for example, restores the territorial integrity of the parent state, it also largely retains the de facto results obtained by the unrecognized state.[676] Settlements might also include some form of power-sharing, as this provides the unrecognized state with guarantees against being out-voted in the reintegrated parent state. In Bosnia, each constituent nation has a representative in the collective presidency and veto rights exist at several levels of the political system.[677] Power-sharing arrange-ments, however, also present problems in the context of unrecognized states. First, there is the problem of size. Anderson has found that with the exception of Somaliland and Northern Cyprus, the popula-tions of the still-existing unrecognized states constitute less than 5 per cent of the parent state.[678] This is likely to mean that power-sharing will either not provide significant protection against being outvoted or if it does (in case of a strong minority veto) it will not prove acceptable to the parent state. Second, a power-sharing agreement ties the unrec-ognized state to the central government, and this may mean a greater degree of reintegration than the regimes are prepared to countenance. Power-sharing is consequently not an essential part of negotiated rein-tegration. Finally, there is a fourth possible outcome: the continuation of the status quo. Even if unrecognized statehood is subject to signifi-cant strain it is, as argued in the previous chapter, likely to be sustain-able in the medium term.

Forceful reintegration is statistically the most likely outcome for unrecognized states,[679] but it comes with significant risks and undeni-able human costs. International recognition is probably the least likely outcome: it is fiercely resisted by parent states and hardly any seces-sionist entities, outside of the colonial context, have been fully recog-nized after the end of World War II. This leaves negotiated reintegration as the normatively most acceptable outcome and the approach does have a certain track record. But there are significant obstacles to suc-cessful conflict resolution in conflicts involving unrecognized states, and breaking the existing stalemate is anything but easy.

Breaking the Stalemate

The way that unrecognized states were created constitutes a key obsta-cle to successful conflict resolution: the legacy of war and the years of separation have created a high level of mistrust between the parent state and the unrecognized state, especially in the cases where de facto independence followed a very bloody war and where there has since been a lack of contact between the two societies. The biggest obstacle to a negotiated settlement, however, is arguably the de facto statehood enjoyed by the unrecognized states.[680] These entities already enjoy the de facto independence and territorial control to which other separatist movements aspire; it is not something they are hoping to achieve in negotiations, they have already obtained de facto independence and are unlikely to give it up. Unrecognized states are not waiting for military victory, they have already won. Important actors therefore have a vested interest in the status quo. As King asks, 'Why be a mayor of a small city if you can be president of a country?'[681] Crucially, these are not just the dreams of separatists; this is the current reality and this is also true for the general population: why agree to a form of autonomy—which could later be abolished—when you presently enjoy de facto independence? Why be a minority in someone else's state when you can be a majority in your own? Sovereignty is regarded as nonnegotiable,[682] it is not a bargaining position, and this has led some analysts to argue that rapprochement is the least likely outcome in conflicts involving unrecognized states.[683]

Even though unrecognized states have won the first round of the conflict, they have not achieved their goal of recognition, and this goal cannot be obtained through military escalation. It depends entirely on the goodwill of their parent state and the wider international community. At the same time the threat of new warfare persists, but the parent state—at least for the time being—also seems unable to reach its goal of reintegration through military escalation. The situation can therefore be described as a stalemate. For the unrecognized states it is, however, a 'soft' stalemate, rather than a hurting one.[684] These entities have 'developed internal and external sources of support that offset the pain of stalemate',[685] or that at least partially make up for the cost of nonrecognition and relative isolation. They moreover feel that time is on their side: they are 'playing the long game, in which not losing means winning'.[686]

But this situation is not necessarily static. In the literature on self-determination conflicts, it is frequently recognized that demands for national self-determination are flexible; they adapt to changing external circumstances, and to dynamics within the community, and what was once a demand for cultural autonomy can radicalize into a demand for full-blown independence.[687] This is a process that almost all of the unrecognized states have been through. What is less explored are the circumstances under which such demands can again move toward more accommodating positions: what turns a soft stalemate into a hurting one that might make the leaders of unrecognized states consider alternative options?

Facing Military Defeat

One possibility is that unrecognized states will only start looking for a 'way out' if the current situation is too hard to sustain and/or is becoming unbearable; if all that has been won would otherwise be lost. This was what happened in the case of Republika Srpska in Bosnia. By the autumn of 1995, the Bosnian Serbs still enjoyed de facto independence, but the statelet was facing the very real prospect of defeat; their statehood was weakening and was becoming increasingly hard to sustain, and this led to a reluctant willingness to accept a—very generous—compromise.[688] Based on this, it is therefore tempting to draw the conclusion that since unrecognized statehood represents a significant obstacle to conflict resolution,[689] it will be easier to reach a compromise if the creation of an effective entity is prevented. This assumption is often underlying the policies pursued by parent states and the tendency by the international community to view and treat these entities as 'rebel territories'. The rationale appears to be that if you deny unrecognized states any form of legitimacy and statehood, then the continued isolation and hardship will force them to compromise, or rather surrender. Such policies are, in part, inspired by the conception of sovereignty analysed in the previous chapters—statehood is not possible anyway—but they also represent a deliberate strategy: 'We can smoke them out.'

Internal Pressures

Intransigence, however, sometimes persists even if the situation is becoming hopeless; as Leon Festinger argues, 'rats and people come to love the things for which they have suffered' and if independence is not achieved then all the sacrifices will have been in vain.[690] While such stubborn intransigence could be written off as irrational behaviour or as misperceptions,[691] it also alerts us to the potential significance of self-interested elite behaviour[692] and to the importance of internal constraints. Stephen Stedman famously pointed to the potential obstacle posed by intracommunal spoilers who try to bring down a settlement,[693] but has also suggested that internal divisions over goals or means provide opportunities for making progress toward a settlement.[694] Timothy Sisk similarly emphasizes the importance of the relative balance of power between moderates and hardliners: are the moderates strong enough to carry a difficult compromise?[695] Separatist movements are not unitary actors and this affects the way in which leaders respond to a change in the military balance.

Internal forces do not only affect whether or not leaders are able to act on an emerging stalemate; I would argue that the *origins* of a ripe moment for conflict resolution, in some instances, can be found in intracommunal dynamics. This is what makes the stalemate painful and persuades the leaders to search for a way out. For example, the military balance had gradually been changing and the Serbs were beginning to lose ground when the Bosnian Serbs finally became willing to negotiate a compromise in the late summer of 1995,[696] but the leaders were also pressured by their kin-state, which had introduced a blockade, and the entity was marred by internal fractionalization. The political leaders were facing significant opposition and were increasingly worried that the army might try to take over power.[697] Not only the survival of the entity, but also their personal power, was therefore at stake and they consequently began searching for a way out and finally agreed to a compromise.[698] This suggests that internal power relations can cause a soft stalemate to become a hurting one. In the case of unrecognized states we have, in the period of relative stability following the ceasefires, seen significant developments in intracommunal dynamics.

Internal and External Factors

The demands made by separatists therefore respond to changes in the conflict context, but the effect of such changes is mediated by internal power relations; will the leaders face powerful spoilers if they initiate settlement negotiations? Not only the military balance, or the perception thereof, appears to matter for the demands made by unrecognized states; international pressures and internal constraints have also led to movements on the issue of full independence. For example, the leaders of both Taiwan and Kurdistan have shown flexibility when it comes to the demands made: do they demand full independence or are other solutions acceptable? In Taiwan this depends significantly on internal politics,[699] while the demands made by the Kurdistan authorities appear to reflect a combination of internal divisions, changes in Baghdad, and the prospect of international support.[700]

Compromise willingness cannot be reduced to either intracommunal or external factors but rather depends on their interplay; for example, whether or not followers can be brought along depends not only on the nature of the leadership, or the balance between hardliners and moderates, but also on what is on offer and the possible repercussions in case compromise is rejected. Separatist demands are often strategic and respond to both internal and external dynamics, although the achievement of de facto independence and years of intransigence tend to reduce their flexibility in unrecognized states compared to other separatist movements.

Promoting Peace Through the Denial of Statehood?

Effective statehood is generally seen as having a positive correlation with peace and stability, but when it comes to unrecognized states, the reverse is often assumed: the less statehood they manage to develop, the greater the chance of conflict resolution. The reluctance to engage with unrecognized states in part reflects the principle of territorial integrity, but it is often also punitive and constitutes a deliberate strategy to undermine the regime.

One of the most extreme examples of this kind of strategy was the brutal eight-year-long air and sea blockade the Papua New Guinea government imposed on Bougainville. All transport was halted *including* medical supplies and humanitarian aid, resulting in great hardship for the Bougainvillean population.[701] A similar approach is found in Gaza, where a cornerstone of Israel's strategy has been to crush Hamas's will to launch attacks by targeting its material base and by undermining its local support base.[702] Gaza has been subject to a full-scale blockade from Israel ever since Hamas seized control in June 2007. From then on, only basic humanitarian items were allowed into Gaza and virtually no exports permitted, and the economy was paralysed as a result. International organizations warned of a humanitarian crisis,[703] but this was denied by Israel, which maintained that this kind of policy was legitimate against a 'terrorist authority'.[704] The situation became even more desperate following the Israeli offensive on Gaza in January 2009. Oxfam subsequently estimated that 'up to 79 per cent of the population of Gaza are living in poverty [less than $2 a day], basic services are facing collapse and malnutrition among children is on the rise'.[705] The UN asserted that 35,000 people were without running water and that more than 20,000 homes had been damaged or destroyed. The situation was made worse by the refusal of Israel to allow building materials into Gaza, since they argued that they could be used for terrorist purposes by Hamas.[706]

This level of blockade is not feasible in most of the unrecognized states analysed in this book, due to their greater degree of territorial control, including control of borders, but some cases nevertheless approach it. Republika Srpska Krajina, for example, was affected by both the international sanctions against its patron state, Serbia, and by the international blockade against the entity that was imposed in 1993. This blockade only excluded 'essential humanitarian supplies including medical supplies and foodstuffs distributed by international humanitarian agencies'; anything else was subject to the authorization of the Croatian authorities.[707] The situation was made worse when Serbia introduced a blockade against the Bosnian Serbs in the late summer of 1994. Nominally this was not targeted at the Serbs in Krajina, but since the only supply route to the western part of the entity went through Bosnia, it nevertheless had a significant impact. As a result, the eastern part of Krajina had to make do with diminishing resources from Serbia, while the western part became reliant on smuggled goods from the Bosnian Serb statelet and emergency aid from international organizations. This was barely enough to survive on and the entity lacked access to vital resources such as petrol, electricity, and certain medicines.[708] Other cases have also been subject to varying levels of blockades. The rationale behind such complete lack of engagement and refusal by the parent state to accept contacts is the same: separate statehood will seem less appealing if these entities are isolated and poor, and both the unrecognized states and their leaderships will consequently be left weakened.

There are, however, several problems with this kind of strategy. Rather than fostering moderation, it risks breeding further intransigence. The increasingly desperate situation in Republika Srpska Krajina initially led the authorities to start negotiating with the Croatia side. In December 1994 the highway between Belgrade and Zagreb, which passed through Krajina, was reopened and the Krajina authorities even agreed to remove signposts and flags from the highway, in exchange for the delivery of parts to the Obrovac electricity plants and the reopening of the northern branch of the Adriatic oil pipeline.[709] The lack of statehood therefore seemingly fostered moderation, out of desperation, and this was precisely the strategy of the international community. The idea was to start normalization in the economic sphere and then this would make way for a political agreement. But there were in fact clear limits to this moderation. In the spring of 1993, some members of the Krajina government had signed the so-called Daruvar agreement with the aim of normalizing life in Western Slavonia. This agreement only amounted to an implementation of the

Vance Plan, which the Krajina leadership had accepted, but the return of refugees was considered a threat to the entity's survival and the negotiators were promptly arrested and charged with treason.[710] The Krajina authorities were opposed to any kind of relations with Croatia, even if it would aid the development of statehood in the entity. Isolation was instrumental for the leadership and the highway did not stay open for long either; a violent incident was used as a pretext for closing it.[711] The Krajina leaders were quick to go back on any kind of moderation if they felt that the entity's de facto independence or their own hold on power was under threat. Once a political solution was proposed that would guarantee extensive Serb autonomy but *within* a Croatian state intransigence returned. This intransigence was, in large part, a consequence of the persistent infighting and lack of central control: the 'men with the guns' were decisive, they could call the shots and saw no reason to negotiate, until it was too late and the Croatian offensive was already underway.[712] The lack of effective statehood that was, in part, a result of the punitive strategy therefore posed an obstacle to a negotiated agreement.

The creation of something approaching 'out of control' areas is generally a bad strategy if the aim is to enhance security, as these areas may come to spread exactly the kind of instability that is generally associated with failed states. Such conditions, in addition, make it less likely that conflict resolution will succeed. Effective conflict resolution requires accountable leaders who are able to bring their followers along, and this is hard to combine with largely anarchical entities. Lack of successful institution-building makes it hard to escape the dominance of warlords and the persistence of infighting and this raises the question: with whom do you negotiate? Shamil Baseyev, the late Chechen warlord, and Arkady Ghukasyan, the former president of Nagorno Karabakh, may, for example, have been equally bent on independence, but whereas the former never established full control over the entity, the latter was firmly in control. I do not think there is much doubt who would have been easier to negotiate with and—more important—who would have been more likely to be able to implement a settlement. As the Croatian envoy said when informed that the prime minister of Republika Srpska Krajina had finally signed a peace agreement: 'but the other nine factions will reject it'.[713] In such a situation, not only willingness but also ability to compromise is likely to be in short supply.

The punitive strategy, moreover, tends to underestimate the strength of ethnic solidarity, or at least the level of internal cohesion in these entities, which only tends to be strengthened by external pressure. Hardship can be blamed on external pressures and this provides a convenient excuse for the leadership ('it is not our fault that your lives are hard') and may cause the population to rally around the flag. Instead of turning against their leaders, the population may reason that they 'may be bastards', but 'they are our bastards'.[714] The case of Republika Srpska Krajina clearly showed that a perception of being 'us against the world' can breed intransigence; it gives credence to the leadership's assertions that it is a question of 'independence or death' and, as Heraclides points out, an almost apocalyptic mood is often prevalent when everything seems lost.[715] In the case of Gaza, rather than undermining support for Hamas, Israel's offensive actually appears to have increased their popular backing. As a wounded Palestinian told the *Washington Post*, 'That is how the Palestinian people are...the more we get hit, the more we become persistent'.[716] This kind of externally produced hardship also confirms existing fears regarding the intentions of the parent state and is hard to combine with a claim to moderation and peaceful agendas. Thus, in addition to underestimating the degree of internal cohesion, this kind of policy also tends to underestimate the genuine fears found in these entities.

Even if lack of effective statehood does serve to undermine popular support, this is not guaranteed to result in greater willingness to compromise. Rather than leading to a shift in allegiance, this situation is likely to cause apathy. Former inhabitants of Republika Srpska Krajina argue that they lived in a ghetto, but also assert that people quickly got used to it, and were comparing it to World War II, saying 'we can get through this too'.[717] These entities have been through wars and the population is often used to hardship, and lack of progress may therefore lead to disillusionment, but not necessarily any attempt to force the leadership to take a different course. To avoid any challenges to their power, the authorities will, moreover, often have a few cards up their sleeves: they can play on genuine fears in the population—the Krajina leaders would, for example, often point to the alleged genocidal intent of the Croatian authorities—and are furthermore not averse to clamping down on expressions of dissent. The Tamil Eelam leadership was, for example, known for its intolerance of internal dissent, even though the entity emphasized its popular backing and—at least rhetorically—prioritized the welfare of the civilian population. So even if the Tamil population withdrew their active support, they were unlikely to be able to force the leaders to compromise.[718] Collective interests are not necessarily decisive and this reduces the effectiveness of a punitive strategy, even if it does succeed in undermining internal cohesion. The entities will be left weakened, but lack of long-term viability does not automatically produce willingness to compromise. In fact, this kind of strategy could likely backfire; not only is it likely to cause further resentment, it also makes the entities more likely to turn to their external patron for support, since all other survival strategies are exhausted and, as the Ottoman army commander said when he had to turn to Russia for help, 'a drowning man clings to a serpent'.[719] The policy recommendation is thus as follows: do not turn unrecognized states into 'black spots' if you want to improve the prospect of conflict resolution. It is indeed notable that the unrecognized states that are currently moving toward some form of compromise or *modus vivendi* with their parent state, such as Taiwan and Northern Cyprus, are *not* the ones without effective statehood.

What the denial of effective statehood might do is make it easier to defeat these entities militarily. Lack of resources will not only erode popular support, but will also make it harder to uphold an effective defence. For all the talk of peaceful solutions, this is often the real motive behind such a strategy. A military solution is tempting for the parent state since it allows the government to save face and demonstrate its strength, and it avoids the need for messy compromises. The problem is that such a solution, for all its seeming simplicity, may not result in lasting peace; it can lead to an even bloodier war than the one that preceded it, the human costs are significant, and the seeds may be sowed for future conflicts. But such considerations are not necessarily decisive for the parent state. Territorial integrity is at the core of statehood and the loss of territory puts the parent state under considerable strain. The status quo may even be perceived as a threat to the very survival of the state, which can therefore not be allowed to persist. As an Azerbaijani man puts it, 'I don't want to hand on this problem to my son, that is why I am for war'.[720] Such sentiments, if sufficiently widespread, might lead to a military attack even if victory—never mind lasting peace—is far from guaranteed. The question is therefore if there are other ways of promoting conflict resolution; other possibilities for moving away from the status quo? Zartman argues that a change in the military balance of power and the threat of imminent defeat is not sufficient for willingness to compromise,[721] but the question is if it is even necessary; could the pressures of unrecognized statehood produce a moderation of demands?

Pressures of Unrecognized Statehood

Absence of statehood is not conducive to peace, but this does not mean that any form of effective statehood eases the path to peace; a militarized, paranoid, puppet regime based on ethnic exclusivity would, for example, not be the most likely candidate for successful conflict resolution. This is the case even though warlords occasionally do agree to peace settlements, and even though hardliners are often thought to be better able to make an agreement stick—due to the lack of more extreme rivals, or perhaps since arguments for compromise must be highly compelling for hardliners to be brought on board. In any case, it seems fair to assume that it matters what *kind* of statehood has developed: what kind of institutions have been built, what kind of political system is in place, and what form of power relations and level of popular legitimacy we find in the entity.

The gradual introduction of democratic reforms that has characterized a number of unrecognized states could potentially have an important effect on attempts to reach a negotiated settlement. Some would argue that this effect is likely to be negative: democratization increases the risk of radicalization,[722] and creates insecurity for incumbent leaders: will they be able to take their followers with them in compromise or should they bolster their domestic position by playing the 'ethnic card'?[723] Successful outbidding should not be automatically assumed,[724] but the increasing openness we have seen in a number of unrecognized states does mean that if leaders agree to a settlement then they will have to consider the possible emergence of a new opposition or the withdrawal of popular support. In these circumstances, compromise might prove extremely difficult, especially given the effort these same authorities have put into convincing their population that the external threat is severe, that the 'enemy' cannot be trusted, and that their choices consequently are limited. Even newly elected leaders are likely to feel constrained, which was illustrated when the opposition gained power in the 2004 elections in Abkhazia; in private the new leaders reportedly conceded that they could imagine future relations with Georgia, but they refrained from publicly making such statements,[725] and progress in the settlement talks never materialized.

One could therefore wonder if a negotiated settlement might have been easier to reach in the immediate postwar period, when a more authoritarian style of leadership was in place in all of these cases. But whether it is easier for an authoritarian leader to agree to a settlement depends on their basis of power, and this was, in many of these cases, not all that secure. For example, in the case of Nagorno Karabakh there was more than one centre of power and increasing conflict characterized the relationship between the military and civilian leaders. This conflict became specifically focused on the issue of a settlement once the civilian leaders tried to oust the obstinate commander. Through one of his mouthpieces, the army commander accused the president of 'preparing the Armenian nation for the military and diplomatic defeat of Karabakh'.[726] Moreover, there was always an underlying expectation of popular sovereignty, and even authoritarian leaders would have worried about defying popular opinion, especially given their dependence on an army that relies on popular mobilization for its strength. An authoritarian regime is therefore not necessarily more able to agree to a settlement, nor is it likely to be more willing. De facto independence may have been less entrenched in these early years, but this did not coexist with greater willingness to consider solutions short of independence. The separatists had won, a large number of people had lost their lives for this victory, and the hope of international recognition was still intact. The leaders were triumphant and had their sights set on full independence; they were in no mood to compromise and actually had little reason to consider it.

Both authoritarian and more democratic leaders of unrecognized states are therefore likely to find themselves constrained if they were to agree to a negotiated settlement. Democratization, however, may have the potential to move the entities away from the dominant military logic and zero-sum thinking and instead introduce a plurality of views on possible solutions.[727] New forces have gained power in a number of those entities and in some cases, as in Abkhazia, the leaderships had their origins in civil society organizations or in the business community, rather than in the military. It is conceivable that such leaders are less likely to view conflict resolution through the prism of 'independence or death' and may be willing to consider alternatives. Protsyk argues that in the case of Transnistria, the democratic opposition would be more willing to accept a compromise solution and Moldova sees democratization as part of a recipe for reaching an agreement on peaceful reintegration. In 2005, the Moldovan parliament appealed to the Council of Europe, the OSCE, and the EU for assistance in democratizing Transnistria. They argued that this would be necessary before the status of the entity can be discussed.[728] This attitude differs significantly from what we find in other parent states, which in part reflects the demography of Transnistria and its large Moldovan population. The proposal comes with important conditions, such as the liquidation of the Transnistrian ministry of state security, which would serve to undermine the powerbase of the existing regime.[729] But it also illustrates the hope that democratization can foster a plurality of views on solving the conflict, and that the regime's maximalist position is not necessarily representative.

The problem is, however, that democratization in unrecognized states is constrained by the context of nonrecognition, the persistence of an external threat, and often the ideology of ethno-nationalism. As a result, the pluralism that results tends to be limited. In the case of Nagorno Karabakh the gradual process of democratization has been based on an underlying consensus on the issue of independence; no matter how much the rivalling elites disagree on other issues, they are united in their support for Karabakh's independence and their rejection of any alternatives. Democratization under such circumstances clearly does not automatically lead to a greater willingness to compromise. On the contrary, leaders indicating any willingness to agree to a difficult settlement may face the very real prospect of being outbid by more extreme rivals.

Even so, the introduction of political reforms does have a potentially significant impact on internal power relations. With democratization it becomes increasingly important to sell the separatist strategy domestically, and although there may be (near) consensus on the demand for independence, this does not mean that there is consensus on how to achieve it. In the first years after de facto independence was achieved, the leaders could bathe in the glory of military victory and make promises of future recognition, but such a consensus may be harder to maintain when recognition is not forthcoming and hardship persists. The context of nonrecognition contains significant tensions and the longer it lasts, the harder it becomes for the authorities to maintain the vision of future international recognition that will bring with it the promised security and prosperity. The external threat can to some extent hold popular dissatisfaction at bay, but the resulting unity might break down if the population becomes concerned that their security is not ensured. In Republika Srpska Krajina, people stopped believing that the entity could survive a military attack and started preparing for defeat,[730] and while this is not the case in Nagorno Karabakh, the war in Georgia shook people's belief in the status quo and led to heightened security fears.[731]

The leaders of unrecognized states will, over time, struggle to convince their populations that their security is protected, that they are moving closer to independence, and that their entity is viable. This creates significant dilemmas for the authorities, such as those experienced by the Nagorno Karabakh leadership, who have problems maintaining the narrative of future recognition, but who are also unable to 'sell' nonrecognition as a viable option. Such dilemmas are also found in entities that have chosen a different strategy, or where a different strategy has been imposed. In Abkhazia debates are ongoing over what kind of entity it should develop into, including the role of Russia.[732] If the authorities have not introduced political reforms, they can largely ignore the creeping popular dissatisfaction, even if it leads to weakened entities, but such a strategy will be more problematic if pluralism has been allowed to emerge. Combining the strained nature of unrecognized statehood with the introduction of political reforms may result in an opportunity for conflict resolution; if status quo becomes increasingly untenable—for internal or external reasons—a cornered leader may conclude that a generous compromise is the least bad option and start to look for alternatives.

While the denial of statehood is therefore not a recipe for conflict resolution, the constrained nature of unrecognized statehood could provide a window of opportunity. The fact that there is an opportunity for conflict resolution does, however, not mean that it will be seized, and there are in fact significant obstacles in the way of a negotiated settlement. The leaders of unrecognized states have for years described independence as a question of physical survival and therefore as non-negotiable, and will find it hard to go back on this.[733] Genuine security, it has been argued, is only possible in an independent state. The population may therefore not feel safe in an unrecognized state, but their security concerns are likely to be even greater when it comes to a possible settlement. The authorities are caught between a rock and a hard place: recognition is increasingly unlikely, they cannot persuade their publics that nonrecognition can be a viable long-term status, but they cannot convince them to support a difficult compromise either. The leaders of unrecognized states must therefore be given a good reason to consider alternatives to the status quo; they must be presented with an attractive way out.

Fudging Sovereignty and Guaranteeing Security

One of the keys to a successful settlement is security: the population of the unrecognized state and other audiences of importance must be assured that their security can be protected by a status that falls short of full independence. Robust security guarantees are consequently needed. It is hard to see how this can be achieved without international involvement, although this does not mean that international peacekeepers should be seen as a panacea. Finding countries willing to send troops is not easy, peacekeepers from interested third parties are often mistrusted by one of the two sides, and unrecognized states are generally mistrustful of the guarantees provided by peacekeepers—after all, as they point out, there were UN peacekeepers in Republika Srpska Krajina when Croatia launched its offensive but it made no difference. One possible strategy could be to make the settlement conditional; for example, Gaugazia wins the right to secede if 'an event out of its own control occurs', that is if Moldova decides to merge with Rumania.[734] Similar safeguards could be included in other agreements, but they again depend on either a sufficient level of trust between the parties or an international guarantee that these terms will be honoured.

Moreover, robust security guarantees may be necessary but they are not sufficient. Unrecognized states are asked not only to give up on their hope for full sovereignty, but also be willing to relinquish some of their power, or at least share it, and possibly also part of the territory they have hitherto controlled. For such a compromise to be feasible they have to be given something in return. They have to be presented with an acceptable way out, and this is likely to mean that conventional mechanisms for conflict resolution will not work: autonomy and/or power-sharing in their conventional forms are simply not enough. As King argues, conflict resolution in the case of unrecognized states is 'not so much about patching together a torn country as about trying to integrate two functionally distinct administrations, militaries and societies'.[735]

A number of scholars have suggested solutions that 'pool' sovereignty and disperse territoriality, for example through various forms of federal or confederal arrangements.[736] As Berg has pointed out, however, it will be difficult for the leaders of unrecognized states to accept postmodern notions of sovereignty and territoriality.[737] Territoriality is embedded in our understanding of sovereignty and it is difficult to imagine authority without it.[738] Territory and security are similarly so closely linked that it will be very hard to untangle them, and territorial control therefore remains a primary concern. Conceptions of sovereignty are deeply ingrained, or conditioned by the international system, and this affects the possibility for conflict resolution. Sovereignty is seen as absolute, and territorial control is seen as crucial for the ability to guarantee security. But even though territoriality remains primary, this does not mean that sovereignty cannot be fudged. For example, the bi-communal, bi-zonal federation that is being discussed for Cyprus may come to include a Turkish security guarantee for the territory that is currently controlled by the Turkish Republic of Northern Cyprus. In order to limit the degree to which this infringes on the territorial integrity of the united island, this could include a need for international approval of any intervention, and it would end if Turkey was to join the EU.[739] China's model for reintegrating Taiwan is based on the same structure that it used for Hong Kong, 'one state, two systems',[740] and it involves a similar fudging of sovereignty: one state, but with two (or more) sovereignties. Such solutions have increasingly been used in protracted conflicts. The leadership of the Bosnian Serb entity, for example, agreed to a solution that fell short of independence, but largely maintained their de facto independence and allowed them to establish links with Serbia.[741] The Good Friday Agreement for Northern Ireland similarly involved elements that fudged sovereignty over the island, such as the creation of a North-South Ministerial Council, which comprises ministers of the Northern Ireland Executive and the Irish Government and was established 'to develop consultation, co-operation and action within the island of Ireland'.[742] These solutions go beyond autonomy and power-sharing and would offer a form of semi-sovereignty to the unrecognized states, but with a promise of a place in the international system as well as security guarantees.

In these examples, the territorial integrity of the parent state was maintained, at least on paper, but the de facto independence enjoyed by the unrecognized state can still be substantial and might even include membership of certain international organizations. Various forms of co-dominions or associated statehood have also been suggested[743] and entities such as Andorra may therefore, after all, provide a model for possible solutions. The key is that we should not limit our search to either sovereignty or nonsovereignty; this is an unhelpful dichotomy that prolongs the stalemate. The international system of sovereign states makes unrecognized statehood unsustainable in the long run, and therefore provides a possible opportunity for compromise, but the solution will—somewhat paradoxically—have to fudge sovereignty. Such an agreement is, however, not easy to reach, as it will be interpreted through the prism of the dichotomy outlined above and seen as a step toward either full reintegration or full independence. Ruth Deyermond argues that the conception of sovereignty that prevailed in the former Soviet Union did allow for two sovereignties on the same territory while also establishing a hierarchy between the two,[744] and this could conceivably make it easier to fudge sovereignty in the post-Soviet space. In the case of Nagorno Karabakh, several

Azerbaijani analysts have suggested that as long as Azerbaijan's territorial integrity is maintained, the entity can have all the de facto independence it wants, perhaps even including special links with Armenia,[745] but even if this does in fact reflect a willingness to fudge sovereignty—and I remain unconvinced that this is the case—international guarantees would still be needed for such an arrangement to be both acceptable and viable.

We therefore see how the international system of sovereign states pressures the leaders of unrecognized states toward maintaining a goal of full, externally recognized, independence; any alternative is too hard to sustain in view of a sceptical public. The appeal of full sovereignty prevents nonrecognition from being seen as an attractive status, but it also presents obstacles to solutions that fudge sovereignty. The strain that characterizes unrecognized statehood may provide a window of opportunity for conflict resolution, but the inherent ambiguity of the possible solutions brings with it a need for strong international assurances. Ambiguity is often recommended when it comes to reaching peace settlements,[746] but may be decidedly unhelpful if a fearful population is to be persuaded to compromise. De Waal quotes a Karabakh Armenian who dismisses the use of constructive ambiguity since, as he puts it, 'death is not an ambiguous concept'.[747] Fudged sovereignty may be the only realistic solution, but it does bring us into largely uncharted territory and would require courageous leadership and committed international involvement.

In most cases, the absence of a negotiated settlement is not due to a lack of imagination when it comes to possible solutions; the same frameworks for agreements have been discussed for years and been rejected by the unrecognized state, the parent state, or by both. The timing has simply not been right for a settlement; status quo is not so painful that an alternative is considered. The calculations made by unrecognized states differ from those made in other secessionist conflicts, since they are not focused on the question of 'can we win?' but rather on, 'can we sustain the current situation?' and this is affected by internal as well as external factors. International practices and norms of recognition affect the extent to which recognition is seen as a likely outcome, and this has a very significant impact on the internal dynamics of these entities. Moreover, the degree of international involvement is important for the sustainability of the status quo and it is also crucial if negotiated solutions short of full sovereignty are to be seen as attractive, or even viable.

The problem is that the strained nature of unrecognized statehood in most cases does not result in an urgent need for change. It may lead to a gradual erosion of the entity's strength and the leaders' powerbase, but they are unlikely to be replaced by anyone with a radically different agenda. Even if the stalemate is therefore becoming more painful, the urgency that Zartman emphasizes is therefore not necessarily present[748] unless the external environment also changes. For example, in the months after the Georgian war there was a great deal of uncertainty on both sides of the Karabakh conflict: would the war spread, had the practice of international recognition changed, how would Russia react to a military offensive? This created a more opportune, but ultimately short-lived, window of opportunity for a settlement.[749] In other cases, conflict resolution will be a slow process, which is hampered by the often-bellicose rhetoric of the parent states and the extreme levels of mistrust that exists between the two sides. A stalemate, even a relatively painful one, can therefore go on for a very long time. But there may be ways of speeding up the process.

Building Trust Through Engagement

One strategy often tried by parent states is to lure unrecognized states back into their arms with promises of increased welfare. Before the August 2008 offensive, Georgia's president, Mikheil Saakashvili, attempted to undermine the internal legitimacy of the South Ossetian leadership and convince the population that they were better off in a Georgian state. To this effect he invested financially in the areas of South Ossetia that were controlled by Tbilisi, organized concerts (with the German disco group Boney M!) and launched other activities meant to showcase the attractiveness of the Georgian state.[750] The intention was apparently to show the population that they would face a better future in Georgia and thereby persuade them to withdraw support for their intransigent leaders. Such economic incentives will, however, be competing with the strength of ethno-national ties and the fear and sense of vulnerability associated with reintegration. Even in the most optimistic scenario, such a strategy will therefore take a long time to have any effect. Moreover, deliberately trying to undermine the powerbase of the unrecognized state may not be conducive to the building of trust. More promising are strategies for two-way engagement between the unrecognized state and the parent state as well as increased international engagement. Such engagement could include trade, civil society exchanges, and even official contacts. Again, this is a long-term strategy but it could gradually change attitudes and make a negotiated settlement more acceptable.[751] The aim is to move closer to a solution of the status issue, by sidestepping it for now.

Isolation is counterproductive; it reinforces a siege mentality and makes unrecognized states even more dependent on their external patron, and engagement strategies are therefore increasingly being considered by international mediators and by some parent states. Since 2004, Northern Cyprus has, for example, seen growing international engagement: the entity now has two representatives in the Council of Europe's Parliamentary Assembly; it has quasi-diplomatic representation in Brussels and lobbying rights in the European Parliament; the Northern Cypriot president has been received by the U.S. Secretary of State and by several other foreign ministers; and the entity's observer status in the Organization of the Islamic Conference has been upgraded from that of a 'community' to that of a 'state', based on the Annan Plan.[752] A similar, if less far-reaching, approach is also tried in the case of Abkhazia and South Ossetia. The EU in 2009 launched its strategy of 'Non-recognition and Engagement', which foresees increased engagement with the unrecognized states, including contacts with civil society and projects related to human rights and economic integration, but combines this with strong support for Georgia's territorial integrity and a consequent reluctance to engage with the Abkhaz leadership.[753] In parallel with this the Georgian government publicized its 'Action Plan for Engagement'.[754] The hope behind this strategy is that increased international engagement, including links with the parent state, will help build trust, strengthen moderate voices, avoid over-reliance on the patron state, and thereby help gain some strategic leverage over the unrecognized state.[755]

The problem with this kind of approach is threefold. First, although the unrecognized states are calling for international engagement, they are likely to be wary of an engagement strategy that is specifically designed to promote reintegration, even if this is a long-term strategy. Second, although more widespread international engagement may offer unrecognized states benefits that they cannot get from their patron states, such as knowledge transfer, it will have to be substantial in order to be able to compete with patron state support, and possibly allow the unrecognized state to loosen its ties. This is especially the case when a patron state provides the unrecognized states with a security guarantee. The required substantial engagement, which for example allows international trade, provides democratization assistance and perhaps even provides certain security guarantees, comes up against the principle of territorial integrity and likely resistance from the parent state. In the case of Georgia, the 'Action Plan for Engagement' is, for example, constrained by the Law on Occupied Territories, which includes travel restrictions and economic restrictions amounting to a blockade.[756] A possible way of getting around this involves using NGOs for some of the more sensitive engagement, such as engagement that involves direct contacts with the de facto authorities.[757] Third, if the engagement is meaningful, then one of the unavoidable side effects is that it makes unrecognized states more sustainable. Even if international actors choose to promote good governance and the rule of law, in the hope that more moderate dynamics will emerge, then this will also help create a more effective and hence more viable entity. The risk is therefore that reaching a negotiated settlement—moving away from the status quo—becomes even less urgent for the unrecognized state.

Even so, there does not seem to be any other way. Isolation has been tried and failed, and engagement could over time make a settlement more likely. But it requires patience, and such patience may be hard for the parent state to muster; status quo is costly for them and they could be led to conclude that a military 'solution' is more attractive. This was what happened in the case of Croatia: limited engagement had been tried, but it did not have the desired effect, so spurred on by U.S. military assistance, the Croatian government opted for a military offensive. For an engagement strategy to work it is therefore important to keep the parent state on board; they must be convinced that engagement follows the Northern Cyprus model and not the Kosovo model; that it leads to greater prospects for conflict resolution and is not a sign of creeping recognition. One possible way of ensuring this would be to make the engagement explicitly part of the peace process, say by linking it to the creation of an interim status for the unrecognized states and to other confidence-building measures, and possibly compromises, for example, on refugee returns. Even if the parties agree to defer the issue of status, then it at least means that they agree that there is an issue to be addressed[758] and the attempt to reach a negotiated settlement has not been completely abandoned.

If All Else Fails: Recognition or Long-Term Nonrecognition?

The de facto independence of unrecognized states is a reality that cannot simply be wished away. Strategies for moving toward peace must take this into account: independence does not just represent an elusive dream, it is the current—albeit not de jure—reality. The denial of statehood through blockades and other punitive strategies should, however, not be associated with improved prospects for conflict resolution. The weakening and isolation of these entities may make their defeat more likely, but the human costs are great and a long-term solution is unlikely to materialize. The unstable nature of unrecognized statehood when combined with the introduction of political reforms does present a possibility for conflict resolution, but in order for this to be anything more than a missed opportunity, international involvement is crucial. Trust has to be established and security guaranteed, and third-party involvement is necessary to convince both sides that a solution that fudges sovereignty is actually feasible and not just a cover for full reintegration or secession.

Negotiating a settlement in conflicts involving unrecognized states is therefore likely to be a slow and arduous process. What if it does not happen, what if the stalemate is not broken—is it then time for recognition? One of the reasons given for recognizing Kosovo's declaration of independence and the result of South Sudan's independence referendum was after all that no other option was feasible; Belgrade and Khartoum had failed to present acceptable alternatives. This is, however, not likely to be the best solution in a number of cases. First, there is the risk of a demonstration effect: the risk that recognition would make other unrecognized states even less likely to accept a compromise solution and would spur on other separatist movements. Given the obstacles to a settlement mentioned above, this is not necessarily very significant, and separatist movements may not need that extra motivation, but there are other potential problems, related to the risk of instability and the normative implications of recognition.

A number of cases have demonstrated that recognition does not necessarily ensure stability; the continued conflict between Ethiopia and Eritrea, for example, illustrates how an intrastate conflict can be turned into an interstate one. This is of course even more likely if the parent state does not consent to the independence. The newly independent states may, moreover, themselves prove to be sources of instability. The image of anarchical badlands has, as argued in this book, been overplayed, but many unrecognized states are small, weak, and lack resources. If their recognition is not based on standards of statehood, then recognition may result in a significant need for international assistance. Finally, we should not forget that some of these entities are founded on ethnic cleansing and other violations of human rights, and recognizing their statehood may set a bad precedent, at least if it does not come with conditions of refugee returns and investigations of war crimes—committed on both sides. If independence is part of a peace agreement, which is accepted by the parent state, then this is clearly a different matter, but it should again come with conditions. For example, the Bougainville settlement includes an independence referendum after ten to fifteen years *if* conditions of good governance have been met.[759]

Recognition is therefore not necessarily the solution, even in cases where de facto independence has been maintained for decades and settlement talks have proved fruitless or where no one is willing to commit the troops needed to provide robust security guarantees. But the solution is also not isolation of the unrecognized state. Instead the international community should pursue a strategy of engagement, which rules out recognition but includes trade relations and other international links. This would, at least, avoid the formal loss of territory and also the creation of 'out of control' areas. Such engagement could possibly be conditioned on democratic developments, which would arguably render these entities less destabilizing, and could perhaps lead to a long-term relaxation of attitudes. This strategy would, as noted above, make nonrecognition more sustainable and thereby reduce the incentive for unrecognized states to compromise, but when such a compromise seems out of reach and the necessary international involvement is not forthcoming, it could provide a form of *modus vivendi* and a greater level of stability. A model for this is the relation between Taiwan and China, which has improved under a 'mutual nondenial' framework that sidesteps the issue of sovereignty for now.[760] It does not result in reintegration, but international engagement may over time make the issue of status less explosive. In the meantime it would create a place for unrecognized states in the international system, it would normalize their anomalous situation, and would thereby fudge sovereignty in a way that does not require a mutual agreement.

7 CONCLUSION

A sigh of relief will accompany the departure from an unrecognized state for many visitors: they are now back on safe, recognized soil where the normal rules of international society apply. When I finished my latest round of fieldwork in Nagorno Karabakh it certainly left my university's ethics committee and head of department relieved; they had not, after all, been foolhardy to give in to my insistence that it was not dangerous to visit an unrecognized state. Even if images of anarchical badlands and imminent warfare are not accepted, there are still significant differences between recognized and unrecognized states. These differences may be particularly pertinent to risk-averse ethics committees and worried relatives, but they also affect the very nature of the forms of statehood that can develop in the context of nonrecognition. The peculiarities of unrecognized statehood may not be immediately obvious: they often look like states and to a large extent function like states; when leaving Nagorno Karabakh and entering Armenia the most noticeable difference is actually the deteriorating condition of the road. If you lose your money or fall ill in an unrecognized state, however, no embassy will be able to help you, and—more important from the point of view of developing statehood—these entities are most often barred from access to international loans and trade.

The exact cost of nonrecognition varies from case to case, depending on the position adopted by the parent state and the unrecognized state's access to alternative sources of external support. But although it is true, as Krasner has argued, that 'nonrecognition does not condemn an entity to death or oblivion',[761] it does come at a price for all unrecognized states; it constrains their ability to create entities that are sustainable in the long term and it puts a strain on their internal legitimacy. This does not mean that there is no variation between these entities. On the contrary, they occupy the entire spectrum from 'failed' unrecognized states such as Chechnya, to (almost) fully functioning and prosperous unrecognized states such as Taiwan and Northern Cyprus. When it comes to their regimes, there is also a world of difference between the regimes of South Ossetia and Transnistria, which are classified as 'non-free', and the 'free' regimes found in Taiwan and Northern Cyprus. Some of this variation is illustrated in Table 2.

The context of nonrecognition may provide powerful incentives for the creation of effective, democratic statehood, but there are significant factors pulling in a different direction, such as the legacy of war, lack of resources, international isolation, infighting warlords, and lack of popular legitimacy. While the creation of effective entities and the introduction of political reforms is therefore by no means guaranteed, it is also not made impossible by the lack of recognition.

Not Simply States-In-All-But-Name

It is important to recognize these differences between unrecognized states. We cannot conclude from Chechnya that all unrecognized states are largely anarchic entities, or from South Ossetia that they are all closely in tune with their patron state. This variation has unfortunately often been missed in the limited literature on unrecognized states, and, in particular, in the media and among policymakers. The fact that these entities vary significantly does not, however, mean that they do not share significant similarities. Despite their different placement on the spectrum of state effectiveness and regime reform, unrecognized states are subject to similar tensions and differ in important respects from their recognized counterparts. The factors that allow unrecognized states to overcome the initial obstacles to state-building are also the factors that constrain their later developments. This results in the specific tensions that characterize statehood without sovereignty: tensions between dependence and independence, and between unity and pluralism. In Nagorno Karabakh this manifests itself in an entity that proclaims its liberal, democratic, and pluralistic nature while also emphasizing its ethnic foundations, internal unity, and strong defence. When it comes to its patron state, Armenia, the entity is similarly torn between insisting on its autonomy and viability as an independent state, while also emphasizing its reliance on ethnic solidarities and its link with the kin-state.

Table 2. Contemporary Unrecognized States at a Glance[762]

Entity	Population size	GDP per capita[763]	Army size[764]			Freedom House ranking
			Standing	Reservists	% population	
Abkhazia	214,016 (2003)	$2,530 (2009)[765]	3,000	45,000	22%[766]	Partly free
Nagorno Karabakh	134,862 (2005)	$2,372 (2010)[767]	18,500	25,000	32%[768]	Partly free
Somaliland	3,000,000 (1997)	$226 (2003)[769]	15,000	0	0.5%	Partly free
South Ossetia	72,000 (2010)	$250 (2002)[770]	2,500	13,500	22%[771]	Non-free
Transnistria	555,347 (2004)	$392 (2003)[772]	4,500	15,000	4%[773]	Non-free
Northern Cyprus	257,000 (2006)	$16,158 (GNP, 2008)[774]	5,000	26,000	12%	Free
Borderline cases						
Kosovo	1,805,000 (2009)	$2,985 (2009)[775]	2,147	0	0.1%[776]	Partly free
Taiwan	23,120,000 (2009)	$16,423 (2009)[777]	290,000	1,657,000	8%	Free

The struggle for recognition remains the raison d'être of these entities—the narrative that legitimizes the regimes—and the promise of
future recognition along with the persistence of an external threat
provide the regimes with a degree of insulation from looming popular
dissatisfaction. It helps the authorities square the circle that is unrecognized statehood. The effectiveness of these arguments, however,
wanes over time, and the regimes find it difficult to replace them with
anything else. Dominant conceptions of sovereignty prevent nonrecognition from being seen as anything but a temporary status, while the
international system of sovereign states acts as an important gatekeeper that prevents these entities from either becoming recognized or
from finding an alternative place in the international system. They
therefore remain caught in an ambiguous position. This, in the long
term, undermines the sustainability of unrecognized statehood.

Unrecognized states are consequently not simply 'states in waiting',
identical to recognized states aside from their lack of recognition. No
matter where they fall on the spectrum between 'failed' and 'strong'
unrecognized states, they are subject to specific tensions that lend them
an almost transient quality. Whereas recognized states are characterized by a certain rigidity, unrecognized states are characterized by their
fluidity. This does not mean that statehood without sovereignty is not
possible, but it does take a specific form. Unrecognized states represent
a partial disconnect between external and internal sovereignty which
challenges dominant conceptions of sovereignty while at the same time
demonstrating the continued power of the paradigm. Even in today's
globalized and increasingly deterritorialized world, it matters if a state
is recognized or not, if it is part of the international system of sovereign
states. Sovereignty still matters, even if this book urges the reader to
rethink how it functions and how it manifests itself. The norms and
practice of state sovereignty still shape and constrain anomalies within
the system. State sovereignty acts as a powerful gatekeeper; anomalies
are either treated as 'honorary insiders' or they are, as outsiders, facing
almost complete isolation. Despite increasing talk of engaging unrecognized states there is presently no niche available for them, and this
affects their long-term sustainability.

Dangerous Vacuum

The position of being 'outsiders' in the international system, moreover,
creates a form of vacuum in the entities; not in the sense of a power
vacuum, as found in failed states, but in terms of international links

and external sources of support. Jakub Grygiel has argued that a vacuum caused by lack of internal sovereignty risks drawing in competing great powers and that this can lead to confrontation, crisis, and even 'vacuum wars'.[778] But a vacuum caused by lack of external sovereignty can also draw in great powers and cement their influence in the region. This was of course illustrated by Russia's recognition of Abkhazia and South Ossetia in August 2008 and its gradual, de facto, incorporation of the two regions. Such a move is often described as being in line with the strategies of the de facto leaderships, but the reality is often far more complex: unrecognized states often deeply resent the undermining of their de facto independence, but the involvement of an external patron may be reluctantly agreed to due to the absence of alternative survival strategies, or it may indeed be imposed by a far stronger neighbour.[779] The fact that these entities are not the anarchical badlands of popular depictions does therefore not mean that their existence cannot constitute a threat to regional stability, but it is crucially the actions of external patrons or parent states that would provide the trigger. This is not to absolve the unrecognized states from any part in subsequent instability, but just to say that they are unlikely to make the first move.

Opportunities for Conflict Resolution

Great power interference or the resumption of warfare is nevertheless far from inevitable. The position of 'outsiders' in the international system also provides a possible catalyst for a compromise solution. The strained statehood found in these entities and their lack of long-term sustainability does not call for urgent action on the part of the de facto authorities and does not automatically produce a willingness to compromise. The decline is gradual. Unrecognized states can survive for a long time, and the leaders are unlikely to be replaced by anyone with a radically different agenda. The only acute danger to the entity comes from the parent state, and the persistence of this external threat provides the regimes with some guarantee against internal dissent, although the case of Republika Srpska Krajina clearly showed that cohesion based on fear and control leads to growing apathy rather than active support and this, in turn, undermines the ability of the entity to mount an effective defence. The de facto statehood in itself constitutes an obstacle to compromise: why give up on what you have already won; 'why be a lieutenant in someone else's army if you can be a general in your own',[780] why replace de facto control with potentially insufficient guarantees? This could lead to the mistaken conclusion that the rejection of effective statehood would make conflict resolution more likely, and such a view has indeed been one of the reasons for isolating these aspiring states: 'if we prevent their de facto independence from becoming entrenched, then they will be more likely to compromise', or 'persistent hardship in the unrecognized state will make the parent state appear more attractive'. Such a strategy, however, underestimates the deep fears found in these entities and overestimates the degree to which collective sentiments are decisive for the decisions made by the leaders. Moreover, authoritarian entities with insufficient central control are hardly conducive to peaceful settlements; the creation of 'black spots' is not a recommended strategy for conflict resolution.

De facto independence is the current reality that cannot simply be wished away. However, the strained statehood characteristic of unrecognized states, along with the gradual introduction of political reforms, nevertheless provides a possible strategy for conflict resolution; what is crucial is the interplay between internal and external dynamics. There is nothing inherently contradictory about democratization in the context of nonrecognition, and in the post-Cold War era, there has even been a perception of a strong external drive to democratize, and political reforms have been observed in the unlikeliest settings. But nonrecognition also creates specific obstacles for democratization, which therefore tends to stagnate at a fairly low level; the desire to democratize has seemingly lost its urgency in cases such as Nagorno Karabakh and Somaliland. This appears to be caused by an overriding emphasis on unity, rather than pluralism and diversity, and by a disappointment with their lack of international recognition. When it comes to the question of whether partition can be said to further democratization, the jury is therefore still out.[781] Even hesitant reforms will affect the internal dynamics of these entities, however; it reduces the manoeuvrability of the leaderships and it could lead to a reluctant acceptance of compromise. The leaders of unrecognized states will, over time, struggle to convince their populations that their security is protected, that they are moving closer to independence, and that their entity is viable. 'Virtual politics' is harder to sustain when the stakes are high and the authorities may find it difficult to put the lid back on political reforms. This does not mean that solutions short of full independence will be embraced, but it does mean that the leaders might be searching for a way out. The leaders will, however, face a trying dilemma: should they try to sell a narrative of de facto statehood with little prospect of recognition and the continuation of an external threat, or can they convince their population to accept a difficult compromise?[782] In order for the leaders to choose the latter, one thing is needed above all: security must be guaranteed. This is not sufficient, but it is necessary.

In order for a solution to prove acceptable to unrecognized states, it will in most cases also have to 'fudge' sovereignty. This would include settlements that on paper restore the territorial unity of the parent state, but in practice allows the unrecognized state to maintain its de facto independence, including links with its patron state. More than one sovereignty would in effect coexist on the same territory. Now this may sound like a paradox: the above analysis has found that there is no place for unrecognized states in the modern international system, so how would the resulting anomalies fit in? The argument is that there is no place for unrecognized states *because* they are seen to violate the principle of territorial integrity; other anomalies are treated as 'honorary insiders' and so would the states resulting from such compromises. A solution that fudges sovereignty would nevertheless be constrained by dominant conceptions of sovereignty, territory, and security. Leaders, as well as the people they represent, would be inclined to see such solutions as either a step toward reintegration or toward full de jure secession. In order for solutions that fudge sovereignty to be viable, international guarantees are needed, but finding states that are willing to commit the necessary troops and other resources may be a tall order indeed.

Engagement: The Least Bad Option

In the absence of such involvement, we are left with four options or scenarios: (1) the status quo continues with a gradual undermining of the unrecognized states running in parallel with an increasingly entrenched sense of separation. This may be accompanied by increasing influence of an external patron. (2) The parent state chooses to use military force to reintegrate its territory. This could result in all-out war, which may draw in neighbouring states, and even if the parent state does win an 'easy' victory, the human costs are likely to be significant and future stability is far from guaranteed. (3) The unrecognized state is recognized without the consent of the parent state. This could result in renewed instability and may set a dangerous precedent. (4) The international community decides to engage with the nonrecognized state, thereby fudging sovereignty in a way that does not require a mutual agreement. The latter option would not prove popular with the parent state, nor with many international actors, and it would even raise concerns among the leaders of unrecognized states who gain some strength from their 'us against the world' rhetoric. Yet if a compromise solution cannot be reached, then it provides a greater level of stability than the other options, especially if combined with demands for democratization and good governance.

The limited long-term sustainability of unrecognized statehood and the degree of popular pressure experienced by the leaders will unfortunately not always make them choose a compromise solution, nor can we be sure that the parent state is willing and able to offer an acceptable settlement or that international actors are willing to provide the necessary guarantees. Otherwise, we have to plan for the longer term and continued isolation does not appear to provide a recipe for success; rather, it risks breeding instability and favours the involvement of patron states. These entities are not merely the puppets of external actors; the relationship is much more complicated and they do not simply mirror great-power interests. But if isolation is maintained for an extended period of time, then the image of the puppet may indeed become a self-fulfilling prophecy. Very small, but recognized, states can survive without patronage, but they can crucially rely on multiple international linkages for their survival. This option is generally not open to unrecognized states, although diaspora support provides some with an alternative source of support while others are permitted limited international engagement. In the absence of such linkages, the entities run out of other options; reliance on the patron state becomes necessary for their continued survival.

We should not fool ourselves: engagement will make unrecognized statehood more viable. It is not possible to just promote more moderate voices, for example through support for good governance, without also aiding the state-building process. Would such a strategy run the risk of encouraging other separatist groups, by sending the signal that even if they cannot achieve full recognition, they might still be eligible for a second prize? It might, but I doubt that the effect would be significant. First of all, secessionist attempts are, as Kaufmann has pointed out, extremely costly[783] and most fail to achieve de facto—let alone de jure—independence. Second, viability and the prospect of success is, contrary to what is often argued in the literature, not necessarily decisive:[784] actions of the parent state are important but so are selfish motivations and intra-group dynamics and these may be more or less independent of what can realistically be achieved.[785] Lee Seymour has, in any case, convincingly shown that almost every resolution to secessionist conflicts since 1975 'has resulted in gains in territorial autonomy and/or legal status for the challenging group';[786] so even though the current international climate is dismissive of secessionist claims, and independence is therefore unlikely to be gained, this does not rule out that separatist attempts will have pay-offs. The prospect of success may therefore improve marginally if the international community opens up for limited engagement with unrecognized status, but it would not fundamentally change the calculations made by aspiring secessionists.

A greater cause for concern is that the prospect of limited international engagement would make it less likely that unrecognized states would agree to an agreement that falls short of full independence. After all, one of the factors that may get the leaders to consider such an agreement in the first place is the limited long-term sustainability of unrecognized statehood. But this problem would be partially solved if they were to be offered a place in the international system. To prevent this form of moral hazard, an end to isolation should only be offered either if all else fails or as part of a phased approach to finding a solution. It should also come with conditions. It should not be offered to 'black spots', ungoverned territories, or to dictatorial regimes. This kind of policy is therefore not problem-free, and would undoubtedly meet with a lot of resistance, yet the current policy based on a rigid conception of sovereignty and territorial integrity is not producing results, so it might be time for a rethink, not only of sovereignty, but also of ways of dealing with unrecognized states. Such a rethink requires us to move away from images of anarchical badlands and instead recognize the variation found among these entities as well as the tensions faced by them. Through in-depth case studies and a re-examination of the links between sovereignty, statehood, and conflict this book has been intended to provide the starting point for precisely such discussions.

NOTES

1 P. Rutland, Frozen conflicts, frozen analysis. Paper presented at the ISA's 48th Annual Convention, Chicago, 1 March 2007.
2 V. Yakubyan, Kosovo-Karabakh—strategic fork, *Regnum*, 13 November 2006. http://www.regnum.ru/english/737310.html.
3 R. Parsons, Russia: Is Putin looking to impose solutions to frozen conflicts? *RFE/RL*, 2 February 2006.
4 For another view of this conflict see S. E. Cornell and S. F. Starr (eds), *The Guns of August 2008: Russia's War in Georgia* (New York, N.Y.: M. E. Sharpe, 2009).
5 D. Medvedev, Why I had to recognise Georgia's breakaway regions, *Financial Times*, 27 August 2008.
6 See, for example, J. A. Camilleri and J. Falk, *The End of Sovereignty?* (Aldershot: Edward Elgar, 1992), 21–5.
7 D. Lynch, *Engaging Eurasia's Separatist States* (Washington, D.C.: United States Institute of Peace, 2004), 18.
8 S. D. Krasner, Sharing sovereignty: New institutions for collapsed and failing states, *International Security*, 2004, 29(2), 87.
9 R. Jackson, *Sovereignty* (Cambridge: Polity, 2007), 150.
10 S. D. Pickering, *Quantifying the Dynamics of Conflict*, Unpublished PhD thesis, Lancaster University 2010.
11 Ibid. 109, 131.
12 A. Boadle, Castro: Cuba not cashing U.S. Guantanamo rent checks, *Reuters*, 17 August 2007.
13 *RIA Novosti*, Russia plans to invest heavily in Sevastopol base, 9 May 2010.
14 On the issue of full independence the population of the Faroe Islands is about evenly split. In 1946 a narrow majority supported independence in a consultative referendum, but the governing coalition could not agree on how to interpret this outcome.

15 J. Crawford, *The Creation of States in International Law* (Oxford: Oxford University Press, 2006), 625.
16 Ibid. 626–8.
17 Ibid. 629–30.
18 This role is to be taken over by the European Union Rule of Law Mission in Kosovo (EULEX).
19 S. D. Krasner, *Sovereignty: Organized Hypocrisy* (Princeton: Princeton University Press, 1999), 234.
20 Both states have been members of the UN since 1993.
21 Constitution of the Principality of Andorra, April 1993. See also Krasner, *Sovereignty*, 16, 230. D. Geldenhuys, *Contested States in World Politics* (Basingstoke: Palgrave Macmillan, 2009), 50.
22 The Treaty between Monaco and France was last renegotiated in 2002 (ratified in 2005). General Consulate of Monaco in New York, Monaco signs new treaty with France, 24 October 2002. http://www.monaco-consulate.com/news_1024.htm.
23 Krasner, *Sovereignty*, 20, 229.
24 See Crawford, *The Creation of States*, 221.
25 Krasner, *Sovereignty*, 232.
26 J. S. Migdal, State building and the non-nation state, *Journal of International Affairs*, 2004, 58(1).
27 R. Jackson, *Quasi-states: Sovereignty, International Relations and the Third World* (Cambridge: Cambridge University Press, 1990), 43.
28 See, for example, S. D. Krasner, Abiding sovereignty, *International Political Science Review*, 2001, 22(3), 231–3. For a further discussion of the difference between contemporary and historical cases of nonrecognition, see Chapter 2.
29 For similar definitions, see P. Kolstø, The sustainability and future of unrecognized quasi-states, *Journal of Peace Research*, 2006, 43(6), 725–6. S. Pegg, *International Society and the De Facto State* (Aldershot: Ashgate, 1998), 26.
30 The different phases of state-building are covered in Chapter 3.
31 http://www.lighthousefoundation.org/alf_lights/boonisland/republicboon_declaration.htm.
32 See, for example, G. B. Helman and S. R. Ratner, Saving failed states, *Foreign Policy*, 1992–3, 89 (Winter). F. Fukuyama, The imperative of state-building, *Journal of Democracy*, 2004, 15(2).
33 I. W. Zartman, Introduction: Posing the problem of state collapse, in *Collapsed States: The Disintegration and Restoration of Legitimate Authority*, ed. I. W. Zartman (Boulder: Lynne Rienner, 1995), 1.
34 See the research project, 'Governance in Areas of Limited Statehood'. Freie Universität Berlin. http://www.sfb-governance.de.
35 B. H. Stanislawski, Para-states, quasi-states, and black spots, *International Studies Review*, 2008, 10(2). For analysis of different degrees of state

failure, see R. I. Rotberg, The failure and collapse of nation-states, in *When States Fail: Causes and Consequences*, ed. R. I. Rotberg (Princeton: Princeton University Press, 2001).

36 See, for example, K. Menkhaus, State collapse in Somalia: Second thoughts, *Review of African Political Economy*, 2003, 30(97). V. Luling, Come back Somalia? Questioning a collapsed state, *Third World Quarterly*, 1997, 18(2). International Crisis Group, *Pakistan's Tribal Areas: Appeasing the Militants* (Islamabad/Brussels, 2006).

37 See also Pegg, *International Society and the De Facto State*, 4.

38 Jackson, *Quasi-states*.

39 Ibid. 40–7.

40 These entities very much exist in a Hobbesian world, rather than in a Lockean or Kantian world. See A. Wendt, *Social Theory of International Politics* (Cambridge: Cambridge University Press, 1999).

41 Katarzyna Pełczynska-Nałęcz and her colleagues use the term 'para-states' to encompass unrecognized states, 'black spots' and states-within-states. K. Pełczynska-Nałęcz, K. Strachota and M. Falkowski, Para-states in the post-Soviet area from 1991 to 2007, *International Studies Review*, 2008, 10(2), 373.

42 See, for example, C. Ross, *Independent Diplomat: Dispatches from an Unaccountable Elite* (London: Hurst, 2007), 194. Kolstø, The sustainability and future of unrecognized quasi-states, 726.

43 International Crisis Group, *Western Sahara: Out of the Impasse* (Cairo/Brussels, 2007), 17 n98.

44 See http://www.president.nkr.am/en/nkr/

45 For Somaliland's disputed territories, see, for example, International Crisis Group, *Somaliland: Time for African Union Leadership* (Hargeisa/Addis Ababa/Brussels, 2006), 8–10.

46 Stanislawski, Para-states, 366, 369.

47 R. W. McColl, The insurgent state: Territorial bases of revolution, *Annals of the Association of American Geographers*, 1969, 59(4).

48 Stanislawski, Para-states, 366.

49 Pegg has argued that including such entities constitutes a potential improvement of his original work. S. Pegg, From de facto states to states-within-states: Progress, problems and prospects, in *States within States: Incipient Entities in the Post-Cold War Era*, eds P. Kingston and I. Spears (New York: Palgrave Macmillan, 2004) 38.

50 A. Heraclides, *The Self-Determination of Minorities in International Politics* (London: Frank Cass, 1991), 1.

51 Even though a desire for independence still exists, the Kurdish leaders have at least for now agreed to a federal Iraq. See, for example, L. Anderson, Reintegrating unrecognized states, in *Unrecognized States in the International System,* eds N. Caspersen and G. Stansfield (London: Routledge, 2010), 198.

52 See Pełczynska-Nałęcz et al., Para-states in the post-Soviet area, 371, 374.

53 See http://www.kosovothanksyou.com/statistics/

54 These cases are examples of what Geldenhuys terms 'zero recognition', 'paltry recognition' and/or 'patron recognition'. Geldenhuys, *Contested States*, 23–4.

55 The population size is contested and likely considerably smaller than the 2003 census results indicate. See, for example, T. Trier, H. Lohm, D. Szakonyi, *Under Siege: Inter-Ethnic Relations in Abkhazia* (London: Hurst, 2010), 30–2.

56 Population data from the Kurdish Regional Government, http://www.krg.org.

57 The process of dissociation was gradual in the case of Montenegro, but by 2000 it had acquired significant state-like attributes and had, for example, introduced the D-Mark as the only legal tender. See N. Caspersen, Elite interests and the Serbian-Montenegrin conflict, *Southeast European Politics*, 2003, 4(2–3), 108–10.

58 The National Statistics Service of Nagorno-Karabakh Republic, http://census.stat-nkr.am/nkr/1-1.pdf. This figure is contested and Azerbaijani sources put it at 120,000 or even lower. See, for example, International Crisis Group, *Nagorno-Karabakh: Viewing the Conflict from the Ground* (Tbilisi/Brussels, 2005), 4.

59 Estimate from *Statistical Yearbook of Republika Srpska* (Banja Luka, 2010).

60 Estimate from F. Švarm, The Krajina economy, *Vreme News Digest*, 15 August 1994.

61 Estimate from Ministry of National Planning & Coordination, *Somaliland in Figures* (Hargeisa, 2003).

62 Estimate from the South Ossetian authorities, which is strongly contested. International Crisis Group, *South Ossetia: the Burden of Recognition* (Tbilisi/Brussels, 2010), 2.

63 Results from http://www.eelam.com/tamil-homeland/statistics.jsp.

64 Results from http://www.minorityrights.com.

65 As in many of the other cases, this number from the 2006 census is contested. International Crisis Group, *Cyprus: Reunification or Partition?* (Nicosia/Istanbul/Brussels, 2009), 20.

66 Estimate from the World Bank, http://data.worldbank.org/country/KV.

67 Population data from 'People and Language', http://www.gio.gov.tw/taiwan-website/5-gp/yearbook/02People&Language.pdf.

68 See Pełczynska-Nałęcz et al., Para-states in the post-Soviet area, 378–81.

69 Ibid.

70 This will be further explored in Chapter 5.

71 Quoted in G. Sørensen, Sovereignty: Change and continuity in a fundamental institution, *Political Studies*, 1999, 47, 590.

72 Jackson, *Sovereignty*, 10. My italics.

73 Quoted in D. Philpott, *Revolutions in Sovereignty: How Ideas Shaped Modern International Relations* (Princeton: Princeton University Press, 2001), 18. See also Jackson, *Quasi-states*, 32.

74 See S. D. Krasner, Rethinking the sovereign state model, in *Empires, Systems and States: Great Transformations in International Politics*, eds M. Cox, T. Dunne and K. Booth (Cambridge: Cambridge University Press, 2001), 17.
75 J. Bartelson, *A Genealogy of Sovereignty* (Cambridge: Cambridge University Press, 1995), 28.
76 O. Tansey, Does democracy need sovereignty? *Review of International Studies*, 2010, 5.
77 Jackson, *Sovereignty*, 12.
78 Tansey, Does democracy need sovereignty, 5.
79 Ibid. See also Crawford, *The Creation of States*.
80 Tansey, Does democracy need sovereignty, 10.
81 M. Cox, T. Dunne and K. Booth, Introduction, in *Empires, Systems and States: Great Transformations in International Politics*, eds M. Cox, T. Dunne and K. Booth (Cambridge: Cambridge University Press, 2001), 4.
82 See D. A. Lake, Reflection, evaluation, integration: The new sovereignty in international relations, *International Studies Review*, 2003, 5(3).
83 Sørensen, Sovereignty, 597.
84 See, for example, C. Weber, *Simulating Sovereignty: Intervention, the State and Symbolic Exchange* (Cambridge: Cambridge University Press, 1995).
85 Krasner, Abiding sovereignty.
86 Bartelson, *A Genealogy of Sovereignty*.
87 See Krasner, *Sovereignty*.
88 Jackson, *Quasi-states*, 29.
89 Rotberg, The failure and collapse of nation-states.
90 Krasner, *Sovereignty*, 4.
91 Tansey, Does democracy need sovereignty. See also Crawford, *The Creation of States*.
92 See also Rotberg, The failure and collapse of nation-states, 3.
93 See also Zartman, Introduction.
94 Krasner, *Sovereignty*, 4.
95 Jackson, *Quasi-states*.
96 S. D. Krasner, Compromising Westphalia, *International Security*, 1995–6, 20(3), 119.
97 Krasner, *Sovereignty*, 228.
98 Pegg, *International Society and the De Facto State*, 128.
99 Crawford, *The Creation of States*, 12.
100 Ibid.
101 Ibid. 12–16. See also Pegg, *International Society and the De Facto State*, 128.
102 Krasner, *Sovereignty*, 39.
103 Ibid.
104 Pegg, *International Society and the De Facto State*, 128.

105 Jackson, *Sovereignty*, 99.
106 See W. Wilson, Fourteen points speech, 8 January 1918, http:// en.wikisource.org/wiki/Fourteen_Points_Speech.
107 Crawford, *The Creation of States*, 112.
108 Jackson, *Sovereignty*, 106.
109 Crawford, *The Creation of States*, 111.
110 Jackson, *Sovereignty*, 108.
111 See, for example, G. C. Paikert, Hungary's national minority policies, 1920–1945, *American Slavic and East European Review* 1953, 13, 204.
112 Crawford, *The Creation of States*, 45ff.
113 Pegg, *International Society and the De Facto State*, 128.
114 Jackson, *Quasi-States*, 17.
115 See also B. Bartmann, Political realities and legal anomalies, in *De Facto States: The Quest for Sovereignty*, eds T. Bahcheli, B. Bartmann and H. Srebrnik (London: Routledge, 2004).
116 Quoted in Pegg, *International Society and the De Facto State*, 127.
117 Ibid.
118 S. Huntington, Foreword to E. A. Nordlinger, *Conflict Regulation in Divided Societies* (Cambridge: Harvard University, 1972), vii.
119 Pegg, *International Society and the De Facto State*, 131.
120 Crawford, *The Creation of States*, 126.
121 Ibid. 142.
122 Ibid. 415–16.
123 M. Weller, *Escaping the Self-Determination Trap* (Leiden: Martin Nijhoff, 2008), 59–60.
124 In its Opinion No. 1 the Arbitration Commission of the Peace Conference on the former Yugoslavia replied that 'the Socialist Federative Republic of Yugoslavia is in the process of dissolution'. A. Pellet, The opinions of the Badinter arbitration committee: A second breath for the self-determination of peoples, *European Journal of International Law*, 1992, 3(1), 183.
125 A. Gardner, Beyond standards before status: democratic governance and non-state actors, *Review of International Studies*, 2008, 34(3).
126 M. Scharf, Earned sovereignty: Juridical underpinnings, *Denver Journal of International Law and Policy*, 2004, 31(3).
127 For Ahtisaari's proposal, see http://www.unosek.org/docref/ Comprehensive_proposal-english.pdf.
128 Council of the European Union, *Press release: 2851st Council meeting, General Affairs and External Relations*, 18 February 2008.
129 V. Kolossov and J. O'Loughlin, Pseudo-states as harbingers of a new geopolitics: The example of the Trans-Dniester Moldovan Republic (TMR), in *Boundaries, Territory and Postmodernity*, ed. David Newman (London: Frank Cass, 1999), 152.
130 European Parliament, *European Parliament ad hoc delegation to Moldova, 5–6 June 2002*, report from the Chairman, Mr Jan Marinus Wiersma.

http://www.europarl.europa.eu/meetdocs/committees/afet/20021007/
473437EN.pdf.

131 A. Kukhianidze, A. Kupatadze and R. Gotsiridze, *Smuggling through
Abkhazia and Tskhinvali region* (Tbilisi: Transnational Crime and
Corruption Center, 2004), 31, 36.

132 A. Etzioni, The evils of self-determination, *Foreign Policy*, 1993, 89.

133 Weller, *Escaping the Self-Determination Trap*, 43.

134 Quoted in C. King, Black Sea blues, *The National Interest*, 2004, 78(5).

135 R. D. Kaplan, The coming anarchy, *Atlantic Monthly*, 1994, 273(2).

136 V. Tishkov, *Chechnya: Life in a War-torn Society* (Berkeley: University
of California Press, 2004), 106, 180.

137 See, for example, F. Švarm, The untouchable dealers, *Vreme News Digest*,
27 September 1993. Švarm, The Krajina economy. M. Vasić, Imitating
life, *Vreme News Digest*, 4 November 1991.

138 See, for example, United Nations Security Council, *Report of the
Secretary-General on the Situation in Abkhazia, Georgia*, S/2006/435
(June 2006). http://www.unomig.org/data/file/843/060626_SG_Report_
eng.pdf.

139 D. Natali, *The Kurdish Quasi-State: Development and Dependency in
Post-Gulf War Iraq* (New York: Syracuse Press, 2010), 44.

140 W. Kemp, Selfish determination: The questionable ownership of autonomy movements, *Ethnopolitics*, 2005, 4(1), 89.

141 Kolstø, The sustainability and future of unrecognized quasi-states, 729.

142 See, for example, I. Khashig, Tangerine fever grips Abkhazia, *Caucasus
Reporting Service*, 21 November 2002.

143 See also N. Caspersen, Separatism and democracy in the Caucasus,
Survival, 2008, 50(4).

144 P. Collier, Doing well out of war: An economic perspective, in *Greed and
Grievance: Economic Agendas in Civil Wars*, eds Mats Berdal and David
Malone (Boulder, CO: Lynne Rienner, 2000).

145 For an article on unrecognized states that tries to move beyond the
dichotomy of greed and grievance, see Kemp, Selfish determination.

146 Pegg, *International Society and the De Facto State*, 230.

147 J. Bartelson, *The Critique of the State* (Cambridge: Cambridge University
Press, 2001).

148 Philpott, *Revolutions in Sovereignty*, 18.

149 See, for example, Pegg, *International Society and the De Facto State*.

150 C. King, The benefits of ethnic war: Understanding Eurasia's unrecognized states, *World Politics*, July 2001, 53.

151 See, for example, P. Kolstø and H. Blakkisrud, Living with non-recognition: State- and nation-building in South Caucasian quasi-states,
Europe-Asia Studies, 2008, 60(3).

152 For important exceptions, see Tansey, Does democracy need sovereignty?
N. Popescu, Democracy in secessionism: Transnistria and Abkhazia's
domestic policies, Center for Policy Studies, August 2006.

L. Broers, The politics of non-recognition and democratization, in *The Limits of Leadership: Elites and Societies in the Nagorny Karabakh Peace Process*, ed. L. Broers (London: Conciliation Resources, 2005).

153 Pegg, *International Society and the De Facto State*. Lynch, *Engaging Eurasia's Separatist States*. T. Bahcheli, B. Bartmann and H. Srebrnik eds, *De Facto States: The Quest for Sovereignty* (London: Routledge, 2004). I. S. Spears and P. Kingston, eds, *States within States: Incipient Political Entities in the Post-Cold War Era* (New York: Palgrave Macmillan, 2004). Geldenhuys, *Contested States*.

154 A couple of excellent books have been written on individual cases, such as Mark Bradbury's book on Somaliland, *Becoming Somaliland* (London: Progressio, 2008), Thomas de Waal's book on Nagorno Karabakh, *Black Garden: Armenia and Azerbaijan through Peace and War* (New York: New York University Press, 2003) and Natali's book on Kurdistan, *The Kurdish Quasi-State*.

155 Decision of the special session of the NKAO Council of People's Deputies, 20 February 1988, http://www.nkr.am/en/decision-of-the-special-session-of-the-nkao-council-of-peoples-deputies-of-xx-session/41/.

156 E. Melander, The Nagorno-Karabakh conflict revisited, *Journal of Cold War Studies*, 2001, 3(2), 59–60.

157 Crawford, *The Creation of States*, 12.

158 It should be noted, however, that France already recognized the new state in 1778 in what also involved a declaration of war against Great Britain. Ibid. 377.

159 Ibid. 370.

160 Ibid. 377–9.

161 Ibid. 130.

162 Ibid. 76, 78.

163 P. Duara, *Sovereignty and Authenticity: Manchukuo and the East Asian Modern* (Lanham Rowman and Littlefield, 2004), 86 n139. I. H. Nish *Japanese Foreign Policy in the Interwar Period* (Westport: Praeger, 2002), 93–5.

164 Crawford, *The Creation of States*, 79. N. K. Kolanović, The NDH's relations with Southeast European countries, Turkey and Japan, 1941–5, *Totalitarian Movements and Political Religions*, 2006, 7(4), 473–92.

165 See, for example, M. Jareb, The NDH's relations with Italy and Germany, *Totalitarian Movements and Political Religions*, 2006, 7(4), 459–72. H. J. Timperley, Japan in Manchukuo, *Foreign Affairs*, 1934, 12 (Jan), 295–305.

166 See Pegg, *International Society and the De Facto State*, 36. The degree of external dependence is analysed in Chapter 3.

167 Kolanović, The NDH's relations, 482.

168 Jackson, *Quasi-states*, 34, 107. Crawford, *The Creation of States*, 129.

169 Crawford, *The Creation of States*, 159.

170 Ibid. 140. See also, C. Warbrick, The recognition of states, *The International and Comparative Law Quarterly*, 1992, 41(2), 474.
171 Crawford, *The Creation of States*, 60.
172 Ibid. 168–9.
173 Krasner, *Sovereignty*, 15.
174 Crawford, *The Creation of States*, 155.
175 J. Brinkley, Pressure on North Korea: U.S. Stealth Jets sent to South, *Washington Post*, 30 May 2005.
176 This is explored in Chapter 3. See also M. Chorev, Complex terrains: Unrecognized states and globalization, in *Unrecognized States in the International System*, eds N. Caspersen and G. Stansfield (London: Routledge, 2010).
177 M. Walls, The emergence of a Somali state: Building peace from civil war in Somaliland, *African Affairs*, 2009, 108 (432).
178 Y. Chu and J. Lin, Political development in 20th century Taiwan, *China Quarterly*, 2001, 117.
179 Ibid. More on this below.
180 International Crisis Group, *Moldova: No Quick Fix* (Chisinau/Brussels, 2003), 1.
181 P. Kolstø and H. Blakkisrud, Separatism is the mother of terrorism, in *Unrecognized States in the International System*, eds N. Caspersen and G. Stansfield (London: Routledge, 2010), 112.
182 International Crisis Group, *Georgia: Avoiding War in South Ossetia* (Tbilisi/Brussels, 2004), 4. Human Rights Watch, *Up in Flames: Humanitarian Law Violations and Civilian Victims in the Conflict over South Ossetia* (New York, 2009), 75.
183 25,000 is the figure used by the U.S. State Department. De Waal, *Black Garden*, 285.
184 S. Kaplan, The remarkable story of Somaliland, *Journal of Democracy*, 2008, 19(3), 148.
185 *ABC News*, Up to 100,000 killed in Sri Lanka's civil war: UN, 20 May 2009.
186 This is a conservative estimate by John Dunlop. Quoted in J. Hughes, *Chechnya: From Nationalism to Jihad* (Philadelphia: University of Pennsylvania Press, 2007), 82.
187 *Global Security*, Biafra war, http://www.globalsecurity.org/military/world/war/biafra.htm.
188 *Vojska*, Republika Srpska Krajina, March 1994.
189 De Waal, *Black Garden*, 285.
190 Numbers from the UNHCR, http://www.unhcr.org/cgi-bin/texis/vtx/page?page=49e48d2e6.
191 De Waal, *Black Garden*, 285.
192 See E. Walker, No peace, no war in the Caucasus: Secessionist conflicts in Chechnya, Abkhazia and Nagorno-Karabakh, Occasional Paper, Belfer Center for Science and International Affairs, 1998.

193 For the importance of autonomous institutions for separatist movements, see S. E. Cornell, Autonomy as a source of conflict: Caucasian conflicts in theoretical perspective, *World Politics*, 2002, 54(2).
194 Kaplan, The remarkable story, 152.
195 Crawford, *The Creation of States*, 412–13.
196 See Chu and Lin, Political development in 20th century Taiwan, 118.
197 See, for example, P. G. Roeder, *Where Nation-States Come From* (Princeton: Princeton University Press, 2007).
198 Pegg, *International Society and the De Facto State*, 5.
199 Act of State Independence of the Republic of Abkhazia, 12 October 1999. http://www.unpo.org/article.php?id=705.
200 Public letter from the RSK Washington office, dated 19 December 1991, from S. Jarčević, ed., *Republika Srpska Krajina: Državna Dokumenta* (Belgrade: Miroslav, 2005), 140–1.
201 Letter from the permanent mission of Yugoslavia addressed to the President of the UN Security Council, dated September 1993, from Jarčević, *Republika Srpska Krajina*, 380.
202 See, for example, Pegg, *International Society and the De Facto State*, 43. Kolossov and O'Loughlin, Pseudo-states as harbingers of a new geopolitics, 166.
203 O. Protsyk, Representation and democracy in Eurasia's unrecognized states: The case of Transnistria, *Post-Soviet Affairs*, 2009, 25(3).
204 P. Kolstø and H. Blakkisrud, From secessionist conflict towards functioning state: Processes of state- and nation-building in Transnistria, *Post-Soviet Affairs* (forthcoming, 2011).
205 Kaplan, The remarkable story, 148.
206 Pegg, *International Society and the De Facto State*, 93.
207 Bradbury, *Becoming Somaliland*, 83.
208 Quoted in Kolossov and O'Loughlin, Pseudo-states as harbingers of a new geopolitics, 160.
209 A. Chun, From nationalism to nationalizing: Cultural imagination and state formation in postwar Taiwan, *The Australian Journal of Chinese Affairs*, 1994, 31(Jan).
210 For further analysis of this principle see, for example, Scharf, Earned sovereignty, 382.
211 Declaration on proclamation of the Nagorno Karabakh Republic, 2 September 1991. http://www.nkr.am/eng/deklaraciya209.html.
212 D. Lynch, Separatist states and post-Soviet conflicts, *International Affairs*, 2002, 4, 837.
213 Quoted in Kolossov and O'Loughlin, Pseudo-states as harbingers of a new geopolitics, 160.
214 LTTE leader in his annual Heroes' Day statement, 27 November 2006. http://www.eelam.com/2006/tamilnationalleader_speech2006.html.
215 See also Caspersen, Separatism and democracy in the Caucasus.

216 See, for example, International Crisis Group, *Abkhazia: Ways Forward* (Tbilisi/Brussels, 2007), 13–15. In the case of Abkhazia, these peacekeepers were nominally representing the Commonwealth of Independent States, while in South Ossetia they were made up of Russian, North Ossetian, South Ossetian and Georgian forces. In practice, however, they functioned as Russian forces.
217 Kolstø and Blakkisrud, From secessionist conflict.
218 F. Švarm, Happy together, *Vreme News Digest*, 4 April 1994. See also the public letter from the leadership of Banija and Kordun, dated 17 January 1992, from M. Rupić, ed., *Republika Hrvatska i Domovinski Rat 1990.-1995: Dokumenti, Knjiga 4* (Zagreb: Hrvatski Memorijalno-Dokumentacijski Centar Domovinskog Rata, 2008), 12–13.
219 Crawford, *The Creation of States*, 404–5.
220 See, for example, Natali, *The Kurdish Quasi-State*.
221 Kolstø and Blakkisrud, From secessionist conflict.
222 Ibid.
223 Kolstø and Blakkisrud, *Living with non-recognition*, 494.
224 Crawford, *The Creation of States*, 163–4.
225 Weller, *Escaping the Self-Determination Trap*, 42.
226 Ibid.
227 Seceding groups are not subject to international law. Ibid. 15.
228 See also Pegg, *International Society and the De Facto State*, 176.
229 N. Caspersen, Belgrade, Pale, Knin: Kin-state control over rebellious puppets? *Europe-Asia Studies,* 2007, 59(4).
230 United Nations Security Council, *Resolution 820 (1993)*, adopted 17 April 1993. http://www.ohr.int/other-doc/un-res-bih/pdf/820e.pdf.
231 See, for example, R. Holbrooke, *To End a War* (New York: Modern Library, 1999), 107.
232 Trier et al., *Under Siege*, 7–8.
233 *RIA Novosti*, Russia lifts trade, economic, financial sanctions on Abkhazia, 6 March 2008.
234 See, for example, T. Hakobian, Turkey keeps Armenia guessing over border blockade, *Caucasus Reporting Service*, 17 April 2009.
235 See, for example, International Crisis Group, *Conflict Resolution in the South Caucasus: The EU's Role* (Tbilisi/Brussels, 2006), 9–10, 18.
236 Ibid. 18.
237 For discussions of the lack of international engagement with these entities, see also Ross, *Independent Diplomat*.
238 Crawford, *The Creation of States*, 380.
239 Nish, *Japanese Foreign Policy*, 93.
240 E. M. Clauss, The Roosevelt Administration and Manchukuo, 1933–1941, *Historian*, 1970, 32(4).
241 Kolanović, The NDH's relations.
242 Crawford, *The Creation of States*, 380.

243 Anyone whose passport contains a stamp from Nagorno Karabakh will, for example, be barred from entering Azerbaijan, since they are deemed to have entered Azerbaijan illegally.

244 Crawford, *The Creation of States*, 167.

245 Ibid. Northern Cyprus passports are, for example, accepted by the U.S. and the UK.

246 Kaplan, The remarkable story, 154.

247 Ibid. 153.

248 Bradbury, *Becoming Somaliland*, 5, 255.

249 Ibid. 204.

250 *Somaliland Times*, CIIR's election observers welcome results of Somaliland parliamentary poll, 2 November 2005. http://www.somalilandtimes.net/198/15.shtml.

251 See, for example, Pegg, *International Society and the De Facto State*, 185.

252 A. Chang, Comparing three ethnic Chinese militaries, *Military Might*, 12 January 2008. For a list of Taiwanese embassies and missions abroad, see http://www.mofa.gov.tw/webapp/lp.asp?ctnode=1864&ctunit=30&basedsd=30&mp=6.

253 Tansey, Does democracy need sovereignty, 11.

254 See Crawford, *The Creation of States*, 201.

255 Krasner, *Sovereignty*, 42.

256 Unrepresented Nations and Peoples Organization. *Declaration: Opening the World Order to de Facto States*, 15 May 2008. http://www.unpo.org/content/view/8133/81/.

257 Crawford, *The Creation of States*, 203–4.

258 Ibid. 25 n105.

259 Ibid. 634.

260 Krasner, *Sovereignty*, 15, 70.

261 Camilleri and Falk, *The End of Sovereignty*.

262 Kolstø and Blakkisrud, From secessionist conflict.

263 See, for example, European Parliament, *European Parliament Ad Hoc Delegation to Moldova*.

264 Quoted in Kolstø and Blakkisrud, Separatism is the mother of terrorism, 125.

265 See, for example, *Somaliland Press*, Police foil terrorist attack in Somaliland, 24 August 2010. http://somalilandpress.com/police-foil-terrorist-attacks-in-somaliland-17895.

266 An exception is Iraqi Kurdistan in whose mountains the Kurdish Workers' Party (PKK) established bases.

267 Kolstø and Blakkisrud, Separatism is the mother of terrorism.

268 Kaplan, The remarkable story, 153.

269 Kolstø and Blakkisrud, From secessionist conflict.

270 See, for example, Kaplan, The remarkable story, 149.

271 For data see http://www.taoyuanairport.gov.tw/

272 Lonely Planet, Introducing Taipei, http://www.lonelyplanet.com/taiwan/taipei.
273 M. Dakić, *Krajina kroz Vijekove* (Belgrade: Vedes, 2001), 55. Author's interview with Savo Štrbac, former RSK government chief-of-staff (Belgrade, 20 February, 2009).
274 Author's interviews with Stanko Momčilović, mayor of Udbina (Zagreb, 1 April 2009) and with Dragan Đević, deputy mayor of Donji Lapac (Donji Lapac, 2 April 2009).
275 Bartmann, Political realities and legal anomalies, 16.
276 See Kolstø and Blakkisrud, From secessionist conflict.
277 Tansey, Does democracy need sovereignty, 16.
278 For the importance of 'utility' in fostering loyalty ties that bind citizens to the state, see J. Meierhenrich, Forming states after failure', in *When States Fail: Causes and Consequences*, ed. Robert I. Rotberg (Princeton: Princeton University Press, 2001).
279 Kolstø and Blakkisrud, From secessionist conflict.
280 B. Buzan, *People, States and Fear: An Agenda for International Security Studies in the Post-Cold War Era* (Hemel Hempstead: Harvester Wheatsheaf, 1991), 70.
281 See, for example Zartman, Introduction.
282 Jackson, *Quasi-States*, 21. I. W. Zartman, Putting things back together, in *Collapsed States: The Disintegration and Restoration of Legitimate Authority*, ed. I. W. Zartman (Boulder: Lynne Rienner, 1995), 273.
283 Zartman, Putting things back together, 272.
284 Author's interview with Slaven Letica (Zagreb, 18 September 2003).
285 United Nations Security Council, *Resolution 820 (1993)*.
286 Macroeconomic indicators from 2009, http://www.gio.gov.tw/taiwan-website/5-gp/yearbook/08Economy.pdf.
287 Bradbury, *Becoming Somaliland*, 162. Reliable macroeconomic indicators for unrecognized states are hard to obtain and this figure is actually an estimate for Somalia as a whole and therefore likely underestimates Somaliland's economic performance.
288 International Crisis Group, *Georgia: Avoiding War*, 11.
289 International Alert, *From War Economies to Peace Economies* (London, 2004), 123.
290 *Abkhazia Today*, GDP per capita in Abkhazia is higher than in Moldova, Uzbekistan, Kirghizia, Mongolia, 7 July 2010. For more GDP per capita data, see Table 2 in the Conclusion.
291 Heraclides, *Self-Determination of Minorities*, 37.
292 Similar arguments are explored in N. Caspersen, Playing the recognition game: External actors and de facto states, *International Spectator* 2009 (Dec), 44(4).
293 See, for example, Kolstø, The sustainability and future of unrecognized quasi-states. Lynch, *Engaging Eurasia's Separatist States*.

294 For kin-state radicalization, see, for example, R. Brubaker, *Nationalism Reframed: Nationhood and the National Question in the New Europe* (Cambridge: Cambridge University Press, 1996).

295 Lynch, *Engaging Eurasia's Separatist States*, 4.

296 Kolstø and Blakkisrud, Living with non-recognition.

297 See, for example, International Crisis Group, *Nagorno-Karabakh*.

298 Kolstø and Blakkisrud, From secessionist conflict.

299 R. Coalson, Russia steps up cooperation with breakaway Georgian regions, *RFE/RL* 30 April 2009.

300 International Crisis Group, *Nagorno-Karabakh*, 10.

301 Even in 1999, it still constituted over 70 per cent of the entity's budget. Data kindly supplied by Levon Zourabian.

302 Author's interview with David Petrosyan, defense analyst (Yerevan, 7 November 2008).

303 Russian passport have been issued in Abkhazia on a limited scale since 2000 and systematically since 2002 when a new law on Russian citizenship was passed. Trier et al., *Under Siege*, 8 n3. See also Cornell and Starr, *The Guns of August 2008*.

304 Kolstø and Blakkisrud, From secessionist conflict.

305 D. Isachenko, Bridging the sovereignty gap in Northern Cyprus, Paper presented at SGIR 6th Pan-European International Relations Conference, Turin, 12–15 September 2007.

306 Geldenhuys, *Contested States in World Politics*, 180.

307 Author's interviews with Drago Kovačević, former mayor of Knin (Belgrade, 20 February 2009).

308 Report on the work of the RSK ministry of foreign affairs, dated 15 March 1993, from the archive of the Croatian Memorial-Documentation Center.

309 Author's interview with Nagorno Karabakh official (Stepanakert, 11 September 2006).

310 J. Kucera, Abkhazia: Bracing for more trouble, *Eurasianet*, 14 June 2007.

311 *RIA Novosti*, 18 September 2006.

312 See N. Caspersen, *Contested Nationalism: Serb Elite Rivalry in Croatia and Bosnia in the 1990s* (Oxford: Berghahn Books, 2010).

313 Author's interview with Filip Švarm, deputy editor of *Vreme* (Belgrade, 24 February 2009).

314 Ibid. Author's interview with Veljko Džakula, former president of SAO Western Slavonia (Zagreb, 23 March 2009).

315 Trier et al., *Under Siege*, 10–11.

316 N. Caspersen, Between puppets and independent actors: Kin-state involvement in the conflicts in Bosnia, Croatia and Nagorno Karabakh, *Ethnopolitics*, 2008, 7(4).

317 Author's interview with David Babayan (Stepanakert, 13 September 2006).

318 R. Panossian, The irony of Nagorno-Karabakh: Formal institutions versus informal politics, in *Ethnicity and Territory in the Former Soviet Union*, eds J. Hughes and G. Sasse (London: Frank Cass, 2002), 152.
319 Kolstø and Blakkisrud, Living with non-recognition, 494.
320 Caspersen, Between puppets and independent actors.
321 Author's interview with David Babayan (Stepanakert, 29 October 2008).
322 Quoted in Chorev, Complex terrains, 34.
323 See, for example, B. Anderson, Western nationalism and Eastern nationalism, *New Left Review*, 2001, 9 (May–June).
324 See, for example, P. Collier and A. Hoeffler, Greed and grievance in civil war, World Bank Policy Research, Working Paper 2355, Washington D.C.). M. Kaldor, *New and Old Wars: Organized Violence in a Global Era* (Cambridge: Polity, 2006).
325 See, for example, K. Stokke, Building the Tamil Eelam state: Emerging state institutions and forms of governance in LTTE-controlled areas in Sri Lanka, *Third World Quarterly*, 2006, 27(6). C. Orjuela, Diaspora identities and homeland politics: Lessons from the Sri Lanka/Tamil Eelam case, Paper presented at the ISA's 49th Annual Convention, San Francisco, March 2008.
326 Several telethons in the U.S. were devoted to raising money for the latter. See http://www.armeniafund.org/telethon/telethon_2004.php.
327 Author's interview with Araik Harutyunyan.
328 Author's interview with David Babayan (2008).
329 Bradbury, *Becoming Somaliland*, 174–5.
330 Bradbury quoted in I. Lewis, *Understanding Somalia and Somaliland* (London: Hurst, 2008), 96.
331 Kaplan, The remarkable story, 150.
332 Bradbury, *Becoming Somaliland*, 148, 177.
333 Ibid. 177.
334 Ibid. 176.
335 See Stokke, Building the Tamil Eelam state.
336 See Orjuela, Diaspora identities and homeland politics.
337 Stokke, Building the Tamil Eelam state.
338 Ibid.
339 Ibid.
340 Orjuela, Diaspora identities and homeland politics.
341 D. Natali, *The Kurds and the State: Evolving National Identity in Iraq, Turkey and Iran* (Syracuse: Syracuse University Press, 2005), 165.
342 International Crisis Group, *Abkhazia Today* (Brussels/Tbilisi, 2006), 17.
343 Trier et al., *Under Siege*, 39–42.
344 Bradbury, *Becoming Somaliland*, 178.
345 See, for example, Collier and Hoeffler, Greed and grievance.
346 See, for example, De Waal, *Black Garden*.
347 Author's interview with Gegham Baghdasaryan, former Karabakh opposition deputy (Stepanakert, 27 October 2008).

348 Kaplan, The remarkable story, 151.
349 Natali, *The Kurdish Quasi-State*, 44.
350 King, The benefits of ethnic war, 548.
351 S. Closson, State weakness in perspective: Strong politico-economic networks in Georgia's energy sector, *Europe-Asia Studies*, 2009, 61(5).
352 Švarm, The untouchable dealers.
353 Ibid.
354 Ibid.
355 F. Švarm, Springtime change, *Vreme News Digest*, 6 March 1995.
356 Author's interviews with Danko Perić and Ninko Mirić, former judge in the RSK (Karlovac, 27 March 2009).
357 Orjuela, Diaspora identities and homeland politics, 15.
358 Author's interview with Branko Lubovac, former RSK deputy prime minister (Belgrade, 17 February 2009).
359 Letter to UNPROFOR, November 1992, from Jarčević, *Republika Srpska Krajina*, 174–5.
360 Quoted in Chorev, Complex terrains, 40 n14.
361 Natali, *The Kurdish Quasi-State*, 42–3.
362 Lewis, *Understanding Somalia and Somaliland*, 96.
363 Bradbury, *Becoming Somaliland*, 157–8.
364 Ibid. 158.
365 Trier et al., *Under Siege*, 14.
366 Stokke, Building the Tamil Eelam state.
367 Kolstø, The sustainability and future of unrecognized quasi-states.
368 See, for example, International Conference on the Former Yugoslavia, *Agreement: Water*, 2 December 1994.
369 See Law on Occupied Territories, 23 October 2008, http://www.venice.coe.int/docs/2009/CDL(2009)004-e.asp.
370 Action Plan for Engagement, 6 July 2010, http://www.smr.gov.ge/uploads/action_plan_en.pdf.
371 Kolstø and Blakkisrud, From secessionist conflict. See also International Crisis Group, *Moldova's Uncertain Future* (Chisinau/Brussels, 2007).
372 Kolstø and Blakkisrud, Separatism is the mother of terrorism, 112–13.
373 International Crisis Group, *Cyprus: Reversing the Drift to Partition* (Nicosia/Istanbul/Brussels, 2009), 19–20.
374 R. S. Ross, Taiwan's fading independence movement, *Foreign Affairs*, 2006, 85(2), 143, 145.
375 *BBC News*, Direct China-Taiwan flights begin, 4 July 2008.
376 See also Chapter 6.
377 Stokke, Building the Tamil Eelam state.
378 Ibid.
379 Kolstø and Blakkisrud, From secessionist conflict.
380 Letter to the deputy chairman of the International Conference on the Former Yugoslavia, dated 10 June 1994, from the archive of the Croatian Memorial-Documentation Center.
381 Author's interview with Veljko Džakula.

382 See, for example, N. Caspersen and A. Herrberg, Engaging unrecognized states in conflict resolution: An opportunity or challenge for the EU? *Crisis Management Initiative*, January 2011.

383 See, for example, M. Miriori, A Bougainville Interim Government (BIG) perspective on early peace efforts, in *Weaving Consensus: The Papua New Guinea – Bougainville peace process*, eds A. Carl and L. Garasu (London: Conciliation Resources, 2002).

384 D. Isachenko, Symptoms of democracy in Transdniestria, *S+F - Sicherheit und Frieden*, 2009, 27(2), 100.

385 Heraclides, *Self-Determination of Minorities*, 69.

386 Macedonia, however, later backtracked and switched its allegiance to Beijing. See A. Casella, Macedonia: Taiwan's lost gambit, *Asia Times*, 11 July 2001.

387 *RFE/RL*, Tiny Nauru in $50 million Russia gambit, 14 December 2009.

388 For the similarity in strategy when it comes to secessionist movements, see Heraclides, *Self-Determination of Minorities*, 42–3.

389 Ibid. 94.

390 For analysis of 'earned sovereignty' see, for example, P. R Williams and F. J. Pecci, Earned sovereignty: Bridging the gap between sovereignty and self-determination, *Stanford Journal of International Law*, 2004, 40(1).

391 *Karabakh Open*, Karabakh has serious grounds for international recognition of sovereignty, 20 February 2008. http://www.armeniandiaspora. com/showthread.php?122518-Karabakh-Has-Serious-Grounds-For-International-Recognition-Of-Sovere

392 Pegg, *International Society and the De Facto State*, 128, 148–9.

393 Krasner, Abiding sovereignty, 238.

394 See Jackson, *Quasi-states*, 72.

395 Ministry of foreign affairs of Nagorno-Karabakh republic, NKR Foreign Minister Georgy Petrossian's interview to *Demo* Newspaper, 4 February 2008. http://www.armtown.com/news/en/aza/20071122/2372/.

396 Author's interview with Natella Akaba (via email, 30 August 2006).

397 Stated at a press conference attended by the author (Stepanakert, 11 December 2006).

398 Bradbury, *Becoming Somaliland*, 131.

399 Chu and Lin, Political development in 20th-century Taiwan, 118.

400 See, for example, R. Paris, *At War's End: Building Peace and Civil Conflict* (Cambridge: Cambridge University Press, 2004).

401 Ibid. 34–5.

402 See, for example, B. B. Ghali, *An Agenda for Democratization* (New York: United Nations, 1996).

403 For example, in 1995 then foreign minister of Nagorno Karabakh, Arkady Ghukasyan, stated, 'I think the Serbs (...) are very close to receiving their desired goals. Of course, this will have an effect on the status of Karabagh.' A. Murinson, The secession of Abkhazia and

Nagorny Karabagh: The roots and patterns of development of post-Soviet micro-secessions in Transcaucasia,' *Central Asia Survey*, 2004, 23(1), 6.

404 Author's interview with Karen Ohanjanyan, co-ordinator of the Nagorno Karabakh 'Helsinki Initiative-1992' (Yerevan, 21 October 2008).

405 As it reads on the website of the U.S. State Department, 'democracy is the one national interest that helps to secure all the others'. http://www.state.gov/g/drl/democ/.

406 The 2002 National Security Strategy famously declared, 'America is now threatened less by conquering states than we are by failing ones'. http://www.whitehouse.gov/nsc/nss/2002/nss.pdf.

407 See, for example, European Commission, *Accession Criteria*. http://ec.europa.eu/enlargement/enlargement_process/accession_process/criteria/index_en.htm.

408 Broers, The politics of non-recognition and democratization, 71.

409 O. Protsyk, Moldova's dilemmas in democratizing and reintegrating Transnistria, *Problems of Post-Communism*, 2006, 53(4), 30.

410 Ibid.

411 Author's interview with Drago Kovačević.

412 Author's interview with Slobodan Jarčević (Zemun, 13 February 2009).

413 Internal report from the RSK president, dated 24 March 1993, from Jarčević, *Republika Srpska Krajina*, 206–11.

414 See, for example, U. Komlenović, The fate of the Krajina, *Vreme News Digest*, 17 October 1994. F. Švarm, Milan Martic's flying circus, *Vreme News Digest*, 13 December 1993. F. Švarm, The return of the district strongman, *Vreme News Digest*, 31 January 1994.

415 Author's interview with Filip Švarm.

416 Tim Guldimann, coordinator of the OSCE mission, quoted in Hughes, *Chechnya*, 95.

417 See, for example, Tishkov, *Chechnya*, 64. Hughes, *Chechnya*, 65.

418 Tishkov, *Chechnya*, 182, 195.

419 Hughes, *Chechnya*, 102.

420 See, for example, Council of the European Union. *2851ˢᵗ Council meeting.*

421 Author's interview with David Babayan (2008).

422 This will be further explored in Chapter 5.

423 *Coconut Revolution: The Bougainville Story*, Documentary Film (Stampede, 2001).

424 See, for example, V. Boege, Bougainville and the discovery of slowness, The Australian Centre for Peace and Conflict Studies, Occasional Papers Series, no. 3, June 2006.

425 G. Tamás, Ethnarchy and ethno-anarchism, *Social Research*, 1996, 63(1), 172, 181.

426 Speech delivered at fund raising dinner in Pasadena, 21 November 2010, http://www.nkr.am/en/news/2010–11–22/314/.

427 Lynch, *Engaging Eurasia's Separatist States*, 63.

174 Notes to pages 76–81

428 Kolstø and Blakkisrud, From secessionist conflict.
429 King, The benefits of ethnic war, 525.
430 See, for example, C. Tilly, War making and state making as organized crime, in *Bringing the State Back In*, eds Peter Evans, Dietrich Rueschemeyer, and Theda Skocpol (Cambridge: Cambridge University Press, 1985).
431 They are, thus, in a very different situation than Jackson's 'quasi-states' that are 'exempted from the power contest at least in part'. Jackson, *Quasi-states*, 23.
432 Tamás, Ethnarchy and ethno-anarchism, 172–3.
433 Kolstø and Blakkisrud, From secessionist conflict.
434 Author's interview with Srđan Radulović, deputy editor of Blic (Belgrade, 10 February 2009).
435 Dakić, *Krajina kroz Vijekove*, 53. Author's interview with Savo Štrbac.
436 Švarm, Milan Martic's flying circus.
437 F. Švarm, Orders from Belgrade, *Vreme News Digest*, 13 March 1995.
438 Author's interviews with Nikola Sužnjevic, former judge in the RSK (Glina, 27 March 2009) and Rajko Ležajić, former speaker of the RSK parliament (Belgrade, 17 September 2004). F. Švarm, Checkmate on Z-4, *Vreme News Digest*, 6 February 1995.
439 Author's interview with Drago Kovačević.
440 Author's interview with Filip Švarm. F. Švarm, Patriots and godfathers, *Vreme News Digest*, 1 March 1993.
441 See J. Braithwaite, H. Charlesworth, P. Reddy and L. Dunn, *Reconciliation and Architectures of Commitment: Sequencing peace in Bougainville* (Canberra: ANU Press, 2010).
442 Tansey, Does democracy need sovereignty, 16.
443 See G. Stansfield, *Iraq* (Cambridge: Polity, 2007), 147.
444 See De Waal, *Black Garden*.
445 See, for example, Hughes, *Chechnya*, 98. K. M. Bakke, After the war ends: violence and viability in post-Soviet unrecognized states, in *Unrecognized States in the International System*, eds N. Caspersen and G. Stansfield (London: Routledge, 2010).
446 See Caspersen, *Contested Nationalism*.
447 Kolstø and Blakkisrud, From secessionist conflict.
448 Ibid.
449 See, for example, De Waal, *Black Garden*.
450 Ibid. 241. *Armenian News Network*, The rise and fall of Samvel Babayan, 6 October 2004.
451 De Waal, *Black Garden*, 245. Author's interview with Karine Ohanyan, journalist (Stepanakert, 3 November 2008).
452 Author's interview with Gegham Baghdasaryan (2006). The president was presented as 'a political leader legitimized by democratic elections

with an ambitious agenda of combating corruption and controlling the power of the military'. R. Giragosian, Nagorno Karabakh democracy, *CACI Analyst*, 26 April 2000.

453 G. Stansfield, Governing Kurdistan: the strengths of division, in *The Future of Kurdistan in Iraq*, eds B. O'Leary, J. McGarry and K. Salih (Philadelphia: University of Pennsylvania Press, 2005).

454 See, for example, Natali, *The Kurdish Quasi-State.*

455 Walls, The emergence of a Somali state.

456 Ibid. 14.

457 Tansey, Does democracy need sovereignty, 16.

458 See Boege, Bougainville. Braithwaite et al., *Reconciliation.*

459 See Boege, Bougainville.

460 Kurdistan constitutes an exception in that institutionalized divisions rather than unity served as basis for stability, but a sufficient degree of unity was nevertheless created by the promise of U.S. protection and the increasing flow of resources. The continued unsettled political climate, in any case, constrained the creation of an effective entity. Natali, *The Kurdish Quasi-State*, 65.

461 Chun, From nationalism to nationalizing, 58, 65. Chu and Lin, Political development in 20th-century Taiwan, 102.

462 Walls, The emergence of a Somali state.

463 Government of Pridnestrovie. http://pridnestrovie.net/government. html.

464 Kolstø, The sustainability and future of unrecognized quasi-states, 725, 727.

465 Kolstø and Blakkisrud, From secessionist conflict.

466 See, for example, W. Reno, *Warlord Politics and African States* (Boulder: Lynne Rienner, 1999), 4.

467 Somaliland constitutes an exception as it has in fact managed to draw migrants from its recognized neighbours. Kaplan, The remarkable story, 149.

468 The precise population sizes are fiercely contested. See, for example, Trier et al., *Under Siege*, 30–2.

469 See Table 1 in the Introduction for population statistics.

470 L. Musaelian, Bid to repopulate Karabakh fraught with problems, *Caucasus Reporting Service*, 19 June 2009.

471 The couples were also given $200 to buy rings and a cow, and were promised lavish financial awards if they have children: $2000 for the first child, which increases to a staggering $100,000 for the seventh child. K. Ohanian, Karabakh's big wedding day, *Caucasus Reporting Service*, 23 October 2008.

472 *RFE/RL*, Mass wedding in Karabakh results in baby boom, 20 August 2009.

473 Protsyk, Moldova's dilemmas.

474 International Crisis Group, *Moldova's Uncertain Future* (Chisinau/ Brussels, 2006), 13.
475 Kolstø and Blakkisrud, From secessionist conflict.
476 Ibid.
477 Hughes, *Chechnya*, 25. Tishkov, *Chechnya*, 62.
478 Hughes, *Chechnya*, 25.
479 Isachenko, Symptoms of democracy. See also A. Wilson, *Virtual Politics: Faking Democracy in the Post-Soviet World* (New Haven: Yale University Press, 2005).
480 Author's interview with Karen Ohanjanyan.
481 Author's interview with Karine Ohanyan.
482 Personal communication in Stepanakert. See also De Waal, *Black Garden*, 243.
483 Caspersen, Separatism and democracy in the Caucasus.
484 Bradbury, *Becoming Somaliland*, 184.
485 Tansey, Does democracy need sovereignty, 17.
486 Bradbury, *Becoming Somaliland*, 187, 190.
487 M. Bradbury, A. Y. Abokor and H. Ahmed, Somaliland: Choosing politics over violence, *Review of African Political Economy*, 2003, 97, 475.
488 Kaplan, The remarkable story, 150.
489 See, for example, I. Khashig, Abkhazia: Government poll landslide contested, *Caucasus Reporting Service*, 8 March 2002. Freedom House, Abkhazia (Georgia), http://www.freedomhouse.org.
490 Popescu, Democracy in secessionism, 17. International Crisis Group, *Abkhazia Today*, 15.
491 Chu and Lin, Political development in 20th-century Taiwan, 118.
492 Bradbury, *Becoming Somaliland*, 204.
493 Author's interview with David Babayan (2008).
494 Isachenko, Symptoms of democracy, 97.
495 See, for example, Panossian, The irony of Nagorno-Karabakh, 149.
496 See, for example, *Armenian News Network*, The rise and fall of Samvel Babayan.
497 See, for example, Tishkov, *Chechnya*, 64. Hughes, *Chechnya*, 65.
498 J. J. Linz and A. Stepan, *Problems of Democratic Transition and Consolidation* (Baltimore: Johns Hopkins University Press, 1996), 17–18.
499 Paris, *At War's End*, 42.
500 Tansey, Does democracy need sovereignty?
501 See, for example, D. Schnapper, Citizenship and national identity in Europe, *Nations and Nationalism*, 2002, 8(1), 2–3.
502 M. Moore, Normative justification for liberal nationalism: Justice, democracy and national identity, *Nations and Nationalism*, 2001, 7(1), 7.
503 C. Kaufmann, Possible and impossible solutions to ethnic civil wars, *International Security*, 1996, 20(4).
504 Moore, Normative justification for liberal nationalism, 7, 18.

505 R. Kumar, The troubled history of partition, *Foreign Affairs*, 1997, 76(1).
506 Etzioni, Evils of self-determination.
507 See Freedom House Index, country reports from 2010. http://www.freedomhouse.org.
508 Kolstø and Blakkisrud, From secessionist conflict.
509 Ibid.
510 International Crisis Group, *Nagorno-Karabakh*, 9.
511 This is higher than heavily militarized, recognized countries such as Israel, Cuba and Iran.
512 Data from International Institute for Strategic Studies, *The Military Balance 2010* (London: Routledge, 2010).
513 Zartman, Introduction, 7.
514 Author's interview with David Babayan (2008).
515 Author's interview with Dragan Đević.
516 Kaplan, The remarkable story, 151.
517 Tansey, Does democracy need sovereignty, 19.
518 G. Nodia, Nationalism and democracy, in *Nationalism, Ethnic Conflict, and Democracy*, eds L. Diamond and M. F. Plattner (Baltimore: Johns Hopkins University Press, 1994), 4.
519 N. Sambanis, Partition as a solution to ethnic war: An empirical critique of the theoretical literature, *World Politics*, 2000, 52, 465, 490.
520 Author's interview with Gegham Baghdasaryan (Stepanakert, 15 September 2006).
521 Author's interview with Karine Ohanyan.
522 Similar stories are heard from monitors of elections in recognized countries, although the overly rosy reports were in these cases prepared by international organizations.
523 Etzioni, Evils of self-determination.
524 Robert Dahl quoted in Paris, *At War's End*, 157.
525 Ibid. 158.
526 Kolstø, The sustainability and future of unrecognized quasi-states.
527 Lynch, *Engaging Eurasia's Separatist States*, 59.
528 Bradbury, *Becoming Somaliland*, 200.
529 Kaplan, The remarkable story, 151.
530 Ibid. 149.
531 Tansey, Does democracy need sovereignty, 18.
532 Kaplan, The remarkable story, 151.
533 M. Gurgulia, Democratisation in conditions of a non-recognized state, Paper presented at the conference *Abkhazia in the Context of Contemporary International Relations*, July 2004. http://www.circassianworld.com/Gurgulia.html.
534 Author's interview with Gegham Baghdasaryan (2008).
535 Protsyk, Moldova's dilemmas, 37.
536 Protsyk, Representation and democracy.
537 Ibid.

538 Protsyk, Moldova's dilemmas, 34. See also Kolstø and Blakkisrud, From secessionist conflict.
539 Quoted in Isachenko, Symptoms of democracy, 98. See also Kolstø and Blakkisrud, From secessionist conflict.
540 E. Owen, Domestic debate marks Karabakh presidential vote, *Eurasianet*, 19 July 2007.
541 Kolstø and Blakkisrud, From secessionist conflict.
542 Popescu, Democracy in secessionism, 19.
543 See, for example, Nodia, Nationalism and democracy, 5.
544 L. Broers, Filling the void: Ethnic politics and nationalities policy in post-conflict Georgia, *Nationalities Papers*, 2008, 36(2), 281.
545 According to the 2003 Abkhaz census which likely overestimates the Abkhaz share of the population. The actual percentage may be as low as 27 per cent. See Trier et al., *Under Siege*, 30–2.
546 Popescu, Democracy in secessionism, 19.
547 Trier et al., *Under Siege*, 95.
548 S. Walker, The phantom parliament: Abkhazia votes, but to what end, *Russia Profile*, 21 March 2007. From *Georgia News Digest*, 22 March 2007.
549 Popescu, Democracy in secessionism, 19.
550 S. Smooha, The model of ethnic democracy: Israel as a Jewish and democratic state, *Nations and Nationalism*, 2002, 8(4), 476–7.
551 Ibid. 482.
552 A. Buchanan, Introduction, in *Secession and Self-Determination*, eds S. Macedo and A. Buchanan (New York: New York University Press, 2003), 5.
553 Kaplan, The remarkable story, 148.
554 Ibid. 150.
555 See, for example, Bradbury, *Becoming Somaliland*, 216.
556 See, for example, Caspersen, Elite interests and the Serbian-Montenegrin conflict.
557 Protsyk, Representation and democracy.
558 Kolstø and Blakkisrud, From secessionist conflict.
559 See, for example, Protsyk, Representation and democracy.
560 Popescu, Democracy in secessionism, 19.
561 P. Rimple, Gali: A key test case for Georgia's separatist Abkhazia region, *Eurasianet*, 5 March 2007.
562 R. Clogg, The politics of identity in post-Soviet Abkhazia: Managing diversity and unresolved conflict, *Nationalities Papers*, 2008, 36(2), 311.
563 Trier et al., *Under Siege*, 74–5.
564 Ibid. 118.
565 Kolstø and Blakkisrud, From secessionist conflict.
566 Constitution of the Nagorno Karabakh Republic. http://www.president.nkr.am/media/documents/constitution/constitution_en.pdf.

567 Interview with David Babayan (2008).
568 Clogg, Politics of identity, 319, 324.
569 Trier et al., *Under Siege*, 95.
570 Ibid. 96.
571 Kolstø and Blakkisrud, From secessionist conflict.
572 Protsyk, Representation and democracy.
573 D. Pollock, The Kurdistan Regional Government in Iraq: An inside story, In *The Future of the Iraqi Kurds*, ed. S. Cagaptay, Washington Institute, Policy Focus #85, July 2008, 2.
574 O. Tansey, Democratization without a state: Democratic regime-building in Kosovo, *Democratization*, 2007, 14(1): 129–50, 140.
575 Interview with Tevan Poghosyan, political analyst (Yerevan, 24 October 2008).
576 Kaplan, The remarkable story, 150–1.
577 See, for example, D. Jama, Somaliland: The end of the democratization process and the return of one party rule, *The Somaliland Globe*, 7 April 2009.
578 Tansey, Does democracy need sovereignty, 18.
579 M. Allen, Afghanistan: Ceding democracy for stability, *Democracy Digest*, 17 March 2009, http://www.demdigest.net/blog/2009/03/afghanistan-ceding-democracy-for-stability/.
580 Protsyk, Representation and democracy. Kolstø and Blakkisrud, From secessionist conflict.
581 2010 country reports from http://www.freedomhouse.org/.
582 For further analysis of ethnic democracy in unrecognized states, see N. Caspersen, Democracy, nationalism and (lack of) sovereignty: The complex dynamics of democratization in unrecognized states, *Nations and Nationalism*, 2011, 17(2): 337–56.
583 For an analysis of how access to resources affects the strategy chosen by rebel movements, see J. Weinstein, *Inside Rebellion: The Politics of Insurgent Violence* (Cambridge: Cambridge University Press, 2006).
584 Unrepresented Nations and Peoples Organization, *Declaration*.
585 Author's interview with Veljko Dzakula.
586 Stanislawski, Para-states, 366.
587 Ibid. Jackson, *Quasi-States*.
588 Jackson, *Quasi-States*, 43, 112.
589 De Waal, *Black Garden*, 246.
590 Stanislawski, Para-states.
591 Kaplan, The remarkable story, 147. See also Walls, The emergence of a Somali state.
592 See, for example, Luling, Come back Somalia.
593 The trade-off between liberty and effectiveness is not a new dilemma and it also preoccupied classical political theorists; see Paris, *At War's End*, 50. However, the dilemma is accentuated by the context of nonrecognition.

594 Author's interview with Arkady Ghukasyan, former NKR president (Stepanakert, 3 November 2008).
595 Zartman, Introduction, 7.
596 Smooha, The model of ethnic democracy.
597 D. Howden, Africa's best-kept secret, *The Independent*, 6 May 2009.
598 Kolstø and Blakkisrud, From secessionist conflict.
599 Natali, *The Kurdish Quasi-State*, 103.
600 See, for example, International Crisis Group, *China and Taiwan: Uneasy Detente* (Seoul/Brussels, 2005), 1.
601 Pełczynska-Nałęcz et al., Para-states in the post-Soviet area, 373.
602 G. Abrahamyan, Armenia: Time for a change on Karabakh? *Eurasia Insight*, 2 May 2008.
603 International Crisis Group, *Abkhazia: Deepening Dependence* (Tbilisi/Brussels, 2010), 9.
604 P. Rimple, Georgia: Ethnic Georgian district in Abkhazia becomes election issue, *Eurasianet*, 14 September 2009.
605 *RFE/RL*, Abkhazia appoints new 'foreign minister', 28 February 2010.
606 See Buzan, *People, States and Fear*, 70.
607 Howden, Africa's best-kept secret.
608 Ibid.
609 See, for example, Associated Press, Russia signs border deal with Abkhazia, S. Ossetia, 30 April 2009. T. Esslemont, Russia pours money into Abkhazia, *BBC News*, 29 December 2008.
610 Kaplan, The remarkable story, 152.
611 Kolstø and Blakkisrud, From secessionist conflict.
612 See Caspersen, Between puppets and independent actors.
613 Bradbury, *Becoming Somaliland*, 178.
614 Author's interview with David Babayan (2006).
615 Bradbury, *Becoming Somaliland*, 151.
616 Ibid. 150.
617 Protsyk, Moldova's dilemmas, 36.
618 Kolstø and Blakkisrud, From secessionist conflict.
619 See, for example, K. Ohanian, Karabakhis' renewed independence hopes, *Caucasus Reporting Service*, 11 September 2008.
620 Author's interviews with Vahram Atanesyan, chairman of the NKR foreign relations committee (Stepanakert, 29 October 2008) and with Ashot Ghulyan, speaker of the NKR parliament (Stepanakert, 27 October 2008).
621 Author's interview with Vahram Atanesyan.
622 Author's interview with Georgy Petrosyan, NKR minister of foreign affairs (Stepanakert, 31 October 2008).
623 Author's interviews with Arkady Ghukasyan, Vahram Atanesyan and Hrachya Arzoumanyan, expert in the NKR foreign ministry (Stepanakert, 1 November 2008).

624 Interview with David Babayan (2008).
625 Interview with Hrachya Arzoumanyan.
626 See E. M. S. Niou, Understanding Taiwan independence and its policy implications, *Asian Survey*, 2004, 44(4).
627 International Crisis Group, *Cyprus: Reversing the Drift to Partition.*
628 International Crisis Group, *Abkhazia: Deepening Dependence*, 11.
629 Ibid.
630 *Tiraspol Times*, Igor Smirnov: 'We have not worked enough with other countries', 20 March 2008.
631 See, for example, V. Socor, Has the Transnistria conflict gone from dead end to wrong turn? *Eurasia Daily Monitor*, 16 April 2008.
632 S. Polkhov, Vladimir Voronon and Igor Smirnov meeting in Bendery: Are the parties ready to make a compromise with each other? *Eurasian Home*, 22 April 2008.
633 King, The benefits of ethnic war.
634 Author's interviews with Karine Ohanyan and Naira Ayrumyan, journalist (Stepanakert, 2 November 2008).
635 Author's interview with Araik Harutyunian.
636 See, for example, Krasner, Abiding sovereignty.
637 See, for example, Bartelson, *The Critique of the State.*
638 Kolstø and Blakkisrud, From secessionist conflict.
639 Protsyk, Moldova's dilemmas, 38.
640 Niou, Understanding Taiwan independence.
641 See, for example, International Crisis Group, *Abkhazia: Deepening Dependence*, 11.
642 Coalson, Russia steps of cooperation.
643 http://www.therepublicofabkhazia.org/pages/issues-points-interview/ sergei-bagapsh.shtml.
644 *RFE/RL*, Abkhazia appoints new 'foreign minister', 28 February 2010.
645 Švarm, Milan Martic's flying circus. Švarm, The return of the district strongman. F. Švarm, Love that'll never die, *Vreme News Digest*, 22 November 1993.
646 Author's interview with Stanko Momčilović.
647 Pegg, *International Society and the De Facto State*, 79.
648 Unrepresented Nations and Peoples Organization, *Declaration.*
649 This suggestion has, for example, been made in *Tiraspol Times*. R. Wadlow, UN membership for the world's phantom republics, *Tiraspol Times*, 25 September 2008.
650 E. Berg, Pooling sovereignty, losing territoriality? Making peace in Cyprus and Moldova, *Tijdschrift voor Economische en Sociale Geografie*, 2006, 97(3).
651 Krasner, Abiding sovereignty, 243.
652 Ibid. 244.
653 Philpott, *Revolutions in Sovereignty*, 20.
654 Jackson, *Quasi-States*, 39–40.

655 Heraclides, *Self-determination of Minorities*, 26.
656 See, Buzan, *People, States and Fear*, 70.
657 See, for example, Paris, *At War's End*. M. Ottaway, Nation-building, *Foreign Policy*, 2002, 132 (Sept-Oct).
658 Address at the G-11 summit, 16 May 2009, from The Official Government News Portal of Sri Lanka. http://www.news.lk/index.php?option=com_content&task=view&id=9679&Itemid=44.
659 Ibid.
660 See, for example, C. Philip, The hidden massacre: Sri Lanka's final offensive against Tamil Tigers, *The Times*, 29 May 2009.
661 M. Weaver and G. Chamberlain, Sri Lanka declares end to war with Tamil Tigers, *The Guardian*, 19 May 2009.
662 *The Jamestown Foundation*, Amnesty International issues reports on disappearances, 24 May 2007.
663 Amnesty International, *Croatia: Operation Storm – Still No Justice Ten Years on* (London, 2005).
664 The United Nations Human Rights Council even passed a resolution which hailed the victory of the Sri Lankan Government and described the conflict as 'a domestic matter that doesn't warrant outside interference'. H. Pidd, UN rejects calls for Sri Lanka war crimes inquiry, *The Guardian*, 28 May 2009.
665 Weller, *Escaping the Self-Determination Trap*, 44.
666 See, for example, *BBC News*, Russia will pay for Chechnya, 7 December 1999.
667 L. Fuller, Three Azerbaijani scenarios for Nagorno Karabakh, *RFE/RL*, Caucasus Report, 8 October 2001.
668 See, for example, L. Yevgrashina, Azerbaijan may use force in Karabakh after Kosovo, *Reuters*, 4 March 2008.
669 Author's interview with Karen Ohanjanyan. The entity's president has even talked about the possibility of a pre-emptive attack if Azerbaijan's actions are seen to present a security threat. International Crisis Group, *Nagorno-Karabakh: Risking War* (Tbilisi/Brussels, 2007).
670 T. de Waal, *The Karabakh Trap: Dangers and Dilemmas of the Nagorny Karabakh Conflict* (London: Conciliation Resources, 2009), 11.
671 Weaver and Chamberlain, Sri Lanka declares end to war.
672 Peter Wallensteen has found that of the wars that ended in outright victory between 1946 and 2004, 20 per cent had recurred after ten years and 50 per cent over the entire period. Quoted in F. Cochrane, *Ending Wars* (Cambridge: Polity, 2008), 71.
673 See, for example, International Crisis Group, *Bosnia's Incomplete Transition: Between Dayton and Europe* (Sarajevo/Brussels, 2009).
674 Anderson, Reintegrating unrecognized states, 198.
675 Ibid. The Bougainville settlement also includes the promise of a self-determination referendum after an interim period. Weller, *Escaping the Self-Determination Trap*, 124.

676 Weller, *Escaping the Self-Determination Trap*, 96.
677 N. Caspersen, Good fences make good neighbours? A comparison of conflict regulation strategies in post-war Bosnia, *Journal of Peace Research*, 2004, 41(5), 569–88.
678 Anderson, Reintegrating unrecognized states, 195.
679 Ibid. 190.
680 Lynch, *Engaging Eurasia's Separatist States*, 6.
681 King, The benefits of ethnic war, 551.
682 Lynch, *Engaging Eurasia's Separatist States*, 51.
683 Berg, Pooling sovereignty, 224.
684 See I. W. Zartman, Ripeness: The hurting stalemate and beyond, in *International Conflict Resolution After the Cold War*, eds P. C. Stern and D. Druckman (Washington: National Academy Press, 2000).
685 Lynch, *Engaging Eurasia's Separatist States*, 8.
686 Ibid. 142.
687 See, for example, Heraclides, *Self-Determination of Minorities*.
688 See Caspersen, *Contested Nationalism*.
689 See, for example, Lynch, *Engaging Eurasia's Separatist States*, 6.
690 Heraclides, *Self-Determination of Minorities*, 35.
691 See, for example, M. Kleibor, Ripeness of conflict: A fruitful notion? *Journal of Peace Research*, 1994, 31(1).
692 See, for example, Kemp, Selfish determination.
693 S. J. Stedman, Spoiler problems in peace processes, *International Security*, 1997, 22(2).
694 S. J. Stedman, *Peacemaking in Civil Wars: International Mediation in Zimbabwe 1974–80* (Boulder: Lynne Rienner, 1991).
695 T. D. Sisk, Peacemaking in civil wars: Obstacles, options and opportunities, in *Managing and Settling Ethnic Conflicts*, eds U. Schneckener and S. Wolff (London: Hurst, 2004), 257.
696 S. Touval, Coercive mediation on the road to Dayton, *International Negotiation*, 1996, 1(3).
697 M. Vasić, Predsednik ili general, *Vreme*, 14 August 1995, 14–15.
698 See Caspersen, *Contested Nationalism*.
699 See, for example, International Crisis Group, *China and Taiwan: Uneasy Detente*.
700 See, for example, Stansfield, *Iraq*, 135, 147–8, 172. Natali, *The Kurds and the State*, 53–69.
701 See, for example, Braithwaite et al., *Reconciliation*.
702 S. Raghavan, At Cairo hospital, injured increasingly voice support for Hamas, *Washington Post*, 14 January 2009, 14. C. McGreal, Israel looks to drive out Hamas, *The Guardian*, 6 January 2009.
703 See, for example, Amnesty International, *Israel/Occupied Palestinian Territories: Israeli Blockade Causes Worsening Humanitarian Crisis in Gaza* (London, 2008).
704 See, for example, G. Myre, Israel plans sanctions as Hamas picks a Prime Minister, *New York Times*, 16 February 2006.

705 See Oxfam, Crisis in Gaza, http://www.oxfam.org/en/emergencies/gaza.
706 J. Bowen, Little hope in Gaza aftermath, *BBC News*, 9 April 2009.
707 United Nations Security Council, *Resolution 820 (1993)*.
708 Author's interviews with Rade Matijaš, former journalist in Knin (Belgrade, 12 February 2009) and Drago Kovačević.
709 F. Švarm and D. Hedl, Bye, bye boys in blue, *Vreme News Digest*, 23 January 1995.
710 U. Komlenović, Mavericks on the road, *Vreme News Digest*, 3 April 1995. U. Komlenović, All Dzakula's arrests, *Vreme News Digest*, 15 May 1995. See also N. Barić, *Srpska Pobuna u Hrvatskoj, 1990–1995* (Zagreb: Golden Marketing, 2005), 3.
711 Author's interview with Veljko Džakula.
712 See, for example, F. Švarm, The view from the fort, *Vreme News Digest*, 7 August 1995.
713 Quote from F. Švarm, *Pad Krajine*, documentary film (Serbia: Vreme Film, 2007).
714 Kemp, Selfish determination, 90.
715 Heraclides, *Self-Determination of Minorities*, 36.
716 Raghavan, At Cairo hospital.
717 Author's interview with Stanko Momčilović.
718 See, for example, Pegg, *International Society and the De Facto State*, 79.
719 Quoted in Heraclides, *Self-Determination of Minorities*, 39.
720 Quoted in De Waal, *Karabakh Trap*, 2.
721 Zartman, Ripeness, 227.
722 See, for example, E. D. Mansfield and J. Snyder, *Electing to Fight: Why Emerging Democracies go to War* (Cambridge: MIT Press, 2005). Paris, *At War's End*.
723 See, for example, E. Nordlinger, *Conflict Regulation in Divided Societies* (Cambridge: Center for International Affairs, Harvard University, 1972).
724 See Caspersen, *Contested Nationalism*.
725 Author's interview with Paata Zakareishvili, political analyst (Tbilisi, 31 August 2006).
726 J. Burke, Armenian paper blames Karabakh leaders for internal political tensions, *Armenia Daily Digest*, 3 February 2000.
727 For the need for a broad approach to conflict resolution that includes different strata of society, see, for example, J. P. Lederach, *Building Peace: Sustainable Reconciliation in Divided Societies* (Washington, DC: United States Institute for Peace, 1998).
728 Protsyk, Moldova's dilemmas, 32–3.
729 Ibid.
730 Interview with Filip Švarm.
731 Author's interviews with Naira Ayrumyan and Karine Ohanyan.
732 I. Khashig, Abkhaz opposition fear growing Russian influence, *Caucasus Reporting Service*, 7 August 2009.

733 As Heraclides argues, such inflexibility is particularly pronounced in cases where independence has been formally declared. Heraclides, *Self-Determination of Minorities*, 35.

734 Weller, *Escaping the Self-Determination Trap*, 123.

735 King, The benefits of ethnic war, 525.

736 Berg, Pooling sovereignty, 223.

737 Ibid.

738 Philpott, *Revolutions in Sovereignty*, 17.

739 International Crisis Group, *Reunifying Cyprus* (Nicosia/Istanbul/Brussels, 2008).

740 See, for example, T. G. Carpenter, Beijing smothers Hong Kong—and drives Taiwan farther away, *Apple Daily* (Hong Kong), 2 June, 2004.

741 See The General Framework Agreement for Peace in Bosnia and Herzegovina. http://www.ohr.int/dpa/default.asp?content_id=380.

742 See http://www.northsouthministerialcouncil.org/.

743 Geldenhuys, *Contested States*, 50–1.

744 R. Deyermond, *Security and Sovereignty in the Former Soviet Union* (Boulder: Lynne Rienner, 2008), 33.

745 Author's interviews with Arzu Abdullayeva, chair of the Helsinki Citizens' Assembly (Baku, 12 June 2009), Rasim Musabekov, political analyst (Baku, 12 June 2009) and Ilgar Mammadov, political analyst (Baku, 19 June 2009).

746 The term 'constructive ambiguity' is generally credited to Henry Kissinger who used it during his attempts to negotiate Arab-Israeli peace.

747 De Waal, *Karabakh Trap*, 8.

748 Zartman, Ripeness, 228.

749 N. Caspersen, Mounting tensions over Nagorno Karabakh, *CACI Analyst*, 7 August 2010.

750 See *BBC News*, Boney M on Georgia's front line, 13 October 2007.

751 See, for example, H. Miall, O. Ramsbotham and T. Woodhouse, *Contemporary Conflict Resolution* (London: Polity, 1999), 164–6.

752 International Crisis Group, *Cyprus: Reversing the Drift towards Partition*, 25.

753 EUSR for the South Caucasus, Non-paper on the parameters for EU's non-recognition and engagement policy for Abkhazia and South Ossetia, 9 December 2009.

754 Action Plan for Engagement, 6 July 2010, http://www.smr.gov.ge/uploads/action_plan_en.pdf.

755 See, for example, A. Cooley and L. A. Mitchell, Engagement without recognition: A new strategy toward Abkhazia and Eurasia's unrecognized states, *Washington Quarterly*, 2010, 33(4).

756 Law On Occupied Territories.

757 Caspersen and Herrberg, Engaging unrecognized states in conflict resolution.

758 Weller, *Escaping the Self-Determination Trap*, 113.

759 Ibid. 124.
760 *China Post*, Ma clarifies 'two areas', reaffirms non-denial, 25 October 2008.
761 Krasner, *Sovereignty*, 228.
762 Due to problems of obtaining statistical information about historical cases, only unrecognized states that still exist have been included in this table.
763 Reliable macroeconomic indicators for unrecognized states are, in most cases, very hard to find, so these figures should at best be considered estimates.
764 These figures do not include foreign forces stationed in unrecognized states, either as peacekeepers or as direct support for the de facto regime. The only exception is the estimate for Nagorno Karabakh which includes soldiers from Armenia proper who serve in the Karabakh army. The data for Somaliland, Northern Cyprus and Taiwan are from International Institute for Strategic Studies, *The Military Balance 2010* (London: Routledge, 2010).
765 *Abkhazia Today*, GDP per capita.
766 Estimates from International Crisis Group, *Abkhazia: Deepening Dependence*, 5.
767 The National Statistics Service of Nagorno-Karabakh Republic, http://www.stat-nkr.am/.
768 Estimates from International Crisis Group, *Nagorno-Karabakh*, 9.
769 This estimate is for Somalia as a whole. Bradbury, *Becoming Somaliland*, 162.
770 Estimate from International Crisis Group, *Georgia: Avoiding War*, 11.
771 Estimates from I. Kramnik, What will be the outcome of the Georgian-Ossetian War? *RIA Novosti*, 8 August 2008.
772 International Crisis Group, *Moldova: No Quick Fix*, 5.
773 Estimates from International Crisis Group, *Moldova: Regional Tensions over Transnistria* (Chisinau/Brussels, 2004), 13.
774 GNP per capita, Turkish Republic of Northern Cyprus, *Economic and Social Indicators 2008*, http://www.devplan.org/Frame-eng.html.
775 Data from the World Bank, http://data.worldbank.org/country/KV.
776 The Kosovo Security Force is still being formed and 800 reservists are yet to be recruited. See Ministry for the Kosovo Security Force, *Stand-up, Challenges and Success* (Pristina, 2010).
777 See Economy http://www.gio.gov.tw/taiwan-website/5-gp/yearbook/08Economy.pdf.
778 J. Grygiel, Vacuum wars: The coming competition over failed states, *The American Interest*, 2009(July/August).
779 See, for example, the current internal debates in Abkhazia. Khashig, Abkhaz opposition.
780 King, The benefits of ethnic war, 551.
781 See also, Sambanis, Partition as a solution to ethnic war.

782 It is not enough for the leaders to be looking for a 'way out', they also have to believe that an acceptable and feasible 'way out' will actually be offered. See, for example, I. W. Zartman, Dynamics and constraints in negotiations in internal conflicts, in *Elusive Peace: Negotiating an End to Civil War*, ed. I. W. Zartman (Washington, DC: The Brookings Institution, 1995).

783 Kaufmann, Possible and impossible solutions.

784 See, for example, Heraclides, *Self-Determination of Minorities*, 12, 20.

785 See Caspersen, *Contested Nationalism*.

786 L. M. Seymour, The surprising success of 'separatist' groups: The empirical and juridical in self-determination, Paper presented at the ISA's 47th Annual Convention, San Diego, CA, 21–6 March 2006.

BIBLIOGRAPHY

ABC News. Up to 100,000 killed in Sri Lanka's civil war: UN, 20 May 2009.

Abkhazia Today. GDP per capita in Abkhazia is higher than in Moldova, Uzbekistan, Kirghizia, Mongolia, 7 July 2010.

Abrahamyan, G. Armenia: Time for a change on Karabakh? *Eurasia Insight,* 2 May 2008.

Action Plan for Engagement. 6 July 2010, http://www.smr.gov.ge/uploads/action_plan_en.pdf.

Allen, M. Afghanistan: Ceding democracy for stability, *Democracy Digest,* 17 March 2009, http://www.demdigest.net/blog/2009/03/afghanistan-ceding-democracy-for-stability/

Amnesty International. *Croatia: Operation Storm—Still No Justice Ten Years on.* London, 2005.

Amnesty International. *Israel/Occupied Palestinian Territories: Israeli Blockade Causes Worsening Humanitarian Crisis in Gaza.* London, 2008.

Anderson, B. Western nationalism and Eastern nationalism, *New Left Review,* 2001, 9 (May–June).

Anderson, L. Reintegrating unrecognized states, in *Unrecognized States in the International System,* eds N. Caspersen and G. Stansfield, London: Routledge, 2010.

Armenian News Network. The rise and fall of Samvel Babayan, 6 October 2004.

Associated Press. Russia signs border deal with Abkhazia, S. Ossetia, 30 April 2009.

Bahcheli, T., B. Bartmann, and H. Srebrnik, eds, *De Facto States: The Quest for Sovereignty.* London: Routledge, 2004.

Bakke, K. M. After the war ends: violence and viability in post-Soviet unrecognized states, in *Unrecognized States in the International System,* eds N. Caspersen and G. Stansfield. London: Routledge, 2010.

Barić, N. *Srpska Pobuna u Hrvatskoj, 1990–1995*. Zagreb: Golden Marketing, 2005.

Bartelson, J. *A Genealogy of Sovereignty*. Cambridge: Cambridge University Press, 1995.

—. *The Critique of the State*. Cambridge: Cambridge University Press, 2001.

Bartmann, B. Political realities and legal anomalies, in *De Facto States: The Quest for Sovereignty*, eds T. Bahcheli, B. Bartmann and H. Srebrnik. London: Routledge, 2004.

BBC News. Russia will pay for Chechnya, 7 December 1999.

—. Boney M on Georgia's front line, 13 October 2007.

—. Direct China-Taiwan flights begin, 4 July 2008.

Berg, E. Pooling sovereignty, losing territoriality? Making peace in Cyprus and Moldova, *Tijdschrift voor Economische en Sociale Geografie*, 2006, 97(3): 222–236.

Boadle, A. Castro: Cuba not cashing U.S. Guantanamo rent checks, *Reuters*, 17 August 2007.

Boege, V. Bougainville and the discovery of slowness, The Australian Centre for Peace and Conflict Studies, Occasional Papers Series, no. 3, June 2006.

Bowen, J. Little hope in Gaza aftermath, *BBC News*, 9 April 2009.

Bradbury, M. *Becoming Somaliland*. London: Progressio, 2008.

Bradbury, M., A. Y. Abokor and H. Ahmed, Somaliland: Choosing politics over violence, *Review of African Political Economy*, 2003, 97: 455–478.

Braithwaite, J., H. Charlesworth, P. Reddy and L. Dunn, *Reconciliation and Architectures of Commitment: Sequencing peace in Bougainville*. Canberra: ANU Press, 2010.

Brinkley, J. Pressure on North Korea: U.S. Stealth Jets sent to South, *Washington Post*, 30 May 2005.

Broers, L. The politics of non-recognition and democratization, in *The Limits of Leadership: Elites and Societies in the Nagorny Karabakh Peace Process*, ed. L. Broers. London: Conciliation Resources, 2005.

—. Filling the void: Ethnic politics and nationalities policy in post-conflict Georgia, *Nationalities Papers*, 2008, 36(2): 275–304.

Brubaker, R. *Nationalism Reframed: Nationhood and the National Question in the New Europe*. Cambridge: Cambridge University Press, 1996.

Buchanan, A. Introduction, in *Secession and Self-Determination*, eds S. Macedo and A. Buchanan. New York: New York University Press, 2003.

Burke, J. Armenian paper blames Karabakh leaders for internal political tensions, *Armenia Daily Digest*, 3 February 2000.

Buzan, B. *People, States and Fear: An Agenda for International Security Studies in the Post-Cold War Era*. Hemel Hempstead: Harvester Wheatsheaf, 1991.

Camilleri, J. A. and J. Falk, *The End of Sovereignty?* Aldershot: Edward Elgar, 1992.

Coconut Revolution: The Bougainville Story. Documentary film. Stampede, 2001.

Constitution of the Principality of Andorra, April 1993.

Carpenter, T. G. Beijing smothers Hong Kong—and drives Taiwan farther away, *Apple Daily* (Hong Kong), 2 June 2004.

Casella, A. Macedonia: Taiwan's lost gambit, *Asia Times*, 11 July 2001.

Caspersen, N. Elite interests and the Serbian-Montenegrin conflict, *Southeast European Politics*, 2003, 4(2–3): 104–21.

—. Good fences make good neighbours? A comparison of conflict regulation strategies in post-war Bosnia, *Journal of Peace Research*, 2004, 41(5): 569–88.

—. Belgrade, Pale, Knin: Kin-state control over rebellious puppets? *Europe-Asia Studies* 2007, 59 (4): 619–39.

—. Between puppets and independent actors: Kin-state involvement in the conflicts in Bosnia, Croatia and Nagorno Karabakh, *Ethnopolitics*, 2008, 7(4): 357–372.

—. Separatism and democracy in the Caucasus, *Survival*, 2008, 50(4): 113–116.

—. Playing the recognition game: External actors and de facto states, *International Spectator* 2009 (Dec), 44(4): 21–34.

—. *Contested Nationalism: Serb Elite Rivalry in Croatia and Bosnia in the 1990s.* Oxford: Berghahn Books, 2010.

—. Mounting tensions over Nagorno Karabakh, *CACI Analyst*, 7 August 2010.

—. Democracy, nationalism and (lack of) sovereignty: The complex dynamics of democratization in unrecognized states, *Nations and Nationalism* 2011, 17(2): 337–56.

Caspersen, N. and A. Herrberg, Engaging unrecognized states in conflict resolution: An opportunity or challenge for the EU? *Crisis Management Initiative*, January 2011.

Chang, A. Comparing three ethnic Chinese militaries, *Military Might*, 12 January 2008.

China Post. Ma clarifies 'two areas', reaffirms non-denial, 25 October 2008.

Chorev, M. Complex terrains: Unrecognized states and globalization, in *Unrecognized States in the International System*, eds N. Caspersen and G. Stansfield. London: Routledge, 2010.

Chu, Y. and J. Lin, Political development in 20th century Taiwan, *China Quarterly*, 2001, 165: 102–29.

Chun, A. From nationalism to nationalizing: Cultural imagination and state formation in postwar Taiwan, *The Australian Journal of Chinese Affairs*, 1994, 31 (Jan): 49–69.

Clauss, E. M. The Roosevelt Administration and Manchukuo, 1933–1941, *Historian*, 1970, 32(4): 595–611.

Clogg, R. The politics of identity in post-Soviet Abkhazia: Managing diversity and unresolved conflict, *Nationalities Papers*, 2008, 36(2): 305–29.

Closson, S. State weakness in perspective: Strong politico-economic networks in Georgia's energy sector, *Europe-Asia Studies*, 2009, 61(5): 759–78.

Coalson, R. Russia steps up cooperation with breakaway Georgian regions, *RFE/RL*, 30 April 2009.

Cochrane, F. *Ending Wars*. Cambridge: Polity, 2008.

Collier, P. Doing well out of war: An economic perspective, in *Greed and Grievance: Economic Agendas in Civil Wars*, eds Mats Berdal and David Malone. Boulder: Lynne Rienner, 2000.

Collier, P. and A. Hoeffler. Greed and grievance in civil war, World Bank Policy Research, Working Paper 2355. Washington DC.

Constitution of the Nagorno Karabakh Republic. http://www.president.nkr. am/media/documents/constitution/constitution_en.pdf

Cooley, A. and L.A. Mitchell. Engagement without recognition: A new strategy toward Abkhazia and Eurasia's unrecognized states, *Washington Quarterly*, 2010, 33(4): 59–73.

Cornell, S. E. Autonomy as a source of conflict: Caucasian conflicts in theoretical perspective, *World Politics*, 2002, 54(2): 245–76.

Cornell, S. E. and S. F. Starr, eds *The Guns of August 2008: Russia's War in Georgia*. New York, NY: M. E. Sharpe, 2009.

Council of the European Union. *Press release: 2851st Council meeting, General Affairs and External Relations*, 18 February 2008.

Cox, M., T. Dunne and K. Booth, Introduction, in *Empires, Systems and States: Great Transformations in International Politics*, eds M. Cox, T. Dunne and K. Booth. Cambridge: Cambridge University Press, 2001.

Crawford, J. *The Creation of States in International Law*. Oxford: Oxford University Press, 2006.

Decision of the special session of the NKAO Council of People's Deputies. 20 February 1988, http://www.nkr.am/en/decision-of-the-special-session-of-the-nkao-council-of-peoples-deputies-of-xx-session/41/

Dakić, M. *Krajina kroz Vijekove*. Belgrade: Vedes, 2001.

De Waal, T. *Black Garden: Armenia and Azerbaijan through Peace and War*. New York: New York University Press, 2003.

—. *The Karabakh Trap: Dangers and Dilemmas of the Nagorny Karabakh Conflict*. London: Conciliation Resources, 2009.

Declaration on proclamation of the Nagorno Karabakh Republic. 2 September 1991, http://www.nkr.am/eng/deklaraciya209.html

Duara, P. *Sovereignty and Authenticity: Manchukuo and the East Asian Modern*. Lanham: Rowman and Littlefield, 2004.

Esslemont, T. Russia pours money into Abkhazia, *BBC News*, 29 December 2008.

Etzioni, A. The evils of self-determination, *Foreign Policy*, 1993.

European Commission. *Accession Criteria*. http://ec.europa.eu/enlargement/enlargement_process/accession_process/criteria/index_en.htm

European Parliament. *European Parliament ad hoc delegation to Moldova, 5–6 June 2002*, report from the Chairman, Mr Jan Marinus Wiersma.

EUSR for the South Caucasus. Non-paper on the parameters for EU's non-recognition and engagement policy for Abkhazia and South Ossetia, 9 December 2009.

Freedom House. Abkhazia (Georgia), http://www.freedomhouse.org
Fukuyama, F. The imperative of state-building, *Journal of Democracy*, 2004, 15(2): 17–31.
Fuller, L. Three Azerbaijani scenarios for Nagorno Karabakh, *RFE/RL*, Caucasus Report, 8 October 2001.
Gardner, A. Beyond standards before status: democratic governance and non-state actors, *Review of International Studies*, 2008, 34(3): 531–552.
Geldenhuys, D. *Contested States in World Politics.* Basingstoke: Palgrave Macmillan, 2009.
General Consulate of Monaco in New York. Monaco signs new treaty with France, 24 October 2002, http://www.monaco-consulate.com/news_1024.htm
Ghali, B. B. *An Agenda for Democratization.* New York: United Nations, 1996.
Global Security. Biafra war, http://www.globalsecurity.org/military/world/war/biafra.htm
Giragosian, R. Nagorno Karabakh democracy, *CACI Analyst*, 26 April 2000.
Grygiel, J. Vacuum wars: The coming competition over failed states, *The American Interest*, 2009 (July/August).
Gurgulia, M. Democratization in conditions of a non-recognized state, Paper presented at the conference *Abkhazia in the Context of Contemporary International Relations*, July 2004, http://www.circassianworld.com/Gurgulia.html
Hakobian, T. Turkey keeps Armenia guessing over border blockade, *Caucasus Reporting Service*, 17 April 2009.
Helman, G. B. and S. R. Ratner. Saving failed states, *Foreign Policy*, 1992–3, 89 (Winter): 3–20.
Heraclides, A. *The Self-Determination of Minorities in International Politics.* London: Frank Cass, 1991.
Holbrooke, R. *To End a War.* New York: Modern Library, 1999.
Howden, D. Africa's best-kept secret, *The Independent*, 6 May 2009.
Hughes, J. *Chechnya: From Nationalism to Jihad.* Philadelphia: University of Pennsylvania Press, 2007.
Human Rights Watch. *Up in Flames: Humanitarian Law Violations and Civilian Victims in the Conflict over South Ossetia.* New York, 2009.
Huntington, S. Foreword to E. A. Nordlinger, *Conflict Regulation in Divided Societies.* Cambridge: Harvard University, 1972.
International Alert. *From War Economies to Peace Economies.* London, 2004.
International Conference on the Former Yugoslavia. *Agreement: Water*, 2 December 1994.
International Crisis Group. *Moldova: No Quick Fix.* Chisinau/Brussels, 2003.
—. *China and Taiwan: Uneasy Detente.* Seoul/Brussels, 2005.
—. *Nagorno-Karabakh: Viewing the Conflict from the Ground.* Tbilisi/Brussels, 2005.
—. *Abkhazia Today.* Brussels/Tbilisi, 2006.

——. *Conflict Resolution in the South Caucasus: The EU's Role.* Tbilisi/Brussels, 2006.

——. *Moldova's Uncertain Future.* Chisinau/Brussels, 2006.

——. *Pakistan's Tribal Areas: Appeasing the Militants.* Islamabad/Brussels, 2006.

——. *Somaliland: Time for African Union Leadership.* Hargeisa/Addis Ababa/ Brussels, 2006.

——. *Abkhazia: Ways Forward.* Tbilisi/Brussels, 2007.

——. *Moldova's Uncertain Future.* Chisinau/Brussels, 2007.

——. *Nagorno-Karabakh: Risking War.* Tbilisi/Brussels, 2007.

——. *Western Sahara: Out of the Impasse.* Cairo/Brussels, 2007.

——. *Reunifying Cyprus.* Nicosia/Istanbul/Brussels, 2008.

——. *Bosnia's Incomplete Transition: Between Dayton and Europe.* Sarajevo/ Brussels, 2009.

——. *Cyprus: Reunification or Partition?* Nicosia/Istanbul/Brussels, 2009.

——. *Cyprus: Reversing the Drift to Partition.* Nicosia/Istanbul/Brussels, 2009.

——. *Abkhazia: Deepening Dependence.* Tbilisi/Brussels, 2010.

——. *South Ossetia: the Burden of Recognition.* Tbilisi/Brussels, 2010.

International Institute for Strategic Studies. *The Military Balance 2010.* London: Routledge, 2010.

Isachenko, D. Bridging the sovereignty gap in Northern Cyprus, Paper presented at SGIR 6th Pan-European International Relations Conference, Turin, 12–15 September 2007.

——. Symptoms of democracy in Transdniestria, *S+F – Sicherheit und Frieden,* 2009, 27(2), 96–101.

Jackson, R. *Quasi-states: Sovereignty, International Relations and the Third World.* Cambridge: Cambridge University Press, 1990.

——. *Sovereignty.* Cambridge: Polity, 2007.

Jarčević, S. ed. *Republika Srpska Krajina: Državna Dokumenta.* Belgrade: Miroslav, 2005.

Jareb, M. The NDH's relations with Italy and Germany, *Totalitarian Movements and Political Religions,* 2006, 7(4): 459–72.

Kaldor, M. *New and Old Wars: Organized Violence in a Global Era.* Cambridge: Polity, 2006.

Kaplan, R. D. The coming anarchy, *Atlantic Monthly,* 1994, 273(2): 44–76.

Kaplan, S. The remarkable story of Somaliland, *Journal of Democracy,* 2008, 19(3): 143–157.

Karabakh Open, Karabakh has serious grounds for international recognition of sovereignty, 20 February 2008, http://www.armeniandiaspora.com/ showthread.php?122518-Karabakh-Has-Serious-Grounds-For-International-Recognition-Of-Sovere

Kaufmann, C. Possible and impossible solutions to ethnic civil wars, *International Security,* 1996, 20(4): 136–75.

Kemp, W. Selfish determination: The questionable ownership of autonomy movements, *Ethnopolitics,* 2005, 4(1): 85–104.

Khashig, I. Abkhazia: Government poll landslide contested, *Caucasus Reporting Service*, 8 March 2002.

—. Tangerine fever grips Abkhazia, *Caucasus Reporting Service*, 21 November 2002.

—. Abkhaz opposition fear growing Russian influence, *Caucasus Reporting Service*, 7 August 2009.

King, C. The benefits of ethnic war: Understanding Eurasia's unrecognized states, *World Politics*, July 2001, 53(July): 524–52.

—. Black Sea blues, *The National Interest*, 2004, 78(5).

Kingston, P. and I. S. Spears, eds, *States within States: Incipient Political Entities in the Post-Cold War Era*. New York: Palgrave Macmillan, 2004.

Kleibor, M. Ripeness of conflict: A fruitful notion? *Journal of Peace Research*, 1994, 31(1): 109–16.

Kolanović, N.K. The NDH's relations with Southeast European countries, Turkey and Japan, 1941–5, *Totalitarian Movements and Political Religions*, 2006, 7(4): 473–92.

Kolstø, P. The sustainability and future of unrecognized quasi-states, *Journal of Peace Research*, 2006, 43(6): 723–740.

Kolstø, P. and H. Blakkisrud. Living with non-recognition: State- and nation-building in South Caucasian quasi-states, *Europe-Asia Studies*, 2008, 60(3): 483–509.

—. Separatism is the mother of terrorism, in *Unrecognized States in the International System*, eds N. Caspersen and G. Stansfield (London: Routledge, 2010), 112.

—. From secessionist conflict towards functioning state: Processes of state- and nation-building in Transnistria, *Post-Soviet Affairs* (forthcoming, 2011).

Kolossov, V. and J. O'Loughlin. Pseudo-states as harbingers of a new geo-politics: The example of the Trans-Dniester Moldovan Republic (TMR), in *Boundaries, Territory and Postmodernity*, ed D. Newman. London: Frank Cass, 1999.

Komlenović, U. The fate of the Krajina, *Vreme News Digest*, 17 October 1994.

—. Mavericks on the road, *Vreme News Digest*, 3 April 1995.

—. All Dzakula's arrests, *Vreme News Digest*, 15 May 1995.

Kramnik, I. What will be the outcome of the Georgian-Ossetian War? *RIA Novosti*, 8 August 2008.

Krasner, S. D. Compromising Westphalia, *International Security*, 1995–6, 20(3): 115–151.

—. *Sovereignty: Organized Hypocrisy*. Princeton: Princeton University Press, 1999.

—. Abiding sovereignty, *International Political Science Review*, 2001, 22(3): 229–251.

—. Rethinking the sovereign state model, in *Empires, Systems and States: Great Transformations in International Politics*, eds M. Cox, T. Dunne and K. Booth. Cambridge: Cambridge University Press, 2001.

—. Sharing sovereignty: New institutions for collapsed and failing states, *International Security*, 2004, 29(2): 85–120.

Kucera, J. Abkhazia: Bracing for more trouble, *Eurasianet*, 14 June 2007.

Kukhianidze, A.; A. Kupatadze and R. Gotsiridze, *Smuggling through Abkhazia and Tskhinvali region*. Tbilisi: Transnational Crime and Corruption Center, 2004.

Kumar, R. The troubled history of partition, *Foreign Affairs*, 1997, 76(1): 22–34.

Lake, D. A. Reflection, evaluation, integration: The new sovereignty in international relations, *International Studies Review*, 2003, 5(3): 303–23.

Law on Occupied Territories. 23 October 2008, http://www.venice.coe.int/docs/2009/CDL(2009)004-e.asp

Lederach, J.P. *Building Peace: Sustainable Reconciliation in Divided Societies*. Washington DC: United States Institute for Peace, 1998.

Lewis, I. *Understanding Somalia and Somaliland*. London: Hurst, 2008.

Linz, J.J. and A. Stepan. *Problems of Democratic Transition and Consolidation*. Baltimore: The Johns Hopkins University Press, 1996.

Luling, V. Come back Somalia? Questioning a collapsed state, *Third World Quarterly*, 1997, 18(2): 287–302.

Lynch, D. Separatist states and post-Soviet conflicts, *International Affairs*, 2002, 4: 831–848.

—. *Engaging Eurasia's Separatist States*. Washington DC: United States Institute of Peace, 2004.

Mansfield, E.D. and J. Snyder. *Electing to Fight: Why Emerging Democracies go to War*. Cambridge: MIT Press, 2005.

McColl, R.W. The insurgent state: Territorial bases of revolution, *Annals of the Association of American Geographers*, 1969, 59(4): 613–31.

McGreal, C. Israel looks to drive out Hamas, *The Guardian*, 6 January 2009.

Medvedev, D. Why I had to recognise Georgia's breakaway regions, *Financial Times*, 27 August 2008.

Meierhenrich, J. Forming states after failure, in *When States Fail: Causes and Consequences*, ed. Robert I. Rotberg. Princeton: Princeton University Press, 2001.

Melander, E. The Nagorno-Karabakh conflict revisited, *Journal of Cold War Studies*, 2001, 3(2): 48–75.

Menkhaus, K. State collapse in Somalia: Second thoughts, *Review of African Political Economy*, 2003, 30(97): 405–22.

Miall, H.O. Ramsbotham and T. Woodhouse. *Contemporary Conflict Resolution*. London: Polity, 1999.

Migdal, J.S. State building and the non-nation state, *Journal of International Affairs*, 2004, 58(1): 17–46.

Ministry for the Kosovo Security Force. *Stand-up, Challenges and Success*. Pristina, 2010.

Ministry of National Planning and Coordination. *Somaliland in Figures.* Hargeisa, 2003.

Miriori, M. A Bougainville Interim Government (BIG) perspective on early peace efforts, in *Weaving Consensus: The Papua New Guinea–Bougainville Peace Process*, eds A. Carl and L. Garasu. London: Conciliation Resources, 2002.

Moore, M. Normative justification for liberal nationalism: Justice, democracy and national identity, *Nations and Nationalism*, 2001, 7(1).

Murinson, A. The secession of Abkhazia and Nagorny Karabagh: The roots and patterns of development of post-Soviet micro-secessions in Transcaucasia, *Central Asia Survey*, 2004, 23(1): 5–26.

Musaelian, L. Bid to repopulate Karabakh fraught with problems, *Caucasus Reporting Service*, 19 June 2009.

Myre, G. Israel plans sanctions as Hamas picks a Prime Minister, *New York Times*, 16 February 2006.

Natali, D. *The Kurds and the State: Evolving National Identity in Iraq, Turkey and Iran.* Syracuse: Syracuse University Press, 2005.

—. *The Kurdish Quasi-State: Development and Dependency in Post-Gulf War Iraq.* New York: Syracuse Press, 2010.

Nish, I.H. *Japanese Foreign Policy in the Interwar Period.* Westport: Praeger, 2002.

Nodia, G. Nationalism and democracy, in *Nationalism, Ethnic Conflict, and Democracy*, eds L. Diamond and M. F. Plattner. Baltimore: Johns Hopkins University Press, 1994.

Nordlinger, E. *Conflict Regulation in Divided Societies.* Cambridge: Center for International Affairs, Harvard University, 1972.

Ohanian, K. Karabakhis' renewed independence hopes, *Caucasus Reporting Service*, 11 September 2008.

—. Karabakh's big wedding day, *Caucasus Reporting Service*, 23 October 2008.

Orjuela, C. Diaspora identities and homeland politics: Lessons from the Sri Lanka/Tamil Eelam case, Paper presented at the ISA's 49th Annual Convention, San Francisco, March 2008.

Ottaway, M. Nation-building, *Foreign Policy*, 2002, 132 (Sept–Oct): 16–24.

Owen, E. Domestic debate marks Karabakh presidential vote, *Eurasianet*, 19 July 2007.

Oxfam. Crisis in Gaza, http://www.oxfam.org/en/emergencies/gaza

Paikert, G. C. Hungary's national minority policies, 1920–1945, *American Slavic and East European Review*, 1953, 13: 201–18.

Panossian, R. The irony of Nagorno-Karabakh: Formal institutions versus informal politics, in *Ethnicity and Territory in the Former Soviet Union*, eds J. Hughes and G. Sasse. London: Frank Cass, 2002.

Paris, R. *At War's End: Building Peace and Civil Conflict.* Cambridge: Cambridge University Press, 2004.

Parsons, R. Russia: Is Putin looking to impose solutions to frozen conflicts? *RFE/RL*, 2 February 2006.

Pegg, S. *International Society and the De Facto State.* Aldershot: Ashgate, 1998.

—. From de facto states to states-within-states: Progress, problems and prospects, in *States within States: Incipient Entities in the Post-Cold War Era,* eds P. Kingston and I. Spears. New York: Palgrave Macmillan, 2004.

Pełczynska-Nałęcz, K., K. Strachota and M. Falkowski, Para-states in the post-Soviet area from 1991 to 2007, *International Studies Review,* 2008, 10(2): 370–87.

Pellet, A. The opinions of the Badinter arbitration committee: A second breath for the self-determination of peoples, *European Journal of International Law,* 1992, 3(1): 178–85.

Philip, C. The hidden massacre: Sri Lanka's final offensive against Tamil Tigers, *The Times,* 29 May 2009.

Philpott, D. *Revolutions in Sovereignty: How Ideas Shaped Modern International Relations.* Princeton: Princeton University Press, 2001.

Pickering, S. D. *Quantifying the Dynamics of Conflict,* Unpublished PhD thesis, Lancaster University, 2010.

Pidd, H. UN rejects calls for Sri Lanka war crimes inquiry, *The Guardian,* 28 May 2009.

Polkhov, S., Vladimir Voronon and Igor Smirnow meeting in Bendery: Are the parties ready to make a compromise with each other? *Eurasian Home,* 22 April 2008.

Pollock, D. The Kurdistan Regional Government in Iraq: An inside story, In *The Future of the Iraqi Kurds,* ed. S. Cagaptay, Washington Institute, Policy Focus #85, July 2008.

Popescu, N. Democracy in secessionism: Transnistria and Abkhazia's domestic policies, Center for Policy Studies, August 2006.

Protsyk, O. Moldova's dilemmas in democratizing and reintegrating Transnistria, *Problems of Post-Communism,* 2006, 53(4): 29–41.

—. Representation and democracy in Eurasia's unrecognized states: The case of Transnistria, *Post-Soviet Affairs,* 2009, 25(3): 257–81.

Raghavan, S. At Cairo hospital, injured increasingly voice support for Hamas, *Washington Post,* 14 January 2009, 14.

Reno, W. *Warlord Politics and African States.* Boulder: Lynne Rienner, 1999.

RFE/RL. Mass wedding in Karabakh results in baby boom, 20 August 2009.

—. Tiny Nauru in $50 million Russia gambit, 14 December 2009.

—. Abkhazia appoints new 'foreign minister', 28 February 2010.

RIA Novosti. Russia lifts trade, economic, financial sanctions on Abkhazia, 6 March 2008.

—. Russia plans to invest heavily in Sevastopol base, 9 May 2010.

Rimple, P. Gali: A key test case for Georgia's separatist Abkhazia region, *Eurasianet,* 5 March 2007.

—. Georgia: Ethnic Georgian district in Abkhazia becomes election issue, *Eurasianet,* 14 September 2009.

Ross, C. *Independent Diplomat: Dispatches from an Unaccountable Elite.* London: Hurst, 2007.

Ross, R. S. Taiwan's fading independence movement, *Foreign Affairs*, 2006, 85(2): 141–8.

Roeder, P. G. *Where Nation-States Come From.* Princeton: Princeton University Press, 2007.

Rotberg, R. I. The failure and collapse of nation-states, in *When States Fail: Causes and Consequences*, ed. R. I. Rotberg. Princeton: Princeton University Press, 2001.

Rupić, M. ed. *Republika Hrvatska i Domovinski Rat 1990–1995: Dokumenti, Knjiga 4.* Zagreb: Hrvatski Memorijalno-Dokumentacijski Centar Domovinskog Rata, 2008.

Rutland, P. Frozen conflicts, frozen analysis. Paper presented at the ISA's 48th Annual Convention, Chicago, 1 March 2007.

Sambanis, N. Partition as a solution to ethnic war: An empirical critique of the theoretical literature, *World Politics*, 2000, 52: 437–83.

Scharf, M. Earned sovereignty: Juridical underpinnings, *Denver Journal of International Law and Policy*, 2004, 31(3): 373–87.

Schnapper, D. Citizenship and national identity in Europe, *Nations and Nationalism*, 2002, 8(1): 1–14.

Seymour, L. M. The surprising success of 'separatist' groups: The empirical and juridical in self-determination, Paper presented at the ISA's 47th Annual Convention, San Diego CA, 21–26 March, 2006.

Sisk, T. D. Peacemaking in civil wars: Obstacles, options and opportunities, in *Managing and Settling Ethnic Conflicts*, eds U. Schneckener and S. Wolff. London: Hurst, 2004.

Socor, V. Has the Transnistria conflict gone from dead end to wrong turn? *Eurasia Daily Monitor*, 16 April 2008.

Smooha, S. The model of ethnic democracy: Israel as a Jewish and democratic state, *Nations and Nationalism*, 2002, 8(4): 474–503.

Somaliland Press. Police foil terrorist attack in Somaliland, 24 August 2010. http://somalilandpress.com/police-foil-terrorist-attacks-in-somaliland-17895.

Somaliland Times. CIIR's election observers welcome results of Somaliland parliamentary poll, 2 November 2005. http://www.somalilandtimes. net/198/15.shtml

Sørensen, G. Sovereignty: Change and continuity in a fundamental institution, *Political Studies*, 1999, 47: 590–604.

Stanislawski, B. H. Para-states, quasi-states, and black spots, *International Studies Review*, 2008 10(2): 366–96.

Stansfield, G. Governing Kurdistan: the strengths of division, in *The Future of Kurdistan in Iraq*, eds B. O'Leary, J. McGarry and K. Salih. Philadelphia: University of Pennsylvania Press, 2005.

—. *Iraq.* Cambridge: Polity, 2007.

Statistical Yearbook of Republika Srpska. Banja Luka, 2010.

Stedman, S. J. *Peacemaking in Civil Wars: International Mediation in Zimbabwe 1974–80*. Boulder: Lynne Rienner, 1991.

—. Spoiler problems in peace processes, *International Security*, 1997, 22(2): 5–53.

Stokke, K. Building the Tamil Eelam state: Emerging state institutions and forms of governance in LTTE-controlled areas in Sri Lanka, *Third World Quarterly*, 2006, 27(6): 1021–40.

Švarm, F. Patriots and godfathers, *Vreme News Digest*, 1 March 1993.

—. The untouchable dealers, *Vreme News Digest*, 27 September 1993.

—. Love that'll never die, *Vreme News Digest*, 22 November 1993.

—. Milan Martic's flying circus, *Vreme News Digest*, 13 December 1993.

—. The return of the district strongman, *Vreme News Digest*, 31 January 1994.

—. Happy together, *Vreme News Digest*, 4 April 1994.

—. The Krajina economy, *Vreme News Digest*, 15 August 1994.

—. Checkmate on Z-4, *Vreme News Digest*, 6 February 1995.

—. Orders from Belgrade, *Vreme News Digest*, 13 March 1995.

—. Springtime change, *Vreme News Digest*, 6 March 1995.

—. The view from the fort, *Vreme News Digest*, 7 August 1995.

—. *Pad Krajine*, documentary film. Serbia: Vreme Film, 2007.

Švarm, F. and D. Hedl, Bye, bye boys in blue, *Vreme News Digest*, 23 January 1995.

Tamás, G. Ethnarchy and ethno-anarchism, *Social Research*, 1996, 63(1): 147–190.

Tansey, O. Democratization without a state: Democratic regime-building in Kosovo, *Democratization*, 2007, 14(1): 129–150.

—. Does democracy need sovereignty? *Review of International Studies*, 2010.

The General Framework Agreement for Peace in Bosnia and Herzegovina. http://www.ohr.int/dpa/default.asp?content_id=380

The Jamestown Foundation. Amnesty International issues reports on disappearances, 24 May 2007.

Timperley, H. J. Japan in Manchukuo, *Foreign Affairs*, 1934, 12(Jan): 295–305.

Tiraspol Times. Igor Smirnov: 'We have not worked enough with other countries,' 20 March 2008.

Tishkov, V. *Chechnya: Life in a War-Torn Society*. Berkeley: University of California Press, 2004.

Touval, S. Coercive mediation on the road to Dayton, *International Negotiation*, 1996, 1(3): 547–570.

Trier, T., H. Lohm, D. Szakonyi. *Under Siege: Inter-Ethnic Relations in Abkhazia*. London: Hurst, 2010.

Turkish Republic of Northern Cyprus. *Economic and Social Indicators 2008*, http://www.devplan.org/Frame-eng.html

United Nations Security Council. *Resolution 820 (1993)*, adopted 17 April 1993, http://www.ohr.int/other-doc/un-res-bih/pdf/820e.pdf.

—. *Report of the Secretary-General on the Situation in Abkhazia, Georgia*, S/2006/435 (June 2006), http://www.unomig.org/data/file/843/060626_SG_Report_eng.pdf

Unrepresented Nations and Peoples Organization. *Declaration: Opening the World Order to de Facto States*, 15 May 2008, http://www.unpo.org/content/view/8133/81/

Vasić, M. Imitating life, *Vreme News Digest*, 4 November 1991.

—. Predsednik ili general, *Vreme*, 14 August 1995, 14–15.

Vojska. Republika Srpska Krajina, March 1994.

Wadlow, R. UN membership for the world's phantom republics, *Tiraspol Times*, 25 September 2008.

Walker, E. No peace, no war in the Caucasus: Secessionist conflicts in Chechnya, Abkhazia and Nagorno-Karabakh, Occasional Paper, Belfer Center for Science and International Affairs, 1998.

Walker, S. The phantom parliament: Abkhazia votes, but to what end, *Russia Profile*, 21 March 2007, from *Georgia News Digest*.

Walls, M. The emergence of a Somali state: Building peace from civil war in Somaliland, *African Affairs*, 2009, 108 (432): 371–89.

Warbrick, C. The recognition of states, *The International and Comparative Law Quarterly*, 1992, 41(2), 473–83.

Weaver, M. and G. Chamberlain. Sri Lanka declares end to war with Tamil Tigers, *The Guardian*, 19 May 2009.

Weber, C. *Simulating Sovereignty: Intervention, the State and Symbolic Exchange*. Cambridge: Cambridge University Press, 1995.

Weinstein, J. *Inside Rebellion: The Politics of Insurgent Violence*. Cambridge: Cambridge University Press, 2006.

Weller, M. *Escaping the Self-Determination Trap*. Leiden: Martin Nijhoff, 2008.

Wendt, A. *Social Theory of International Politics*. Cambridge: Cambridge University Press, 1999.

Williams, P. R. and F. J. Pecci, Earned sovereignty: Bridging the gap between sovereignty and self-determination, *Stanford Journal of International Law*, 2004, 40(1): 1–40.

Wilson, A. *Virtual Politics: Faking Democracy in the Post-Soviet World*. New Haven: Yale University Press, 2005.

Wilson, W. Fourteen points speech, 8 January 1918, http://en.wikisource.org/wiki/Fourteen_Points_Speech.

Yakubyan, V. Kosovo-Karabakh—strategic fork, *Regnum*, 13 November 2006, http://www.regnum.ru/english/737310.html

Yevgrashina, L. Azerbaijan may use force in Karabakh after Kosovo, *Reuters*, 4 March 2008.

Zartman, I. W. Dynamics and constraints in negotiations in internal conflicts, in *Elusive Peace: Negotiating an End to Civil War*, ed. I. W. Zartman. Washington DC: The Brookings Institution, 1995.

—. Introduction: Posing the problem of state collapse, in *Collapsed States: The Disintegration and Restoration of Legitimate Authority*, ed. I. W. Zartman. Boulder: Lynne Rienner, 1995.

—. Putting things back together, in *Collapsed States: The Disintegration and Restoration of Legitimate Authority*, ed. I. W. Zartman. Boulder: Lynne Rienner, 1995.

—. Ripeness: The hurting stalemate and beyond, in *International Conflict Resolution after the Cold War*, eds P. C. Stern and D. Druckman. Washington: National Academy Press, 2000.

Author's interviews

Abdullayeva, Arzu. Chair of the Helsinki Citizens' Assembly. Baku, 12 June 2009.

Akaba, Natella. Chair of Sukhumi city council. Via email, 30 August 2006.

Arzoumanyan, Hrachya. Expert in the Karabakh foreign ministry. Stepanakert, 1 November 2008.

Atanesyan, Vahram. Chairman of the Karabakh foreign relations committee. Stepanakert, 29 October 2008.

Ayrumyan, Naira. Journalist. Stepanakert, 2 November 2008.

Babayan, David. Advisor to the Karabakh president. Stepanakert, 13 September 2006.

—. Stepanakert, 29 October 2008.

Baghdasaryan, Gegham. Former Karabakh opposition deputy. Stepanakert, 15 September 2006.

—. Stepanakert, 27 October 2008.

Đević, Dragan. Deputy mayor of Donji Lapac. Donji Lapac, 1 April 2009.

Džakula, Veljko. Former president of SAO Western Slavonia. Zagreb, 23 March 2009.

Ghukasyan, Arkady. Former Karabakh president. Stepanakert, 3 November 2008.

Ghulyan, Ashot. Speaker of the Karabakh parliament. Stepanakert, 27 October 2008.

Harutyunyan, Araik. Karabakh prime minister. Stepanakert, 30 October 2008.

Jarčević, Slobodan. Former Krajina foreign minister. Zemun, 13 February 2009.

Kovačević, Drago. Former mayor of Knin. Belgrade, 20 February 2009.

Letica, Slaven. Former advisor to President Franjo Tuđman. Zagreb, 18 September 2003.

Ležajić, Rajko. Former speaker of the Krajina parliament. Belgrade, 17 September 2004.

Lubovac, Branko. Former Krajina deputy prime minister. Belgrade, 17 February 2009.

Mammadov, Ildar. Political analyst. Baku, 19 June 2009.

Matijaš, Rade. Former journalist in Knin. Belgrade, 12 February 2009.
Mirić, Ninko. Former judge in Krajina. Karlovac, 27 March 2009.
Momčilović, Stanko. Mayor of Udbina. Zagreb, 1 April 2009.
Musabekov, Rasim. Political analyst. Baku, 12 June 2009.
Ohanjanyan, Karen. Chair of Karabakh 'Helsinki Initiative-1992'. Yerevan, 21 October 2008.
Ohanyan, Karine. Journalist. Stepanakert, 3 November 2008.
Petrosyan, David. Defence analyst. Yerevan, 7 November 2008.
Petrosyan, Georgy. Karabakh minister of foreign affairs. Stepanakert, 31 October 2008.
Poghosyan, Tevan. Political analyst. Yerevan, 24 October 2008.
Radulović, Srđan. Deputy editor of *Blic*. Belgrade, 10 February 2009.
Štrbac, Savo. Former RSK government chief-of-staff. Belgrade, 20 February 2009.
Sužnjevic, Nikola. Former judge in the RSK. Glina, 27 March 2009.
Švarm, Filip. Deputy editor of *Vreme*. Belgrade, 24 February 2009.
Zakareishvili, Paata. Political analyst. Tbilisi, 31 August 2006.

INDEX